Asian Territorial and Maritime Disputes

A Critical Introduction

EDITED BY

MOISES DE SOUZA, GREGORY COUTAZ
& DEAN KARALEKAS

E-INTERNATIONAL
RELATIONS
PUBLISHING

E-International Relations
Bristol, England
2022

ISBN 978-1-910814-63-5

Production: Michael Tang
Cover Image: Pupes/Shutterstock & Nik Merkulov/Shutterstock

A catalogue record for this book is available from the British Library.

E-International Relations

Editor-in-Chief and Publisher: Stephen McGlinchey
Books Editor: Bill Kakenmaster
Editorial Assistance: Fian Sullivan Sweeney, Kaiqing Su, Naman Karl-Thomas Habtom

E-International Relations is the world's leading International Relations website. Our daily publications feature expert articles, reviews and interviews – as well as student learning resources. The website is run by a non-profit organisation based in Bristol, England and staffed by an all-volunteer team of students and academics. In addition to our website content, E-International Relations publishes a range of books. As E-International Relations is committed to open access in the fullest sense, free electronic versions of our books, including this one, are available on our website.

Find out more at https://www.e-ir.info/

Abstract

This volume is designed to be a practical, yet critical, introduction to the main maritime and territorial disputes in the Indo-Pacific region. It covers the most controversial disputes, including those in the South China Sea, the Senkaku/ Diaoyu Islands, Dokdo/Takeshima, the Kuril Islands, Taiwan, and Sino-India border issues. In addition, the role of the key actors in the region is examined, offering various perspectives on the disputes along with the basic rationales behind claimant nations' diplomatic approaches. With a team of contributors made up of both senior and early-career scholars, diplomats, and legal specialists, the book provides a wide range of insights that go beyond what is provided in the media.

About the editors

Moises de Souza, obtained his PhD from the International Doctoral Program in Asia-Pacific Studies (IDAS) at Taiwan's National Chengchi University. Currently, he is Lecturer in Asia Pacific Studies at the School of Humanities, Language and Global Studies and Chair of the Northern England Policy Centre for the Asia Pacific (NEPCAP) at the University of Central Lancashire (UCLan). He is also Researcher in Asia Studies at the International Relations Research Centre of the University of São Paulo (NUPRI-GEASIA) and deputy-director of the South China Sea Think Tank (SCSSTT). Additionally, he is also *Asia Pacific Viewpoint Journal* Editor-in-Chief (SCCI).

Gregory Coutaz is a Swiss political scientist. He holds an MA in Political Science from the University of Lausanne and a MAS in Asian Studies from the University of Geneva. Living in Taiwan since 2008, he received his PhD from the National Chengchi University and currently works as an Assistant Professor at the Department of Diplomacy and International Relations at Tamkang University. His major areas of research include comparative politics, conflict resolution, and non-traditional security. He is the author of *Coping with Disaster Risk Management in Northeast Asia* (2018).

Dean Karalekas is a research fellow at the Centre of Austronesian Studies at the University of Central Lancashire, having earned his PhD from the International Doctoral Program in Asia-Pacific Studies at Taiwan's National Chengchi University. He is the author of *The Men in No Man's Land: A Journey into Bir Tawil* and *Civil-Military Relations in Taiwan: Identity and Transformation*. He is also an ethnographic and narrative filmmaker, having produced, written and directed several award-winning films on a diversity of subjects, from the Canadian experience in World War II to indigenous mythology.

Contributors

Yoichiro Sato is a Professor at Ritsumeikan Asia Pacific University and is the dean of the Department and the Graduate School of Asia Pacific Studies. He earned his Ph.D in Political Science from University of Hawaii. Previously, he has taught at the U.S. Department of Defense's Asia-Pacific Center for Security Studies, Auckland University, Kansai Gaidai Hawaii College, and the University of Hawaii. His publications include *The Rise of China and International Security* (co-edited with Kevin Cooney, Routledge, 2008), *The U.S.-Japan Security Alliance* (co-edited with Takashi Inoguchi and G. John Ikenberry, Palgrave, 2011), *Regional Institutions, Geopolitics and Economics in the Asia Pacific* (co-edited with Steve Rothman and Utpal Vyas, Routledge, 2017), *Re-Rising Japan* (co-edited with Hidekazu Sakai, Peter Lang, 2017), and *Identity, Culture and Memory in Japanese Foreign Policy* (co-edited with Michal Kolmaš, Peter Lang, 2021).

Serafettin Yilmaz (Yao Shifan), PhD, is an Associate Professor in School of Political Science and Public Administration at Shandong University, China. His research interests include energy security, global governance, and East Asia regional development. His articles have appeared in *Asian Politics & Policy*, *Asian Perspective*, *Pacific Focus*, *Asia Europe Journal*, *Energy Strategy Reviews*, *International Relations of the Asia Pacific*, *Europe-Asia Studies*, *Journal of Chinese Political Science*, *Issues and Studies*, and *International Critical Thought*.

Bhaso Ndzendze, PhD, is Senior Lecturer and Head of Department: Politics and International Relations at the University of Johannesburg (UJ). His scholarship on China, Taiwan and Africa has been published in numerous journals and books, in addition to the popular press and policy briefs. His forthcoming volume (Palgrave) *The Political Economy of Sino-South African Trade in the Context of Asia-Pacific Regional Competition* examines the influence of disputes in the Asia- and Indo-Pacific on Asian states' trade with external regions.

Mark Henderson is currently a Presidential Management Fellow for the U.S. Department of State. He is serving in the role of Foreign Affairs Officer in the Bureau of East Asian and Pacific Affairs, Office of Taiwan Coordination. He received his PhD at the National Chengchi University (NCCU) in Taipei, Taiwan, where he focused on topics in political economy in the Asia Pacific region, specifically related to international economic development through local government policy. Previously, he served for several years as an International Relations Specialist for the International Relations Office at the City of San Antonio in Texas.

Adam Gerval is an Economist with the U.S. Department of Agriculture. He serves as an analyst researching macroeconomic trends in Asian markets, including East Asian nations (i.e. Japan, South Korea, Hong Kong, and Taiwan), in addition to emerging economies in Southeast Asia and sub-Saharan Africa. He has received Master's degrees in economics and international studies from George Washington University and The Ohio State University.

Duan Xiaolin is an Assistant Professor in the Global Studies Programme at the Chinese University of Hong Kong (Shenzhen). He received his PhD in Public Policy from Lee Kuan Yew School of Public Policy at the National University of Singapore in 2017. His research interests mainly focus on Chinese foreign policy, East Asian Security and nationalism.

Alana Camoça is an Adjunct Substitute Professor at the Defense and International Relations Department of the Federal University of Rio de Janeiro. Her scholarly interests include international political economy, Sino-Japanese relations, international security, and East Asian Security and Economic Relations. She received her bachelor degree in Political Science from Federal State University of Rio de Janeiro, her MA degree in International Political Economy from Federal University of Rio de Janeiro and her PhD degree in International Political Economy from Federal University of Rio de Janeiro. She also acted as a Visiting Scholar at the Department of History at Columbia University in New York in the USA and the Department of International Public Policy at the University of Osaka in Osaka in Japan.

Valentina Maljak is an international lawyer, with special expertise in public international law and international dispute settlement. She holds a master law degree from University of Zagreb, Croatia and an Advanced LL.M. in Public International Law and Dispute Settlement from Leiden University, the Netherlands. She has written and presented at conferences several papers concerning the South China Sea maritime disputes and its challenges. Valentina also worked in domestic and international law firms where she gained litigation skills and experience. She passed her bar exam in December 2021 and moved to Athens, Greece where she aims to continue and deepen her research and expertise in international maritime disputes, the field of law she is most passionate about.

Gleice Miranda is a social science researcher. Her main interests are on water policies and security, as well as on maritime disputes and its intricacies. She holds a bachelor's degree in International Relations from Pontifical Catholic University of Rio de Janeiro, and a master's degree in Transnational Security from Royal Holloway, University of London. She has written and presented papers in several conferences regarding freshwater securitization and the South China Sea maritime disputes. Currently, Gleice is pursuing a PhD in Geography at King's College London, with focus on water justice and the coexistence of conflict and cooperation in the water field.

Mayuri Banerjee is a Research Analyst with the East Asia Centre at the Manohar Parrikar Institute for Defence Studies and Analyses (MP-IDSA), New Delhi. Her research focus is on India-China relations. She primarily looks at the role of memory and trust in India-China relations after the 1962 war and Indian media's perception of China. Currently, she is pursuing PhD at the Department of International Relations at Jadavpur University, Kolkata. Her doctoral thesis deals with "Remembering 1962 war: War Memory and Trust-Deficit in India-China Relations". She received the Indu Bhushan Putatunda and Shanti Shudha Putatunda Memorial Award in 2013 from Jadavpur Alumni Association and Certificate of Merit in Political Science in 2014 from Jadavpur University. She was also a recipient of the Sasakawa Young Leaders Fellowship Fund (SYLFF) Masters' Fellowship in 2015. Her work has been published in MP-IDSA, ORF Expert Speak, South Asian Voices (Stimson Center, USA), and The Kootneeti.

Leticia Simões is Assistant-Professor at the La Salle University (Rio de Janeiro). She receives her PhD in International Relations from the Graduate Program in International Relations at Rio de Janeiro State University (PPGRI-UERJ). She also obtained her master's in international Relations at the same institution.

Astha Chadha is a Japanese Government MEXT Scholar pursuing PhD at Ritsumeikan Asia Pacific University and is a researcher at the university's Center for Democracy Promotion. She holds MSc in International Relations (Ritsumeikan Asia Pacific University), MA in Economics (Jawaharlal Nehru University) and BA (Hons) in Economics (University of Delhi). Her research is focused on India-Japan relations, security, and defense analyses of regional powers in the Indo-Pacific, South Asian rivalries, and conflict resolution etc. She has previously published in Global Affairs, Contemporary Japan, South Asian Popular Culture, Ritsumeikan Journal of Asia Pacific Studies, and has contributed to The Diplomat, Khabarhub, Kootneeti and others.

Contents

Introduction

MOISES DE SOUZA, DEAN KARALEKAS AND GREGORY
COUTAZ

This volume is designed to be a practical yet critical introduction to the main maritime and territorial disputes in the Indo-Pacific region. Through each chapter, the authors outline the foundations of each dispute, followed by an analytical discussion that will provide the reader with a more in-depth understanding, allowing them to go one step further beyond a mere descriptive perspective on these intricate geopolitical questions.

As with many geopolitical disputes, nationalistic passions arise from all sides. The editors of this volume have therefore endeavoured to provide the various opposing viewpoints on the disputes from a position of neutrality, with the intention of reaching a more sober and balanced account of the events involved. Given the editorial scope and inevitable space limitations, many other analytical possibilities could have been explored, but it was our primary intention to provide the necessary background information enabling the reader to grasp the conditions on the ground, and hence to be armed with the tools needed to confidently access more theoretical and technical studies on the subject of the region's nuanced maritime and territorial disputes.

Moreover, decisions were made regarding which of the region's many disputes to include, as it would not have been possible to cover all of the myriad territorial controversies in the Indo-Pacific. Questions related to Tibet's status; China's actions on the border with Bhutan; the contentious Socotra rock between South Korea and China; the controversial occupation of the Nepalese Rui Village by China; these are some examples of important territorial disputes that did not make the cut. While the editors recognize the importance of these conflicts, it was our intention to provide a book that offers the student of international relations and Indo-Pacific conflict an overview of the disputes with the geopolitical weight and strategic implications to threaten the peace and stability of the region, and that today have the potential to redraw the map. Eventually, we are hopeful that a second (or updated) volume will be able to help fill this gap.

The topics covered herein include the maritime and territorial disputes in the South China Sea and East China Sea. Gleice Miranda and Valentina Maljak provide the foundations of these conflicting and overlapping claims along with the important role played by the United Nations Convention on the Law of the Sea (UNCLOS) to better understand the legal complexities of each country's claims. At the same time, Leticia Simões outlines the important discussion concerning the role of the Association of Southeast Asian Nations (ASEAN) as a regional organization and its place as a possible mediator in the disputes.

The rationale and interpretations behind China and Japan's territorial disputes are discussed by specialists from these two countries. Yoichiro Sato and Astha Chadha offer a comprehensive analysis of the Diaoyu/Senkaku Island dispute between Japan and China using aspects of territorial and maritime sovereignty, international law, natural resource exploitation, and the role of the United States, as well as the geopolitical implications of the same. The Chinese rationale for the disputes in the East China Sea is described by Duan Xiaolin, who focuses his discussion on the general behavioural patterns of China's leaders in their quest for territorial integrity, additionally exploring the implications for the DSI dispute. Duan argues that the relative-gains concept and the instrumental value of disputed territories both fail to provide coherent explanations for China's territorial strategies. Rather, what matters most are the political meanings of disputed territories within the context of China's grand strategy.

The implications of the presence and interest of the United States in both disputes are analysed by Adam Gerval and Mark Henderson, who clarify how Washington sees its role in the region vis-à-vis the maritime claims of each nation involved. As much as the United States, the specificity of the presence of Taiwan's position is discussed by Dean Karalekas, who calls attention to the differences between the East and South China Sea claims pressed by Taipei and those by Beijing, despite their common origin. Going up to the Northeast part of the map, Serafettin Yilmaz offers a summary of the intricacies surrounding Japan's twin disputes with South Korea and Russia related to control over Dokdo/Takeshima Islands and Kuril Islands, respectively.

The territorial claims and counterclaims that so threaten peace and security in the region go beyond just island disputes. Mayuri Banerjee addresses the origin of the Sino-Indian border dispute, along with India's colonial legacy, and the factors that have contributed to the flare-ups of kinetic conflict along the frontier that have arisen in recent years. Finally, while the region is currently abundant in quarrels over territory, other disputes – equally complex

– have nevertheless been resolved in the not-too-distant past, making them worthy of revisiting. Bhaso Ndzendze looks at the history of the Chinese methods of dealing with disagreements over sovereignty by examining three distinct case studies: Mongolia, Shandong, and Macau. Ndzenze explains that the Mongolian declaration of independence during the 1911 Xinhai Revolution, which brought down China's last imperial dynasty, remains the only successful case of secession by a former Chinese colony, and suggests that this event may hold clues to how disputes might be peacefully resolved today.

It is our hope that students and members of the general public will find this volume useful in their exploration of the many maritime and territorial disputes that help define the Asia-Pacific geopolitical landscape. Now, more than ever, it is necessary first to seek to understand the many facets of the contentious disagreements in the region, and the historical conditions that led to the predicament the region finds itself in today. This book is an effort in this direction.

1

The Role of United Nations Convention on the Law of the Sea (UNCLOS) in the South China Sea Disputes: The Challenges to Conflict Resolution

GLEICE MIRANDA AND VALENTINA MALJAK

> *The dark oceans were the womb of life: from the protecting oceans life emerged. We still bear in our bodies – in our blood, in the salty bitterness of our tears – the marks of this remote past* – Arvid Pardo.

Interstate conflicts have shaped the destiny of nations since the very beginning of their formation. Wars between and within states have played a role in forging the current international system, creating new laws and governments, and solidifying ancient ones. However, conflicts also jeopardize peace and security around the world, especially when they do not receive due attention from the international community. One such conflict is currently underway in the South China Sea (SCS). The tensions are territorial in nature, with some parties claiming the rights to islands based on international law and conventions, and others asserting their claims as historical rights. Overtime, as tensions increased, the parties have attempted to settle their dispute with the help of international bodies, such as the Permanent Court of Arbitration (PCA), and the application of United Nations Convention on the

Law of the Sea (UNCLOS). However, little to no success has been achieved in decreasing the conflict in the region. The purpose of this chapter is threefold: (1) to provide a geopolitical and legal overview of the SCS disputes, focusing on the importance of the region and identifying the different territorial claims; (2) to explain the major attempt at conflict resolution in the region made through UNCLOS and the PCA; and (3) to critically analyse the impact of UNCLOS on the SCS disputes, highlighting its merits and shortcomings in the region's main attempt at conflict resolution.

The second section of this chapter provides a background on the SCS conflict, focusing on the reasons and the details for it. It examines the strategic importance of the region, as well as analyses the various territorial claims, explaining the assertions made by the primary claimant states. The third section reflects on the dispute settlement mechanism under the auspices of UNCLOS, providing an overview of the convention to guide the discussion. Then, it investigates the arbitration between the Philippines and China, which was brought before the PCA. The fourth section provides a brief analysis of the UNCLOS conflict resolution mechanism in light of the *South China Sea Arbitration*.

Dispute Background

The SCS encompasses several hundred small islands, reefs, and atolls, almost all uninhabited and uninhabitable, within a 1.4 million square mile area (Bader 2016). Two island groups – the Spratly and Paracel Islands – have been the primary focus of the disputes for decades due to their significance to the coastal countries surrounding them.

First, the region is rich in oil and natural gas reserves, but accurate estimates are difficult to find. According to the US Energy Information Administration (EIA), the area contains 11 billion barrels of untapped oil and 190-500 trillion cubic feet of natural gas (EIA 2013), while the Ministry of Geological Resources and Mining of the People's Republic of China (PRC) has estimated that the number of barrels may be as high as 130 billion (Kaplan 2015). Second, the area is a major trading route. Namely, it is considered as one of the busiest shipping lanes in the world with an annual trade of US$5.3 trillion passing through the region (CFR 2017). This number represents half of the world's annual merchant fleet tonnage and a third of all maritime traffic globally (Kaplan 2015).

Additionally, the oil transported through the South China Sea coming from the Indian Ocean is three times greater than the amount that transits the Suez Canal and 15 times more than what goes through the Panama Canal. The main cause for this has been the increase in China's oil consumption, as well as a large part of South Korea, Japan, and Taiwan's energy supplies coming through the region. Hence, it is no surprise that control of the area is of extreme importance. For instance, China has dubbed the South China Sea its Second Persian Gulf: not only does 80% of the country's crude oil imports pass through the region, but also a huge assortment of goods (Kaplan 2015; CFR 2017).

This aspect of the region is one of the major causes for the contentions regarding the islands, since many of them lie in the exclusive economic zones (EEZ) of Vietnam, Malaysia, and the Philippines. Thus, it is not surprising that these coastal states, along with China, Brunei and the Republic of China (ROC) in Taiwan, are pushing forward with their own territorial claims in the area. Each wants to secure its own national interests by asserting their rights to exclusive exploitation of the region through the utilization of international law and other mechanisms to assure those are protected and exercised.

Furthermore, the South China Sea has some of the world's richest reef systems, with more than 3,000 indigenous and migratory fish species. It also constitutes more than 12% of worldwide fishing (Greer 2016). Thus, the region offers abundant fishing opportunities, and whoever has control over its waters will have the potential to support and further develop its fishery sector. This aspect of the SCS has already led to many clashes in the region between the Philippines and Chinese fishing vessels (Kaplan 2015; EIA 2016).

Moreover, competition over fisheries in the area has been escalating, and it tends to increase more over time once fishing in the region becomes more jeopardized. In 2008, it was already estimated that the fishery stocks in the region were becoming depleted, with 25% being over-exploited and 50% fully exploited without any attempts at developing sustainable fishing practices in the region (Greer 2016).

Territorial Claims

The claims in the SCS are twofold; while some allegations are based on historical rights, others appeal to provisions of UNCLOS. These multiple territorial claims indicate a lack of agreement among the parties, which resulted in a regional conflict that has been happening for decades. The analysis of these claims (Figures 1.1 and 1.2) will be made in light of UNCLOS guidelines from 1982, since all coastal states in Southeast Asia have ratified it. Thus, an overview of most claimant parties will be conducted, to clarify their allegations and highlight the leading issues in the conflict, focusing on claims made by China and the Philippines, to better establish the case studied in this chapter.

Vietnam

Hanoi claims the Spratly and Paracel Islands along with the Gulf of Thailand. However, unlike China, Vietnam has not written its extended claims over the South China Sea in official texts or maps. As far as the Spratly Islands are concerned, in the 1970s, Vietnam established them as an offshore district of the Khanh Hoa Province, occupying several islands. That same decade, China seized the archipelago in a military engagement known as the Battle of the Paracel Islands (EIA 2013; Tonnesson 2000). In a bid to solidify its claims, Vietnam employed archaeologists to provide evidence to support the country's long historic presence in the SCS. It was asserted that the state has actively dominated both the Paracels and the Spratlys since the 17th Century (BBC 2016). Consequently, China, Brunei, Malaysia, and the Philippines oppose Vietnam's claims.

Vietnam and Malaysia jointly submitted their territorial claims in the South China Sea to the UN Commission on the Limits of the Continental Shelf in 2009 (CLCS 2009). The submission was considered legitimate, and the countries had to clarify their positions on the legal status of features and limits of their claims in the region (EIA 2013; Nguyen 2020). Vietnam also adopted a maritime law in 2012 in which it claimed jurisdiction over the Paracel and Spratly Islands, requiring that all naval ships from foreign states register with Vietnamese authorities when passing through the region (EIA 2013).

Malaysia

Kuala Lumpur's participation in the SCS disputes started in 1979, when the Malaysian Department of Mapping and Survey unveiled an official map placing the Spratly Islands within the country's continental shelf (Roach 2014). This map overlapped the EEZ and continental shelf of Malaysia and other states, which drew protests from neighbours including China, Indonesia, Vietnam, and the Philippines. Although Malaysia's claim was considered weak by some legal analysts (EIA 2013; Roach 2014), it was not inferior to China or Vietnam's claims to the entire Spratly archipelago.

In 2009, pursuant to Article 76, paragraph 8 of UNCLOS[1], Malaysia and

---

[1]   In Article 76, paragraph 8 of the UNCLOS it is provided that information on the limits of the continental shelf beyond 200 nautical miles from the baselines from which the breadth of the territorial sea is measured shall be submitted by the coastal State to the Commission on the Limits of the Continental Shelf set up under Annex II on the basis of

Vietnam jointly submitted to the CLCS information on the limits of the continental shelf beyond 200 nautical miles from the baselines from which the breadth of the territorial sea is measured in respect of the southern part of the South China Sea (CLCS 2009). To date, the CLCS did not make any recommendations on matters related to the establishment of the outer limits of their continental shelf. Nevertheless, the actions of these two countries can be regarded as steps within international law to solidify their claims.

A decade later, in 2019, Malaysia made a partial submission to the CLCS for the remaining portion of states' the continental shelf beyond 200 nautical miles in the northern part of the SCS (Malaysia 2017). Previously, Malaysia's position on the dispute had often been characterised as subdued: practicing quiet diplomacy and demonstrating a willingness to strengthen bilateral ties with China, rather than confronting Beijing publicly (Parameswaran 2016). Following their latest submission, Kuala Lumpur's strategy seemed to change, leaning towards compliance with UNCLOS and departing from an alignment with China's position. Additionally, Malaysia has also used diplomatic, political, and economic measures to sustain its claims by improving its ties with the United States and supporting a united front on the part of the Association of Southeast Asian Nations (ASEAN) (Parameswaran 2016; Nguyen 2020).

Brunei

After it gained independence in 1984, Brunei released maps in which it declared a 200-nautical mile EEZ overlapping the Chinese nine-dash line and a continental shelf extending to a hypothetical median with Vietnam. In so doing, the Brunei government claimed part of the Spratly Islands archipelago closer to its EEZ in the north of Borneo (Rüland 2005). Perceived for years as a silent claimant, Brunei bases its claims on UNCLOS (EIA 2013; Putra 2021).

Brunei has often adopted a cooperative, neutral stance regarding the SCS disputes, being in favour of a collective approach to providing maritime security and resolving disagreements (Brunei's Ministry of Defence 2011). At times, however, the sultanate has sided with China's preference for bilateral agreements, due to its weaker military power and dependency on oil reserves to sustain its economy and monarchical rule (Putra 2021).

---

equitable geographical representation. Further, the Commission shall make recommendations to coastal States on matters related to the establishment of the outer limits of their continental shelf and such established limits shall be final and binding (United Nations 1982).

China

The People's Republic of China bases its claim to the Spratly and Paracel Islands on historical naval expeditions dating back to the 15th century (EIA 2013). In 1947, the Kuomintang – then, the party in control of China – drew a line around the aforementioned islands, calling it the nine-dash line map (Figure 1.3). In doing so, China declared its sovereignty over all islands enveloped by this line (Nguyen 2015). After the Communist Party ascended to power in 1949 and established the PRC, the new government continued to use this map in official correspondence and claimed rights to the waters within it. Currently, China maintains its claim over the SCS based on this and other historical evidence (EIA 2013).

In 2009, following the joint submission of Vietnam and Malaysia to the Commission on the Limits of the Continental Shelf (CLCS), China submitted the nine-dash line map to the CLCS, seeking to solidify its claim and legitimize it beyond 200 nautical miles.[2] China's claims resulted in Malaysia, Vietnam, Brunei, and the Philippines also declaring rights over the islands and various zones in the SCS, directly contesting the Chinese claims (EIA 2013). However, the nine-dash line map is not in accordance with the provisions of UNCLOS. Namely, the Convention stipulates guidelines on baselines, the width of territorial waters, the regime of islands[3], the low-tide elevations, the exclusive economic zone, the continental shelf, the maritime boundary delimitation, and dispute settlement, which are all applicable to the South China Sea (United Nations 1982). Hence, the foundation of the Chinese claims over the islands is unsubstantiated because it fails to follow the Convention's determinations and does not provide sufficient historical evidence.

Nevertheless, aiming to reclaim land in the South China Sea, China has engaged in island-building, increasing the size of islands and turning islets

---

[2]   UNCLOS gives states the right to declare EEZs that extend 200 nautical miles from a continental shoreline or around islands that can be habitable. In the South China Sea, the application of this provision resulted in the overlapping of EEZs of other coastal states. In this kind of situation, Article 74 of UNCLOS offers a solution: the demarcation of EEZs between States with opposite or adjacent coasts shall be affected by agreement on the basis of international law in order to achieve an equitable solution (United Nations 1982).

[3]   UNCLOS in Article 121 defines an island as a naturally formed area of land, surrounded by water, which is above water at high tide. It further provides that the contiguous zone, the exclusive economic zone and the continental shelf of an island are determined in accordance with the provisions of this Convention applicable to other land territory. The exception of the latter are rocks which cannot sustain human habitation or economic life of their own and which, therefore, have no exclusive economic zone or continental shelf (United Nations 1982).

and other features into full-fledged islands in order to produce an EEZ extending 200 nautical miles (CFR 2017). Therefore, the PRC is claiming its rights over and around islands that cannot naturally support habitation, as well as building new ones to expand the area that would be under its sovereignty.

These actions go against UNCLOS, which states in Article 121, paragraph 3 that 'rocks which cannot sustain human habitation or economic life of their own shall have no exclusive economic zone or continental shelf.' Unsurprisingly, China's position and operations have complicated Beijing's relationships with its neighbours, which also have claims in the region. As a result, the disputes have escalated tremendously, leading to situations where vessels have been sunk, and military exercises have been performed to assert sovereignty (EIA 2013).

The Philippines

Manila's claims are both legal and historical over the Scarborough Shoal and the Kalayaan Island Group (KIG), which is comprised of 50 features of the Spratly islands (Rosen 2014). These claims clash with China's declarations of ownership. In 1956, the Philippine government began explorations in the SCS, legitimizing those by claiming that the islands and the shoal were *terra nullius*, or no man's land, and furthered it by occupying several of the Spratly Islands and naming them the Kalayaan Island Group. In addition, the Philippines declared the aforementioned islands and shoals as a special regime of islands that, in spite of being distinct from the rest of the Philippine archipelago, belongs to Manila (EIA 2013).

Under the provisions of UNCLOS, Philippine sovereignty appears stronger, because an EEZ can be declared up to 200 nautical miles from the baseline. Both groups of islands are 400 nautical miles closer to the Philippines than to China, are within the Philippines EEZ and are recognized as such under UNCLOS. In spite of being consistent with the provisions of UNCLOS, China, Malaysia, and Vietnam have objected to the Philippines' claims, which led to an increase of tensions in the SCS (CFR 2017).

Attempts at Resolution: UNCLOS and *South China Sea Arbitration*

In the attempt to find a peaceful resolution, bilateral and multilateral agreements were pursued by the claimant parties, and some were signed.[4]

---

4   In most cases, the parties involved were China and ASEAN. Agreements regarding peaceful coexistence in the region were attempted. One of them was the 2002 Declaration on the Conduct of the parties in the South China Sea, in which the parties

Due to the scope of this chapter, we will forgo the investigation of such agreements, and hereby examine the UNCLOS mechanism for dispute settlement and its role in the SCS conflict.

United Nations Convention on the Law of the Sea

The first call for a 'constitution of the seas' was brought forth on 1 November 1967 by Arvid Pardo, then Ambassador to the United Nations. In his speech at the General Assembly, he addressed the issues of emerging rivalry between states, which was spreading to the oceans; the pollution of the seas; the conflicting legal claims and their collateral effects on stability and order; and the potential richness of the seabed (United Nations 1967; United Nations 1998).

After three UN conferences on the Law of the Sea, UNCLOS was created. The UNCLOS III came into effect on 14 November 1994 precisely 21 years after the first meeting and one year after ratification by the sixtieth state (GRID-Arendal 2014). To date, there are 168 state-parties to the agreement (United Nations 2020). One of the main purposes of UNCLOS III is to strengthen peace, security, cooperation, and friendly relations among all nations in conformity with the principles of justice and equal rights (United Nations 1982). The unique dispute resolution system under UNCLOS is one of the most notable features of the Convention.

Dispute Resolution Mechanism under UNCLOS

Professor Natalie Klein, dean of Macquarie Law School in 2014, started her assessment of the 20 years of dispute settlement under UNCLOS stating that one should always reach for the stars, and if one only reaches the rooftops, then at least one had gotten off the ground (Klein 2014). Such ambition can be found in the idealized version of the dispute settlement mechanism of UNCLOS, once it aimed to be compulsory and indispensable to the solution of all maritime disputes. The result was a politically realistic system with various dispute settlement means, exceptions and limitations, but still compulsory and indispensable to some disputes. Thus, it can be argued that 'it is not possible to conclude that UNCLOS dispute settlement regime has reached the stars, but we can have a healthy debate as to what level rooftop has been reached' (Klein 2014, 359).

---

reaffirmed their goal to commit to the principles and purposes of the UN and UNCLOS Charters and recognized such principles as guidelines to the relationship among states (ASEAN and PRC 2002, 1). It was expected that tensions would decrease and that the conflict would end if all parties had followed the provisions of the Declaration. However, this did not happen, as the states continued to press their territorial claims and continued to seize each other's fishing vessels (Bader 2014).

The limitations and exceptions to compulsory dispute settlement were set out in Part XV, Section 3 of UNCLOS (Churchill 2017). For instance, before resorting to compulsory dispute settlement under Part XV, Section 2, the parties had to first try to resolve their dispute by the means provided in Part XV, Section 1. Articles 279–285 of said Section 1 lay out the obligation to settle disputes by peaceful means. It gives parties the option to settle disputes by any peaceful means[5] they choose; sets out a procedure for when no settlement can be reached by the parties; refers to obligations under general, regional, or bilateral agreements; sets out rules for conciliation; and provides for the application of this section to disputes submitted pursuant to Part XI - the Area (United Nations 1982).[6]

Additionally, under Article 283 of UNCLOS, states have an obligation to exchange views regarding settlement of disputes concerning the interpretation or application of UNCLOS by negotiation or other peaceful means. Furthermore, the parties shall continue to exchange views even when the dispute has not been solved through peaceful means, but it requires consultation on the manner of implementing the settlement (United Nations 1982).

Only after such attempts at dispute settlement have proven to be unsuccessful can one resort to Part XV, Section 2 of UNCLOS, which sets out rules for the resolution of disputes between State Parties arising out of the interpretation or application of UNCLOS (Tribunal 2018). Pursuant to Article 287(1) of UNCLOS, when signing, ratifying, or acceding to UNCLOS, a state may make a declaration choosing one or more of the following means for settling such disputes:

- the International Tribunal for the Law of the Sea (ITLOS) in Hamburg, Germany;
- the International Court of Justice (ICJ) in The Hague, The Netherlands;
- ad hoc arbitration (in accordance with Annex VII of UNCLOS); or
- a "special arbitral tribunal" constituted for certain categories of disputes (established under Annex VIII of UNCLOS).

The variety of choices for dispute settlement forums was a necessary precondition for state parties to accept the compulsory jurisdiction, even more so as they were unable to agree on a single forum (Churchill 2017).

---

[5] Namely, Article 279 of UNCLOS clarifies that 'peaceful means' refers to settling any dispute concerning the interpretation or application of UNCLOS in accordance with Article 2.3 of the Charter of the United Nations where disputing parties shall seek a solution by the means indicated in Article 33, paragraph 1, of the Charter.
[6] Which under Article 1 of UNCLOS means 'the seabed and ocean floor and subsoil thereof, beyond the limits of national jurisdiction.'

Additionally, it is set out in Article 287(3) of UNCLOS that arbitration under Annex VII is the default means of dispute settlement in cases where a state has not declared a preference for a dispute resolution mechanism available under Article 287(1) of UNCLOS, or when a state has not made any reservation or optional exceptions pursuant to Article 298 of UNCLOS.

Pursuant to Article 287(5) of UNCLOS, if the parties have not accepted the same procedure for the settlement of disputes, the dispute can only be submitted for arbitration under Annex VII. However, as stated above, there are limitations and exceptions to the compulsory dispute settlement.

In Part XV, Section 3, Article 297, limitations and exceptions to the aforementioned dispute settlement fora leaves a possibility for states when signing, ratifying, or acceding to this Convention – or at any time thereafter – to declare in writing that it does not accept one or more of the provided procedures. Such a statement can be made with respect to one or more disputes concerning maritime boundaries with neighbouring states or those involving historic bays or titles, disputes concerning military activities, and certain kinds of law enforcement activities in an EEZ and/or disputes over which Security Council is exercising its duties under the UN Charter (United Nations 1982; Churchill 2017)[7].

It is also provided in Article 297 that there is no obligation for a coastal state to accept referral by another state to legally binding dispute settlement concerning the exercise of its rights in the fisheries and marine scientific research (Churchill 2017). Nevertheless, some of the disputes that are exempted from compulsory dispute settlement are subject to compulsory conciliation. Hence, the compulsory dispute settlement system under UNCLOS is one of its biggest assets, despite the difficult road travelled to reach it.

Permanent Court of Arbitration (Tribunal) – South China Sea Arbitration

As mentioned above, a member state of UNCLOS may choose the ITLOS, the ICJ, an ad hoc arbitration, or a 'special arbitral tribunal' to settle its dispute. After failing to solve the dispute through negotiations, the Philippines

---

[7]   To date, only 54 of the 168 states parties to UNCLOS made such a declaration: China, in 2006, and Malaysia, in 2009, are two of them. Their declarations excluded disputes concerning interpretation or application of articles 15, 74 and 83 relating to sea boundary delimitations, or those involving historic bays or titles, and by non-acceptance of any of the procedures provided for in Part XV, Section 2 of the Convention with respect to all the categories of disputes referred to in paragraph 1 (a) (b) and (c) of Article 298 of the Convention (United Nations 2021).

elected to bring its dispute against China on the SCS before the Tribunal. The arbitration started on 22 January 2013 under the compulsory dispute settlement provisions of UNCLOS. It is important to stress that UNCLOS does not address the sovereignty of states over land territory which the Tribunal itself has also underlined in the final award brought in the case at hand.

The arbitration deals with disputes between the parties regarding the legal basis of maritime rights and entitlement in the SCS; the status of certain geographic features in the SCS; and the lawfulness of certain actions taken by China in the SCS. The Tribunal in its final award sorted the Philippines' requests into four categories to be resolved:

1. dispute concerning the source of maritime rights and entitlement in the SCS;

2. dispute concerning the entitlement to maritime zones that would be generated under the UNCLOS by Scarborough Shoal and certain maritime features in the Spratly Islands claimed by both the Philippines and China;

3. series of disputes concerning the lawfulness of China's actions in the SCS;

4. to find that China has aggravated and extended the disputes between the parties during the course of this arbitration by restricting access to a detachment of Philippine marines and by engaging in the large-scale construction of artificial islands and land reclamation at seven reefs in the Spratly Islands.

From the beginning, China made it clear that it refused to participate in the arbitration or to comply with the final award. China communicated this position in public statements and in many diplomatic *Notes Verbales*, both to the Philippines and to the Tribunal. Furthermore, in 2006, China made a declaration to exclude maritime boundary delimitations from its acceptance of a compulsory dispute settlement. This is one of the objections that China expressed in its Position Paper on the Matter of Jurisdiction in the South China Sea, sent to the Tribunal on 12 July 2014, where it offered an extensive legal analysis of each of its objections and expressed its refusal to comply with the Tribunal's decision (PRC 2014).

In its Award on Jurisdiction and Admissibility, the Tribunal found that it could not agree with China's arguments and concluded that it indeed had jurisdiction over the case. Moreover, even though China insisted that its communication should not be interpreted as participation, the Tribunal, during adjudication, took all this into account.

The Tribunal overwhelmingly ruled in favour of the Philippines in the award released on 12 July 2016. It concluded that, in the matter of China's claims of historical rights and its nine-dash line, China had no legal basis to claim historical rights to resources within the sea areas falling within the nine-dash line. The Tribunal found that China and other states had historically made use of the islands in the SCS, but it found no evidence that China had historically exercised exclusive control over the waters and their resources (Tribunal 2016).

The Tribunal also concluded that the Spratly Islands could not generate its own EEZ because they were not inhabited and it was historically impossible for them to be inhabited, and under the provision of UNCLOS: '[r]ocks which cannot sustain human habitation or economic life of their own shall have no exclusive economic zone or continental shelf.' Thus, the Tribunal declared that the areas are within the EEZ of the Philippines, stating that 'those areas are not overlapped by any possible entitlement of China' (Tribunal 2016, 10).

Post-Award Developments

After the award was released, China continued to oppose the ruling and did not recognize the award. The Chinese Ministry of Foreign Affairs stood behind the state's interpretation that since the Tribunal proceeded with the arbitration despite China's refusal to participate, this voided and nullified the award (Philips et al. 2016). As such, the Chinese government stated that China's territorial sovereignty and maritime rights in the region remained unaffected by the ruling.

In the Philippines, meanwhile, there was a reversal of policy. Following the election of Rodrigo Duterte as president in 2016 on an anti-American, pro-China platform, Manila declared that it wanted to 'set the award aside' and renegotiate the dispute settlement directly with China (The Guardian 2016). This capitulation to Beijing was an indication of Duterte's ambition to boost Sino-Filipino ties in a bid to attract Chinese investment (Camba 2018). Duterte also stressed his intention to decrease the Philippines' dependence on the United States, going as far as to no longer consider America an ally, and turning toward China for economic partnership (The Guardian 2016; BBC 2017).

However, in 2019, Duterte began to show signs of standing up to Chinese forays into the Philippine territory, especially after tensions rose due to

People's Liberation Army Navy incursions and the gathering of Chinese fishing vessels near the Philippines' Pag-asa Island – the administrative centre of the Kalayaan group and located 932 kilometres southwest of Manila. Duterte declared tensions could escalate to armed conflict to protect the island if necessary (The Guardian 2019). In 2020, Duterte delivered a speech to the 75th UN General Assembly in which he expressed support for the Hague's ruling, stating that the award is 'part of international law, beyond compromise and beyond the reach of passing governments to dilute, diminish, or abandon' (Duterte 2020). Additionally, Duterte asserted that any attempts by China to undermine the award would be rejected and fought off. To support this position, the United States stated that in the event of an armed attack, it would come to the Philippines' aid, notwithstanding the current shaken state of their relationship (Strangio 2020). These developments, and the maintenance of claims by both China and the Philippines, further complicate the chances for peaceful resolution of the dispute.

Thus, the SCS disputes continue to rage on and to draw the attention of the international society. This unresolved territorial feud has the potential to escalate to armed conflict, which would bring insecurity and instability to the region. Having in mind the importance of the region, it is of high priority to settle this dispute peacefully, avoiding any kind of armed conflict.

Analysing the Dispute Settlement Mechanism under UNCLOS in South China Sea

States are generally amenable to the UNCLOS system because it enables them to retain control over the dispute and negotiate the conditions of a resolution rather than to find themselves bound by strict rules of law. Furthermore, the unpredictability of international litigation also favours negotiation (Churchill 2017). As such, the choice between diplomatic means of dispute settlement and settlement through litigation is a matter of economic, political, and public reputation strategy. States will rarely choose to litigate when they are aware the chances of losing the dispute are reasonably high. Moreover, dispute resolution through diplomatic means is cheaper, could be faster, and gives states enough space to mitigate the negative publicity that could result from litigation (Churchill 2017).

Nevertheless, there are cases where negotiations have failed to generate a settlement or to maintain an agreed-upon settlement as such. The disputes in the SCS fall into the latter category[8]. The UNCLOS mechanism gives states,

---

[8]   Negotiations failed in maintaining bilateral agreements, such as the 2002 Declaration on the Conduct of the Parties in the South China Sea at the 8th ASEAN

especially weaker ones, comfort and protection in cases where one of the parties to a dispute – like China in the SCS – consistently insists on only addressing disputes through bilateral negotiations, because it enjoys significant advantages over other countries. It is notable that the Tribunal in the award in the *South China Sea Arbitration* acknowledged the importance of negotiation in dispute settlement, stressing that the parties were free to use other methods of dispute settlement but only if those were in accordance with international law (Nguyen 2018).

One of the advantages of compulsory dispute settlement mechanism is the variety of dispute settlement forums from which states can choose, all of which have positive and negative aspects. As seen, arbitration under Part VII is a default dispute settlement mechanism in case disputing parties chose different fora. Furthermore, arbitration is a forum more flexible than, for example, the ICJ or ITLOS, since the appointment of arbitrators and decisions about procedures and rules of arbitration remains under the control of the disputing parties (Singh 2016). One of the main disadvantages is the high financial cost of such arbitration, since both parties must pay high fees to arbitrators and court registrars, pay to rent the premises in which proceedings are held, and pay for secretarial and interpreting services. Another challenge for arbitration is its perceived lower status when compared with other fora. For instance, it has been argued that arbitration does not possess the same prestige as the ICJ does, which is reflected in the higher rates of compliance with ICJ decisions compared to arbitral tribunal awards (Singh 2016).

Such issues of non-compliance can be highlighted in China's declared non-participation, disobedience, and disregard toward the arbitral award issued in the *South China Sea Arbitration*. It is indisputable that the award failed to settle the dispute or mitigate its escalation. Nevertheless, it would be a mistake to completely categorize it as a failure. The award has, for the first time in international jurisprudence, provided clarification on the meaning of historic rights claims and the regime of islands pursuant to Article 121 of UNCLOS (Nguyen 2018, 105). Moreover, by rejecting China's claims based on the nine-dash line, the Tribunal has also showed its stance toward excessive claims and reduced the maritime areas subject to the dispute. By doing so, the Tribunal provided clarification of disputed areas and lawful overlapping claims. This is important because, prior to the award, disputant states in the region had not defined which features they believed were islands and what maritime zones they are entitled to claim from such islands (Nguyen 2018, 104). Therefore, it is reasonable to expect that a significant number of states will clarify their claims based on the definitions provided in the award. Such can already be seen in Malaysia's 2019 partial submission, in which the

---

Summit in Phnom Penh, Cambodia, on 4 November 2002 (for more information, see ASEAN and PRC, 2002; Bader 2014; Khoo 2016).

state defined the extent of its northern and southern continental shelfs (Malaysia 2017). In doing so, Kuala Lumpur showed implicit support to the 2016 Tribunal award and strengthened the Tribunal's stance. This could consequently lead to more states doing the same and, at last, to some form of dispute settlement.

Lastly, enforcement of and compliance with decisions made under international law is not a new challenge. Nevertheless, history has shown that sometimes the non-compliance rhetoric of a state does not always reflect its actions and behaviour in the field, which indicates that lack of an enforcement mechanism does not necessarily translate to non-compliance (Nguyen 2018). Furthermore, even in cases where dispute settlement mechanisms have failed to generate compliance or mitigate the escalation of a dispute, it still provided some clarification on the interpretation and application of the relevant provisions, which could be crucial in a final dispute settlement.

Conclusion

The South China Sea disputes have been shaping relationships among nations for various decades. Not only are the states directly involved in the disputes impacted, but also those outside of it, who have been trying to reduce the tensions and find agreements on the multiple overlapping claims. The abundant natural resources in the area and its strategic geography put the disputes at the very centre of the states' national interests. As presented, the disputes are territorial, and the parties used historical (mostly China) and legal arguments (Philippines, Brunei, Malaysia and Vietnam) to support their claims.

Throughout the years, there have been attempts to decrease tensions and solve the SCS conflicts through bilateral and multilateral agreements. Due to failure in the maintenance of such agreements, the Philippines took their dispute with China to the Permanent Court of Arbitration, one of the UNCLOS dispute settlement mechanism. The Tribunal found that the disputed area fell within the Philippines' EEZ, which made China's claims legally and historically unsubstantiated. However, China's refusal to recognize the Tribunal's jurisdiction and final award highlighted the struggle of international law to resolve the dispute. Nevertheless, this chapter presented that compulsory adherence to the dispute settlement system and the multiple fora are two of the advantages of the UNCLOS. However, such are challenged by non-compliance and the lack of enforcing apparatuses within international law.

Additionally, when negotiations are the preferred method of settling disputes, such dispute resolution should definitely have a priority. However, it is important to ensure that this kind of mechanism is used properly to give voice and security to smaller states in the international arena. Hence, it provides a balance to the power dynamics of the international system, once less-influential states have the option of resorting to compulsory dispute settlement fora under UNCLOS to resolve conflicts. Moreover, it was shown that even when an attempt to settle a dispute through a judicial forum fails, it may still create a significant legacy in form of interpretation and clarification, which could lead to conflict resolution within and without such legal settings.

Figure 1.1. Maritime claims and UNCLOS exclusive economic zones (blue) in the South China Sea. Source: Goran tek-en/Wikimedia commons. https://upload.wikimedia.org/wikipedia/commons/4/4a/South_China_Sea_vector.svg

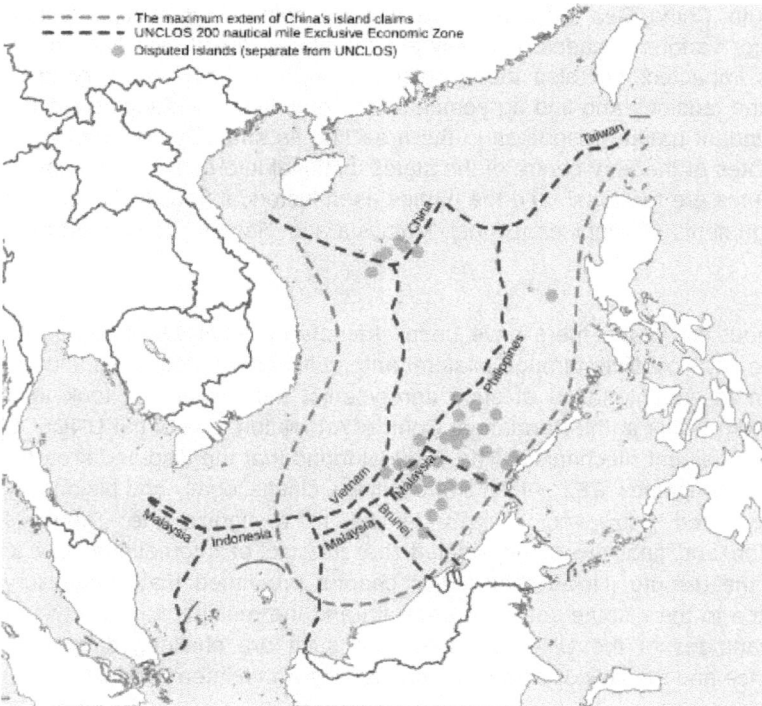

Figure 1.2. States' Individual Maritime Claims (IILSS 2021). Source naturalflow/Flickr.
https://www.flickr.com/photos/70693287@N00/14221014032

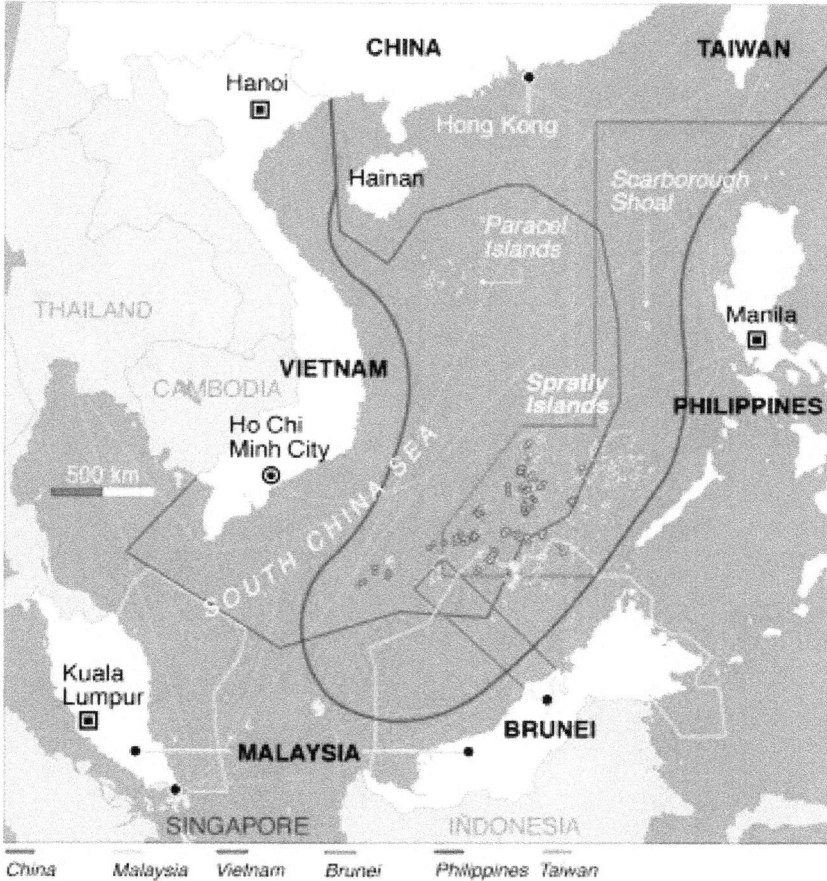

Figure 1.3. Nine-Dash Line Map attached to *Note Verbale* CML/17/2009 (PRC 2009). Source: United Nations/Wikimedia commons. https://commons. wikimedia.org/wiki/File:China%27s_2009_nine-dash_line_map_submission_ to_the_UN.pdf

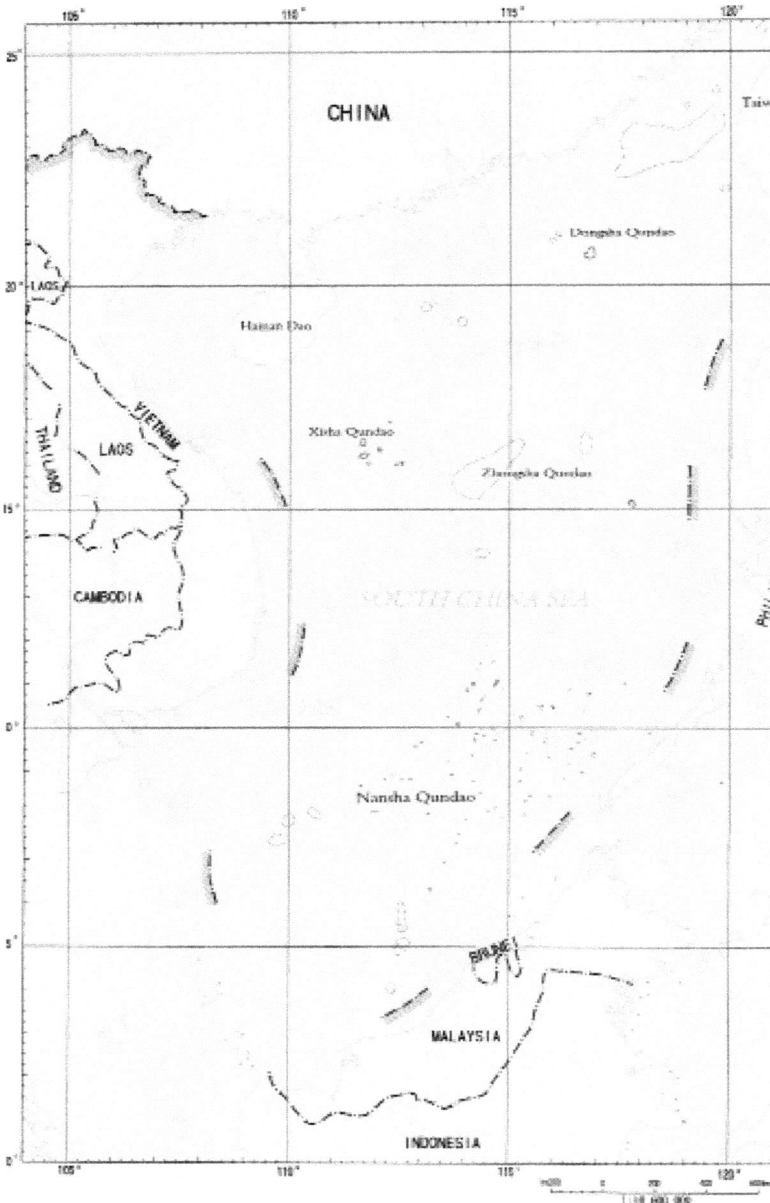

References

ASEAN [Association of Southeast Asian Nations] and PRC [People's Republic of China]. 2002. "2002 Declaration on the Conduct of Parties in the South China Sea." Accessed February 12, 2021. https://cil.nus.edu.sg/rp/pdf/2002%20Declaration%20on%20the%20Conduct%20of%20Parties%20in%20the%20South%20China%20Sea-pdf.pdf

Bader, Jeffrey A. 2014. "The U.S. and China's Nine-Dash Line: Ending the Ambiguity." Accessed February 9, 2021. https://www.brookings.edu/opinions/the-u-s-and-chinas-nine-dash-line-ending-the-ambiguity

BBC. 2016. "Why is the South China Sea Contentious?" February 10, 2021. http://www.bbc.co.uk/news/world-asia-pacific-13748349

_____. 2017. "South China Sea: Philippines' Duterte Sends Troops to Unoccupied Islands." https://www.bbc.com/news/world-asia-39519160

Brunei's Ministry of Defence. 2011. "Defence White Paper: Defending the Nation's Sovereignty. Expanding Roles in Wider Horizons." Accessed July 19, 2021. https://www.mindef.gov.bn/Defence%20White%20Paper/DWP%202011.pdf

Camba, Alvin. 2018. "Assessing Duterte's China Investment Drive." Accessed February 12, 2021. https://www.lowyinstitute.org/the-interpreter/assessing-dutertes-china-investment-drive

Churchill, Robin. 2017. "The General Dispute Settlement System of the UN Convention of the Law of the Sea: Overview, Context and Use." *Ocean Development and International Law* 48, no. 1: 216–238.

CFR [Council on Foreign Relations]. 2017. "Territorial Disputes in South China Sea". Accessed November 26, 2021, available in http://www.cfr.org/global/global-conflict-tracker/p32137#!/conflict/territorial-disputes-in-the-south-china-sea

CLCS [Commission on the Limits of the Continental Shelf]. 2009. Outer Limits of the Continental Shelf beyond 200 Nautical Miles from the Baseline. Submissions to de Commission: Joint Submission by Malaysia and the Socialist Republic of Viet Nam. Accessed February 26, 2022. https://www.un.org/depts/los/clcs_new/submissions_files/submission_mysvnm_33_2009.htm

Duterte, Rodrigo. 2020. "President Duterte's Speech at 75th UN General Assembly." https://www.rappler.com/nation/full-text-duterte-unga-speech-2020

EIA [US Energy Information Administration]. 2013. "South China Sea." Accessed February 9, 2021. https://www.eia.gov/beta/international/regions-topics.cfm?RegionTopicID=SCS

Greer, Adam. 2016. "The South China Sea is Really a Fishery Dispute." *The Diplomat*, July 20, 2016. https://thediplomat.com/2016/07/the-south-china-sea-is-really-a-fishery-dispute

GRID-Arendal. 2014. "Continental Shelf Programme: Background to UNCLOS." Accessed February 11, 2021. http://www.continentalshelf.org/about/1143.aspx

IISLL [International Institute for Law of the Sea Studies]. 2021. International Law in the South China Sea. Accessed February 28, 2022. http://iilss.net/international-law-in-the-south-china-sea/

Kaplan, Robert D. 2015. "Why the South China Sea is so Crucial." Accessed February 10, 2021. http://www.businessinsider.com.au/why-the-south-china-sea-is-so-crucial-2015-2

Khoo, Nicholas. 2016. "Manila's phyrrhc victory: ASEAN in disarray over the South China Sea". Accessed March 1, 2022. https://amti.csis.org/manilas-pyrrhic-victory-asean-disarray-south-china-sea/

Klein, Natalie. 2014. "The Effectiveness of the UNCLOS Dispute Settlement Regime: Reaching for the Stars?" In *Proceedings of the Annual Meeting (American Society of International Law)* 108, 359–364. Cambridge: Cambridge University Press.

Malaysia. 2017. *Malaysia Partial Submission to the Commission on the Limits of the Continental Shelf pursuant to Article 76, paragraph 8 of the United Nations on the Law of the Sea1982 in the South China Sea.* Kuala Lumpur: Malaysia. https://www.un.org/Depts/los/clcs_new/submissions_files/mys85_2019/20171128_MYS_ES_DOC_001_secured.pdf

Nguyen, Hong Thao. 2020. "Extended Continental Shelf: A Renewed South China Sea Competition." *Maritime Issues*, April 19, 2020. http://www.maritimeissues.com/uploaded/Nguyen%20Hong%20Thao_Extended%20Continental%20Shelf-A%20Renewed%20South%20China%20Sea%20Competition.pdf

Nguyen, Lan Ngoc. 2018. "The UNCLOS Dispute Settlement System: What Role Can it Play in Resolving Marine Disputes in Asia?" *Asian Journal of International Law* 8, no. 1: 91–115.

Nguyen, Thi Lan Anh. 2015. "Origins of the South China Sea Dispute." In *Territorial Disputes in the South China Sea,* edited by Jing Huang and Andrew Billon, 15–38. London: Palgrave Macmillan.

PRC [People's Republic of China]. 2009. *CML/17/2009 Submission by the PRC to the UN Commission on the Continental Shelf.* New York: United Nations. https://www.un.org/depts/los/clcs_new/submissions_files/mysvnm33_09/chn_2009re_mys_vnm_e.pdf

_____. 2014. *Position Paper of the Government of the People's Republic of China on the Matter of Jurisdiction in the South China Sea Arbitration Initiated by the Republic of the Philippines.* Beijing: People's Republic of China.

Putra, Brama A. 2021. "Comprehending Brunei Darussalam's Vanishing Claims in the South China Sea: China's Exertion of Economic Power and the Influence of Elite Perception." *Cogent Social Sciences* 7. DOI: 10.1080/23311886.2020.1858563.

Roach, Ashley J. 2014. "Malaysia and Brunei: An Analysis of their Claims in South China Sea." *CNA Occasional Paper*. https://www.cna.org/cna_files/pdf/iop-2014-u-008434.pdf

Rosen, Mark E. 2014. "Philippine Claims in the South China Sea: A Legal Analysis." *CNA Occasional Paper.* https://www.cna.org/cna_files/pdf/iop-2014-u-008435.pdf

Rüland, Jürgen. 2005. "The Nature of Southeast Asian Security Challenges." *Security Dialogue* 36, no. 4: 545–563. https://doi.org/10.1177/0967010605060453

Singh, Vinai K. 2016. "Analysis of Advantages and Disadvantages of Forums Prescribed Under the UNCLOS and State Practice: The Way Ahead for India." *Revista de Direito Internacional* 13, 319–336.

Strangio, Sebastian. 2020. "In UN Speech, Duterte Stiffens Philippines' Stance on the South China Sea." *The Diplomat*, September 23, 2020. https://thediplomat.com/2020/09/in-un-speech-duterte-stiffens-philippines-stance-on-the-south-china-sea

The Guardian. 2016. "Philippines to 'Set Aside' South China Sea Tribunal Ruling to Avoid Imposing on Beijing." December 17, 2016. https://www.theguardian.com/world/2016/dec/17/philippines-to-set-aside-south-china-sea-tribunal-ruling-to-avoid-imposing-on-beijing

_____. 2019. "South China Sea: Duterte Warns Beijing of 'Suicide Missions' to Protect Disputed Islands." April 5, 2019. https://www.theguardian.com/world/2019/apr/05/south-china-sea-duterte-warns-china-of-suicide-missions-to-protect-disputed-island

Tonnesson, Stein. 2000. "Vietnam's Objective in the South China Sea: National or Regional Security?" *Contemporary Southeast Asia* 22, no. 1: 199–220.

United Nations. 1967. *United Nations General Assembly Twenty-Second Session.* New York: United Nations.

_____. 1982. "United Nations Convention on the Law of the Sea." Accessed January 31, 2021. http://www.un.org/depts/los/convention_agreements/texts/unclos/unclos_e.pdf

_____. 1998. "Oceans and Law of the Sea - The United Nations Convention on the Law of the Sea - A Historical Perspective." Accessed February 11, 2021. https://www.un.org/Depts/los/convention_agreements/convention_historical_perspective.htm#Historical%20Perspective.

_____. 2020. "Chronological Lists of Ratifications of, Accessions and Successions to the Convention and Related Agreements." Accessed February 11, 2021. https://www.un.org/Depts/los/reference_files/chronological_lists_of_ratifications.htm

_____. 2021. "United Nations - Treaty Collection - Law of the Sea." Accessed February 11, 2021. https://treaties.un.org/Pages/ViewDetailsIII.aspx?src=TREATY&mtdsg_no=XXI-6&chapter=21&Temp=mtdsg3&clang=_en#EndDec

Welch, David A. 2016. The Hague's South China Sea Ruling: Implications for East Asian Security. Accessed February 11, 2022. https://www.asiapacific.ca/canada-asia-agenda/hagues-south-china-sea-ruling-implications-east-asian

2

The Role of ASEAN in the South China Sea Disputes

LETICIA SIMÕES

After the Cold War came to an end, the South China Sea (SCS) gradually rose in importance in terms of international security. Several countries have claimed islands, rocks, and adjacent waters there, and these claims are fiercely disputed even today. The SCS is one of the most important sea lines of communication (SLOCs) in the world, strategically positioned in terms of military and trade flow, and replete with marine natural resources, estimates of which are likely to increase exponentially once the studies regarding oil and gas resources in the region are complete and full extraction operations are underway. Four of the primary claimants (Vietnam, Malaysia, the Philippines, and Brunei) are members of the Association of Southeast Asian Nations (ASEAN). Of the two remaining claimants – the People's Republic of China (PRC) and the Republic of China (ROC) on Taiwan – Beijing has been the most dangerous to ASEAN members, having been responsible for a series of incidents since 1974. Hence, China's counterclaims against the ASEAN states, and its behaviour in prosecuting said counter-claims, will be the focus of this chapter, as the specifics of the ROC claims are discussed in separate chapter of this volume.

This chapter aims to analyse the position of ASEAN toward the SCS maritime disputes. In the first section, we present a brief history of the process known as the ASEAN Way, and the importance of the United Nations Convention on the Law of the Sea (UNCLOS), and how this is connected to the SCS disputes. In the second section, we show how ASEAN has reacted to the disputes, either collectively or individually as member-states, as well as how ASEAN members' policies on the disputes influence the association's decision-making process. In this section we aim to answer this specific question: What are the positions of ASEAN members, individually and as a whole, regarding the SCS disputes? In the third part we attempt to explain ASEAN's behaviour regarding the SCS issue aiming to answer these questions: Why has ASEAN failed to reach a common position, and how will the ASEAN Way affect the association's future development, in security terms?

The ASEAN Way and the South China Sea Disputes

Using the Bandung Conference of 1955 as inspiration, many Southeast Asian countries began attempting to establish supranational groups for regional solidarity. The Philippines proposed an anti-communist group, and this would be followed by many similar propositions from Manila. Most of these early attempts had an ethnic or religious component, which ended up narrowing the membership and not advancing the regionalisation project as quickly as expected. However, all these movements showed an interest in moving the region toward some sort of integration process (Ba 2009).

In 1961, despite a number of conflicts and rivalries deriving from a post-colonial sense of nationalism, the Association of Southeast Asia (ASA) was created, consisting of Thailand, the Philippines, and Malaya. In 1963, in the same spirit of seeking cooperation and solidarity among the Malay race, the Greater Malayan Confederation, or Maphilindo, was created, consisting of the Philippines, Indonesia, and Malaya (now Malaysia). Neither effort stood the test of time, however. Maphilindo failed to accommodate the rivalry between two of its members, and the ASA was weakened due to the lack of official relations between two of its three members. Once again, rival nationalisms would stand in the way of a Southeast Asian regional association (Ba 2009).

In 1967, an agreement between groups devoted to transnationalism and to forming an alternative type of regionalism enabled the creation of ASEAN. This was aided by the emergence of new ways of thinking about concepts such as nationalism and regionalism (Ba 2009).[1] At the time, regionalism and nationalism were largely mutually exclusive, at least in the eyes of many Southeast Asian leaders. Ideas of self-determination, national interest, and an ethic of non-interventionism – so strong in the immediate post-colonial era – were becoming allied to ideas such as unity, solidarity, and regional cohesion. This meant there was a search to end the conflicts between nations in the region, and led to the conditions necessary for a coalition of Southeast Asian States to arise (Ba 2009).

---

[1]   ASEAN was founded by the Bangkok Declaration in 1967. Its member countries are Malaysia, Philippines, Indonesia, Thailand and Singapore (1967), Brunei (1984), Vietnam (1995), Myanmar and Laos (1997), and Cambodia (1999).

Because of those conditions, ASEAN was founded under the following principles: non-interference; quiet diplomacy; no use of force; and decision-making through consensus – in other words, the ASEAN Way (Hazmi 2009). These principles have allowed the association, united through a regional proposal, to have a loose enough framework to accommodate countries with old rivalries so as not to threaten their continued sovereignty (Haacke 2002).

Today, the same ASEAN Way that was fundamental to the association's creation and establishment is responsible for hampering any emphatic action from the group in the face of maritime territorial claims against its members in the SCS. Those claims are directed connected to UNCLOS, created 15 years after ASEAN's foundation and impacting at least half of its members.

UNCLOS and the ASEAN Way

In 1982, the United Nations Convention on the Law of the Sea resulted in an agreement on the matter of nations' responsibilities and rights on the world's waterways. The competing claims in the SCS region began in earnest after World War II, but it received a new boost after the launch of UNCLOS and the promulgation of its rules governing the definition of territorial seas, exclusive economic zones (EEZ), and continental shelves, which would enable countries to expand their coastal territory and open new possibilities for the exploration of natural resources and maritime patrols (Beckman 2014).

UNCLOS established parameters for the exploration of resources, freedom of navigation, territorial rights, and dispute settlement. The treaty addresses issues including coastal states' sovereignty rights over sea territory and airspace,[2] and provides a conflict resolution mechanism in cases of disputes based on overlapping claims. It entered into force in 1994, by which time the Philippines (1984) and Vietnam (1994) had already ratified the treaty. Few years later, Malaysia and Brunei (1996) ratified it. Other ASEAN members have also ratified the treaty, including Indonesia (1986), Singapore (1994), Myanmar (1996), Laos (1998) and Thailand (2011). Cambodia signed the treaty in 1983 but never ratified it. China, which is not a member of ASEAN – but which has extensive relations with the bloc and has intense maritime and territorial disputes with them in the SCS – ratified the treaty in 1996.

UNCLOS is not the only mechanism through which to address ASEAN members' claims in the SCS. In 2002, ASEAN and China signed the Declaration on the Conduct of Parties in the South China Sea (DOC) that

---

[2]   Territorial sea: 12 nautical miles (nm) from the land; contiguous zone: 12nm from the end of a territorial sea; EEZ: up to 200nm from the land; continental shelf: up to 350nm from the end of a territorial sea. UNCLOS does not recognize claims based on historical arguments when it comes to territorial seas or EEZs.

applies the same principles as the 1967 ASEAN Charter to territorial disputes and uses UNCLOS as a basis for dealing with claims and disputes between ASEAN members and China. The DOC is a non-binding document, however, and does not have a dispute resolution mechanism, leaving its signatories to resolve their disagreements on a voluntary basis without taking the disputes to international institutions. The DOC was unable to gather a common position among ASEAN countries on China's claims against ASEAN members' territory, due largely to those members having different interests in the matter (Severino 2014).

Thus, without being able to move toward the desired Code of Conduct (COC), which has been under negotiation since 1999, and which would be binding and include dispute resolution mechanisms, the DOC remains an ineffective instrument. China is the main obstacle to the adoption of a COC, since any such code would restrict Beijing's claims (Thayer 2012). Given the level of tensions in the last few years, principally between the Philippines and China, as well as between Vietnam and China, a new attempt was made in 2017 to reach a basic agreement on the nature and scope of a new COC. In August of that year, the foreign ministers of ASEAN and their Chinese counterpart endorsed a framework for an updated version of a Code of Conduct for the South China Sea largely based on the 2002 DOC. Despite the fact that it specifically addressed conflict prevention and the assurance of freedom of navigation, the draft of the document still indicates that it, like its predecessor, would not be legally binding (Storey 2017).

The various disputes and claims in the SCS involve ASEAN members and actors that have direct relations with ASEAN. Therefore, such disputes and claims need to be analysed on an individual basis, but also on how they influence ASEAN's decision-making, carried out through consensus.

ASEAN Members' Individual Strategies.

The main claims in the SCS, defined as a semi-enclosed body of water, involve the Paracel and Spratly Islands. While the Paracel archipelago has been controlled by the PRC since 1974 and is claimed by Vietnam and the ROC, the Spratly Islands possess the greatest number of overlapping claims in the region, with China and the ROC making claims against islands held by Vietnam, the Philippines, Malaysia, and Brunei (Emmers 2003). A broad overview of those claims is provided in Table 2.1.

ASEAN members have different individual positions on the SCS issue. Only some members of the bloc are claimants, and among these there remain some border disputes, even if China is not included. Meanwhile, the Chinese economic and political influence affects every ASEAN country, though this effect is not homogeneous. Some members, especially non-claimants, put more emphasis on the bilateral relationship with China, and are less interested in negotiating with Beijing as a bloc. This effectively prohibits the ASEAN members from unifying their influence in a joint effort to solve territorial disputes collectively.

China's Position and Claims in the South China Sea

China is the most active claimant in the SCS and has the most territorial demands. The PRC government claims the SCS almost entirely, according to the nine-dash line map that Beijing submitted to the United Nations in 2009 when the Philippines, Vietnam, and Malaysia presented technical information in order to make submissions asking for permission to extend their continental shelf. The PRC government relies on a historical argument to justify its claims over the islands and what the PRC sees as adjacent waters (Beckman 2014).

China's demands exceed the legal claims established by UNCLOS, even though that treaty was ratified by Beijing. The PRC claims are based in a map named 'Map of Chinese Islands in the South China Sea,' originally issued in 1947 and therefore pre-dating the existence of the PRC and based on supposed historical rights dating back to the quasi-legendary Xia dynasty (c. 2070-1600 BC) – the very first dynasty to emerge in ancient China (Baumert and Melchior 2014). The PRC claim based on this ancient inheritance is for the entire area enclosed by the lines to be considered Chinese territorial waters. This runs counter to the 12 nautical miles conferred by UNCLOS rules on overlapping EEZ claims, territorial seas, and areas adjacent to several other countries in the region. It is worth noting that China is not the only actor in the SCS that is a signatory to UNCLOS and whose claims exceed what that document establishes as legal.

ASEAN Members Claims in the South China Sea

Vietnam

The South China Sea is Vietnam's lifeline. The country has fought several conflicts with neighbouring China over the years over the issue of sovereignty in the SCS. Like the PRC, Vietnam's claims include the Spratly and Paracel Islands.

Sino-Vietnamese relations have historically been tense. Although land border disputes between the two have been settled (Fravel 2008), the same cannot be said about their maritime disputes. The most contentious issue may be that of the Paracel Islands, which were controlled by Hanoi until China seized them during the Battle of the Paracel Islands (1974). Today, many of the Vietnamese claims overlap those of Malaysia and the Philippines. Vietnam joined ASEAN almost 20 years after its beginning and its influence as a major player in the institution took a long time to solidify.

What differentiates the Vietnamese and Chinese claims, beyond the total area, which in the case of Vietnam is slightly smaller, is that unlike China, which demands every area as its own territorial sea, Vietnam claims it as an EEZ (Elmore 2013). In the case of Vietnam, as with China, the region claimed by that country is bigger than what would be allowed by UNCLOS.

Considering the threat posed by China, Vietnam has not truly trusted ASEAN as an effective tool for dealing with the SCS disputes. In fact, in the case of the Spratly Islands, Vietnam leaned toward the internationalization of the issue, seeking help from several organizations and asking for the participation of other countries (including the United States, Japan, and India) in an effort to establish a wide arc, based on the UNCLOS perspective, which if successful would result in the dilution of Chinese power (Collinson and Roberts 2013). Also, Vietnam tried to take the issue to international arbitration in 2013, but this effort was blocked by China. At the same time, Vietnam has been enhancing its military position and strengthening its Navy and Coast Guard (Vuving 2014).

The Philippines

The Philippines does not claim the entire SCS, as do China, and to an extent Vietnam, but Manila also extrapolates upon what UNCLOS stipulates as its legal claims. The Philippines makes territorial demands of EEZs that represent an effort to expand its fishing industry, as claims are concentrated mainly in the abundant fishing zone area to the west of the country.

The Philippines launched territorial demands over some of the Spratly Islands, which puts it in conflict with China and Vietnam. The presence of Philippine fishing vessels in areas also claimed by China has been the catalyst for much of the confrontation between the two countries (Elmore 2013).

The Philippines was the first ASEAN member to be directly affected by China's military expansion in the SCS, and Manila appealed to the organization to help deal with the issue in 1995.[3] The Mischief Reef Incident of 1995, in which China built an installation on the Philippine-owned Mischief Reef, resulted in a remark included in the 1995 ASEAN Foreign Ministers' Meeting (AMM) Joint Communiqué condemning the unilateral Chinese action. Since then, the Philippines has employed many strategies to navigate the SCS border disputes (Severino 2014); one of them is pressing ASEAN to establish a Code of Conduct. As described above, this has only gone as far as a weaker Declaration of Conduct, which is non-binding.

Another strategy is looking for outside support to reaffirm the use of UNCLOS as the basic tool to achieve a solution. In 2014, taking a page from Vietnam's playbook of the previous year, Manila filed complaints in the Permanent Court of Arbitration at The Hague against Chinese assertiveness in the region. Despite a 2016 award that ruled in favour of the Philippines' position, China has so far refused to abide by the tribunal's ruling. Moreover, since the election of the China-friendly politician Rodrigo Duterte as president, the government of the Philippines has declined to press its rights as conferred by The Hague, and has largely adopted policies that are favourable to closer ties with China. This has reduced conflict on the disputed areas and led to Chinese promises of joint resource exploitation by both nations. Duterte's stance on the issue remains at odds with much of the electorate, as well as the country's political elite.

Malaysia

Malaysia's claims in the SCS involve the waters surrounding the eastern border of Peninsular Malaysia and East Malaysia (Sabah and Sarawak, on the island of Borneo) (Mahadzir 2014). Kuala Lumpur has avoided levelling too much public criticism at China, due in part to the influential ethnic Chinese group in that country (in 2020, 22.6% of Malaysia's population was classified as Chinese, with 69.6% Bumiputera, or ethnic Malay), as well as China's outsized influence on the Malaysian economy (Kaplan 2014; Hirschmann 2021). Although Kuala Lumpur has always sought a unified ASEAN position on the SCS border disputes, it has not shirked its responsibility to continue modernizing its military force while strengthening its military and economic ties with the United States (Mahadzir 2014).

Malaysia also makes EEZ claims over parts of the Spratly Islands, which unlike the Philippines, Vietnam, and China, are consistent the rules set down by UNCLOS. However, Malaysia claims that the islands of the Spratly archipelago that are within its EEZ should be considered Malaysian territory,

---

[3]   Although the Paracel Islands were seized from Vietnam in the 1970s, that country only became part of ASEAN in 1995.

which deviates somewhat from a strict reading of UNCLOS, as those islands are not inhabited and therefore are not covered.

Brunei

Like Malaysia, Brunei is careful not to criticize China in public, although the nine-dash line comes uncomfortably close to that country's shores. Therefore, its EEZ would be severely diminished if Chinese claims were considered valid. Inside ASEAN, Brunei has supported a unified position on the issue, but stresses much more the economic benefits of maintaining a relationship with China rather than focusing on the occasional incidents of Chinese belligerence against its neighbours in the SCS.

The only disputed feature for Brunei is Louisa Reef, although there is a difference of opinion on whether it constitutes an island or a rock (Roach 2014). Brunei recognizes that the whole SCS issue should be solved using a multilateral approach (Storey 2005). Some interpretations claim that Brunei, in 2018, abandoned its maritime claims in the SCS in exchange for Chinese funding (Hart 2018). However, there are researchers that still claim that while Brunei maintains a low profile on the Louisa atoll issue, it has not necessarily given up those bases (Tiezzi 2018). Due to the geographical proximity, there are overlapping claims between Brunei's EEZ with the EEZ of Indonesia, Malaysia, and the Philippines (Elmore 2013).

ASEAN Members Without Claims in the SCS

Indonesia

Indonesia is the biggest country in ASEAN, both by population and by GDP. Therefore, it should be expected that it would undertake a leadership role in steering the organization. That potential guidance suffered a setback with the 1997 Asian financial crisis and the fall of the Suharto government after three decades in power. Since then, Indonesia has tried to play a tertiary role in the many of the main issues in ASEAN, and the SCS disputes are no exception.

Even before the 1997 crisis or the 1995 Mischief Reef Incident, Indonesia had already tried to defuse the security challenges involving the SCS. Not an official claimant to any part of the disputed areas – although China's nine-dash line overlaps the Indonesian Natuna gas fields – Jakarta is more concerned with maritime security and freedom of navigation. In trade terms, China has invited Indonesia to be an essential part of the so-called Maritime Silk Road (Tiezzi 2014).

Indonesia does not have disputes with China in the SCS, and its demands are within the stipulations prescribed under UNCLOS as legal, and are solely for economic purposes. Indonesia's EEZ is very close to those of Brunei, Vietnam, Malaysia, and the Philippines, however (Elmore 2013). On the other hand, it is important to highlight that tensions with Beijing have been rising due to constant incursions into the area by Chinese vessels caught fishing illegally in the waters off the Natuna Islands. According to Jakarta, these islands are located within the country's 200-nautical-mile EEZ. However, this area overlaps with the southernmost dash in China's nine-dash line. So far, Indonesia has adamantly refused to recognize that the area is in dispute. At the same time, it has disclosed videos showing the sinking of Chinese fishing boats and beefed up its maritime forces to keep Chinese fishermen out of the area (Chew 2021).

Singapore

Although Singapore is a small city-state, it represents a potent diplomatic and military force among ASEAN members due to its high GDP per capita (Kaplan 2014). In the SCS disputes, Singapore adopts a conciliatory tone – a position that is helped by the fact that it is not directly affected by the disputes. Singapore has close military ties with the United States, however, and defends maritime security and freedom of navigation in the area.

Thailand

Due to Bangkok's strong economic ties with China and the fact that it has no claims in the SCS, Thailand usually adopts a soft approach toward SCS issues, and refrains from blaming China.

Laos and Myanmar

Like Thailand, both Laos and Myanmar enjoy major economic ties with China. Moreover, they share borders with that country. Since they are not party to any disputes in the SCS, they therefore usually defer to Chinese pressure and assist in deflecting attempts by other ASEAN members to introduce harsh remarks against Beijing in the association's reports and communiqués.

Cambodia

Not located in the SCS, Cambodia strongly supports China due to economic ties and as a tool to minimize Hanoi's influence, Phnom Penh's main geopolitical rival. In practice, Cambodia has been the main supporter of

Chinese discourse within ASEAN, especially when the discussion turns to the DOC and COC. Cambodia supports China's desire for a more flexible document to govern the approach to disputes and overlapping claims in the SCS (Thayer 2012).

Bilateral relations between Beijing and Phnom Penh are not new, and there is cooperation between the two countries in the political, economic, cultural, and military realms. This approach has recently been called the Comprehensive Strategic Partnership of Cooperation between the People's Republic of China and the Kingdom of Cambodia (Siphat 2015).

For China, Cambodia is a central ally in Southeast Asia. For Cambodia, China is the main source of foreign assistance as well as foreign capital. In addition, the Chinese have become managers and investors in Cambodian state-owned enterprises and bilateral economic interactions have increased, which may explain Cambodia's support for China in matters related to the disputes in the SCS, including in the ASEAN decision-making process (Siphat 2015).

Countries' Influence in ASEAN's Decision Making

ASEAN's decision-making is done by consensus at annual meetings such as the aforementioned AMM. The association's loose structure, which is an essential component of its success and indeed its very genesis, derives from the ASEAN Way, and while it can be seen as an asset, it is as a weakness.

The member states of ASEAN usually focus strongly on their individual priorities, and with few exceptions are not really reaping the benefits (or the costs) of being part of a supranational organization. To analyse the association's decision-making process, seven important ASEAN meetings that dealt with difficult decisions regarding the SCS disputes will be examined.

The 1992 25th AMM, Manila

Issued in the Philippine capital, the Manila Declaration (ASEAN 1992), while vague, called for a peaceful resolution of any territorial disputes in the SCS and for cooperation in many areas, along with a Code of Conduct to be further developed. The conference took place against the backdrop of rapid Chinese militarisation, its assertive behaviour around the Spratly Islands, and Beijing's passage on 25 February 1992 of the Law of the People's Republic of China on the Territorial Sea and the Contiguous Zone, which essentially laid claim to the entire SCS. Indonesia and the Philippines (as chair and host of the meeting, respectively) wanted to deal directly with the issue, but Malaysia and Brunei resisted the issuance of a more assertive statement that might have raised Beijing's ire. Since there were only six members in attendance at that conference, and the consensus of opinion was that Chinese opposition to the meeting could derail it, the watered-down declaration that was issued after the meeting, while calling for restraint and joint exploration, completely omitted any mention of the issue of sovereignty (Emmers 2003; Garofano 2002).

The 1995 28th AMM, Bandar Seri Begawan

After the political weakness exhibited at the Manila AMM, things slowly began to improve. Three years later, member countries of ASEAN exhibited the capacity to work together, especially with Vietnam newly installed as the seventh ASEAN member after having suffered at the hands of Chinese aggression in the Mischief Reef incident described above. This time, the incident was not ignored, but made it into the text of the Joint Communiqué (ASEAN 1995), though the representatives from Hanoi had to exert significant pressure to accomplish this (Emmers 2003). The other members in attendance claimed the incident was irrelevant; their governments having been placated by Chinese promises that it was a one-time thing, and would not happen again.

The 2002 35th AMM, Bandar Seri Begawan

While the quest for a Code of Conduct has been underway since the 1992 Manila Declaration, and the idea consistently received praise in successive AMM Joint Communiqués, building up expectations that it would serve as the ideal final step toward solving the SCS disputes once and for all, it has yet to be achieved. An important step in this direction – some might say a compromise – was made the following decade, however. In 2002, at the 35th AMM hosted by Brunei, the idea of non-binding DOC was adopted, after being proposed by Malaysian Foreign Minister Syed Hamid Albar.

The idea was designed to break the political deadlock between ASEAN member states, which each had concerns and stipulations on what they wanted to see in a COC. Vietnam, for example, wanted the code to encompass the entire South China Sea, whereas Malaysia wanted to restrict its scope to the Spratly Islands. No agreement could be reached on the issues of new occupation and military exercises, either. Moreover, while the Philippines pushed hard to validate a COC, Malaysia was against it on the grounds that it would likely freeze any new construction on the disputed features – a practice that Malaysia was engaged in. The non-binding declaration not only represented a compromise, in the time-tested manner of the ASEAN Way, but China's acceptance of the DOC hinted that Beijing might be softening its stance against multilateral negotiations (having long employed the divide-and-conquer approach of insisting on bilateral negotiations) and could be enticed to work together with ASEAN (Mahadzir 2014; Emmers 2003; Thuy 2009).

The 2010 43rd AMM, Hanoi

Vietnam tried to use its position as chair of the meeting to internationalize the SCS question, with the aid of the United States, which declared that it was one of its diplomatic priorities and that it could play the role of mediator (Collinson and Roberts 2013). China, of course, was upset at the notion. As for the implementation of the 2002 DOC, Vietnam resumed the work of the ASEAN-China Joint Working Group, but only after China (through Cambodia) made sure that any activity or project would be duly reported to the ASEAN-China Ministerial Meeting (Collinson and Roberts 2013).

The 2012 45th AMM, Phnom Penh

The 45th AMM marked the first time that ASEAN failed to reach a consensus and did not issue a Joint Communiqué. The drafters of the document insisted on including a paragraph elaborating upon the SCS disputes. Cambodia, which was both host and chair of the meeting, vetoed the move, blaming the Philippines and Vietnam for the failure to reach a consensus. During the meeting, the Filipino representative spoke of the Chinese expansion and aggression since the 1990s, and how Beijing's actions were disrespecting the DOC and the principles of UNCLOS. The Vietnamese representative described his worries about the Chinese imposition of the nine-dash line and mentioned violations of Vietnamese sovereignty and jurisdiction over its territorial waters, EEZ, and continental shelf (Thayer 2012). Both Vietnam and the Philippines asked the meeting chair to include in the final Joint Communiqué mention of the Chinese aggressions in these two cases, but Cambodia refused. In addition to Cambodia, Thailand, Brunei, Laos and Myanmar were also against mentioning the SCS aggressions, since it could jeopardize peaceful relations between ASEAN and China, and hence imperil regional stability. On the other hand, the Philippines, Vietnam, Singapore, Indonesia, and Malaysia insisted that a paragraph be included in the Joint Communiqué remarking on the incidents.[4] With that split decision, and amid acrimonious debate, no Joint Communiqué was issued that year.

---

[4]   This vote tally was achieved after reading Thayer's (2012) transcripts of the Meeting and interpreting each Minister's position. Nevertheless, it should be stressed that, according to Thayer, 'each of these documents was provided to the author by sources that must remain confidential' (2012).

The 2014 47th AMM, Nay Pyi Taw

At the meeting in Myanmar, Indonesia supported Manila's requests for a freeze on activities that would escalate tensions in the SCS, the completion of COC, and the use of international arbitration to settle disputes (Tiezzi 2014). The Joint Communiqué was detailed over the issue and expressed serious concerns about the situation. Nevertheless, the ASEAN position was much less assertive than what the Philippines and Vietnam had hoped for, as both countries had been embroiled in incidents involving Chinese incursions into what they considered to be their waters.

In Vietnam's case, China had deployed its Hai Yang Shi You 981 oil platform to waters near the disputed Paracel Islands in South China Sea, and while Vietnamese vessels attempted to prevent the platform from assuming a fixed position, Chinese ships began ramming into them and firing water cannon. The incident came to be known as the Hai Yang Shi You 981 standoff, and led to anti-Chinese protests in Vietnam that escalated into riots. Meanwhile, tensions between the Philippines and China had been escalating as well, after the arrest by Philippine law enforcement of 11 Chinese poachers for harvesting endangering turtles, even as China had been using its Salami slicing tactics to drive Philippine fishermen away from disputed areas (The Guardian 2014).

The 2020 53th, AMM, Vietnam – Video Conference

The Joint Communiqué, despite the escalation of the COVID-19 pandemic, was very similar to the 2019 Joint Communiqué and indicated that the search was still on for a full implementation of the DOC. It emphasized the importance of cooperative relations between China and ASEAN and the efforts made to continue the second reading of the Single Project of the COC Negotiating Text, which started the previous year. However, there were moments of tension as activities in the SCS were raised at the meeting, which displeased certain states and raised tensions.

External ASEAN Member's Influence in ASEAN's Decision-Making Process

Until 1984, the five original members of ASEAN shared a number of characteristics, one of which was staunch anti-communism, with led to a deep distrust of the PRC's expansionism. This pattern continued with Brunei, a former British protectorate, but after the Cold War, such a stance became less important, at least in ideological terms. Nevertheless, the fear of uncontrolled Chinese expansionism subsisted and was taken seriously by the ASEAN's hard-core original members.

This changed with the admission of Vietnam, Laos, Myanmar, and Cambodia – all of which are either communist, authoritarian, or some mixture thereof – into the group, blending the core's relatively waning mistrust of Beijing with the newcomers' deep economic and political dependence on China. Even hard-core members, such as Thailand, gradually softened their position toward the PRC, as they enjoyed soaring trade and investment with China and were not SCS claimants.

It is worth mentioning that ASEAN's geographical concentration was diminished somewhat after the entrance of Laos, Myanmar, and Cambodia, which do not have a shoreline on the SCS, while all of the other seven members (with the exception of Thailand) have at least some manner of maritime border there. It is not random chance that Laos, Myanmar, Cambodia, and Thailand tend to vote more often for a compromise with China.

ASEAN's Behaviour in the South China Sea: The Lack of an Assertive Position

ASEAN has been successful in bringing peace to a troubled region since its inception in 1967. The ASEAN Way transformed Southeast Asia 'into a *de facto* security community, where it is almost inconceivable for any member-nation to wage war against another. Preventive diplomacy and cooperative security are the name of the game in ASEAN. However, when it comes to the SCS disputes, involving ASEAN members and China, the regional body has yet to craft an optimal response' (Heydarian 2015, para 11).

ASEAN and its own unique take on regionalism cannot be fully explained by classic regional integration theories such as neofunctionalism (Haas 1958) or regime theory, (Kasner 1982) or through newer approaches such as institutional bargaining (Aggarwal and Koo 2008; Aggarwal and Dupont 2005). Nevertheless, those theories can give us interesting insights into the reasons behind ASEAN's lack of assertiveness on the issue of the SCS disputes.

It was the activities of various interest groups pushing integration, as presented by Ba (2009) that were instrumental in ASEAN's creation in the first place. At the regional level, these interest groups' activities were mostly connected to trade and economic issues. The role of governments is much more important than the role of supranational institutions; mainly because of the dynamics of the ASEAN Way. As for the region's political parties, they did not carry any weight when it came to the establishment of ASEAN's brand of regionalism. All of these elements are central to classic neofunctionalist theory to explain the success of regional integration inside and outside Europe (Ruggie et al. 2005).

The creation of supranational institutions and organizations inside of a bloc is a central characteristic of neofunctionalist theory. ASEAN does not possess supranational institutions because supranationalism requires that the supranational organization have enforcement power over its members, which is absent in ASEAN.

The mechanism of loyalty transfer presented by Haas (1958) as the last step in neofunctionalist theory is the furthest ASEAN is from, and the reason for this is very well exemplified in the SCS disputes. Even with the economic integration that ASEAN has experienced, there will not be loyalty transfer from the national to the supranational level. First, this is because in ASEAN there is no supranational organization in the strict sense of the term. Second, ASEAN members have old but latent rivalries that would act against any such identification. The third reason is that member-states are not ready to give up any part of their sovereignty to the supranational level.

In the case of the SCS disputes that ASEAN members have with China, ASEAN behaviour and actions are weak. This is not only because of the ASEAN Way, but also because of the individualist positions of the association's members and their fear of giving over any sovereignty to the kind of strong regional institutions, led by ASEAN, that could represent their interests in such negotiations.

Analysing ASEAN's position through the lens of regime theory (Krasner 1982), we can assume that principles, norms, rules and decision-making procedures within an institution help actors' expectations converge in a given issue-area. In the case of the SCS disputes, it can be said that, after more than 20 years trying to craft a common, assertive position to solve the problem, ASEAN has achieved little. The disputes still stand, even among some of its own members. This is worsened by the intractability of the Chinese stance.

In this sense, ASEAN exhibits discernible principles: striving for the stability of the region, usually through the non-use of violence. But the ASEAN Way, with its loose approach to most of the matters concerning members' individual positioning vis-à-vis the organization, is a rarefied set of norms, which offers little in terms of obligations and in terms of rights, especially as regards security issues. That is, any specific problem menacing one or some of the members is not necessarily seen by the others as a problem for the whole organization.

Such a loose set of norms results in a lack of rules, and therefore hampers the organization's ability to elaborate prescriptions for action. In fact, the most common decision taken by ASEAN in dealing with SCS disputes has been to exhort all the claimants to calm down, abide by the DOC, and await the coming of the COC. With this porous institutional architecture, the decision-making process does not seem well-enough equipped to cope with problems like the SCS disputes.

Unlike what regime theory would suggest, these decision-making procedures achieve a limited collective choice in ASEAN, since it is so heavily influenced by each member's individual interests. In this manner, it stands in the way of the formation of a real regime, according to the theory. With this dynamic, it is no surprise that those ASEAN members that are claimants in the SCS disputes have started looking for other alternatives, outside the association itself.

Interpreting ASEAN and its position regarding the SCS disputes through the institutional bargaining approach is interesting. Institutional bargaining tries to measure the degree of integration in different processes and institutions, and can be applied to understanding different situations that a group as ASEAN has to face. This is why there is weight given to factors such as number of participants, strength, and institutional delegation – factors that can be objectively measured (Aggarwal and Koo 2008; Aggarwal and Dupont 2005).

In terms of participants, ASEAN has doubled in size since its inception – from the original five members to ten. Although in theory, this should lead to a more robust institution, in the case of ASEAN it has wrought a worsening of the decision-making process. After all, ASEAN employs a consensus-based procedure to reach decisions. Therefore, building a consensus with ten members is more difficult than it is with five.

Therefore, by this factor alone, the greater number of participants would make it more difficult to reach consensus. But the presence of members that are influenced by China, due to its economic and political power, only worsens the prospects for swift and assertive decision-making, especially in issue areas where a security problem might arise that would affect China or its interests. So, in terms of the number of participants, the enlargement only brought greater inefficiency and an inability to achieve a more assertive solution, at least regarding the SCS disputes.

From the perspective of strength, which includes the degree to which agreements are binding, the ASEAN Way surely harms – or at least does not help – the interests of ASEAN members when dealing with the SCS disputes. Individual interests are put ahead of collective ones and any enforcement is hardly conceivable. This feature demonstrates that if the ASEAN Way was the innovation needed to heal a rivalry-stricken developing region in the 1960s, it has since become a clear obstacle to tackling security issues derived from foreign pressure.

As to the issues described by Aggarwal and Dupont (2005), institutional delegation is minimal, which promotes almost no autonomy of institutional organs. That lack of autonomy, and investing too much decision-making power in the ASEAN Ministerial Meetings and Summits, only highlights the importance of the latter. As we have seen, however, the SCS issue has been systematically swept under the rug due to the characteristics of the process already described.

Conclusion

ASEAN has been successful in diluting security rivalries between members and avoiding new conflicts among them. But the deepening of the integration process came in the economic area. In other areas, like cultural relationships, anti-piracy measures, and disaster management, there has been only tepid development. In political terms, the process has somehow stalled, especially in terms of achieving common guidelines to deal with critical problems derived from external pressure. In those cases, it seems that it is not the organization's cohesion or consensus which is important to most countries, but rather their individual interests.

ASEAN can be described as an inward-looking institution, in political terms, looking to ease internal tensions. Therefore, it is not surprising that it faces many problems when trying to deal with external confrontations. As Heydarian points out, 'when it comes to the SCS disputes, involving ASEAN members and China, the regional body has yet to craft an optimal response [...] ASEAN isn't equipped with the legal mandate and bureaucratic capacity to enforce compliance with regionally accepted principles and rules' (2015, para 12).

The ASEAN Way was instrumental in creating ASEAN from scratch by putting together regional concepts and national issues to reach a stable political environment in Southeast Asia. But this characteristic is an obstacle to enforcing common views about external pressures.

Moreover, ASEAN has not been successful in solving the border disputes among its members, and even less successful in dealing with the border disputes between those members and China. Full implementation of the DOC, which would ideally lead to a COC, seems infeasible in the short term.

Finally, we can answer the three questions presented at the beginning of this chapter, and which are central to understanding ASEAN's dilemma. The position of ASEAN's ten members regarding the disputes in the SCS are quite different, and vary slightly according to their geographical position (how close they are to the SCS), their territorial or economic claims in the region (balancing defence and economic concerns) and the type of relationship they have with China. This wide variation in conditions also directly impacts the association's position on how to address the conflicts in the SCS. This posture is linked to the ASEAN Way which, due to its very nature, leads to a reinforcement of individual interests over collective or supranational ones.

As for the last two questions, it is worth mentioning that the many different positions on the disputes and the loose structure of the association that prevents ASEAN from taking a more assertive stance on issues related to the SCS. In this sense, the ASEAN Way will very likely continue to weaken the association in terms of security and defence, despite its strength in establishing economic and socio-political ties in the region, thus forcing its members to seek other mechanisms, outside of the institution, to deal with such matters.

Table 2.1. Number of occupied features in the disputed Spratly Islands, Paracel Islands and others (2021). Sources: Banlaoi (2009) and AMTI.CSIS (2021)

Countries	Spratly	Paracel	Others
Vietnam	21	-	6 (DK1 Stations)[5]
Philippines	9	-	-
PRC	7	20	1 (Scarborough Shoal)
Malaysia	5	-	-
ROC	1	-	-

---

[5]   The Dịch vụ-Khoa (DK1), also called economic, scientific, and technological service stations, are a series of isolated sea platforms built by Hanoi in the southern Spratly Islands. The 14 platforms are steel structures that support logistics and living facilities and are operated by the Vietnam Navy (AMTI.CSIS 2021).

References

Aggarwal, Vinod K., and Cedric Dupont. 2005. "Collaboration and Coordination in the Global Political Economy." *Global Political Economy*, 28–49.

Aggarwal, Vinod K., and Min Gyo Koo. 2008. "Asia's New Institutional Architecture: Evolving Structures for Managing Trade, Financial, and Security Relations." In *Asia's New Institutional Architecture*, 1–34. Heidelberg: Springer.

AMTI [Asia Maritime Transparency Initiative]. 2021. "Island Tracker Archive." https://amti.csis.org/island-tracker

ASEAN [Association of Southeast Asian Nations]. 1992. "1992 Declaration on the South China Sea."

_____. 1995. "Joint Communique 28th ASEAN Ministerial Meeting."

Ba, Alice D. 2009. *(Re) Negotiating East and Southeast Asia: Region, Regionalism, and the Association of Southeast Asian Nations*. Stanford: Stanford University Press.

Banlaoi, Romme C. 2019. "Renewed Tensions and Continuing Maritime Security Dilemma in the South China Sea: A Philippine Perspective." In *The South China Sea: Cooperation for Regional Security and Development*, edited by Tran Truong Thuy, 143–159. Hanoi: Diplomatic Academy of Vietnam.

Baumert, Kevin, and Brian Melchior. 2014. "China: Maritime Claims in the South China Sea (Limits in the Seas No. 143)." US Department of State Bureau of Oceans and International Environmental and Scientific Affairs.

Chew, Amy. 2021. "Indonesia Arms Maritime Force Amid Chinese, Vietnamese Fishing Boat Incursions." *South China Morning Post*, January 10, 2021. http://archive.today/pP10B.

Collinson, Gary, and Christopher B. Roberts. 2013. "The Role of ASEAN." *The South China Seas and Australia's Regional Security Environment*, no. 5: 35–39.

Elmore, Tom. 2013. "The South China Sea: Every Nation for Itself." Army Command and General Staff Coll Fort Leavenworth Ks School of Advanced Military Studies.

Emmers, Ralf. 2012. *Cooperative Security and the Balance of Power in ASEAN and the ARF*. New York: Routledge.

Fravel, Taylor. 2008. *Strong Borders, Secure Nation: Cooperation and Conflict in China's Territorial Disputes*. Princeton: Princeton University Press.

Garofano, John. 2002. "Power, Institutions, and the ASEAN Regional Forum: A Security Community for Asia?" *Asian survey* 42, no. 3: 502–521.

Haas, Ernst B. 1958. *The Uniting of Europe: Political, Social, and Economic Forces, 1950-1957*. Stanford: Stanford University Press.

Hart, Michael. 2018. "Brunei Abandons South China Sea Claim for Chinese Finance." *Geopolitical Monitor*, April 4, 2018.

Hazmi, Adli. 2020. "What is 'ASEAN Way'?" Seasia, January 20, 2020. https://seasia.co/2020/01/21/what-is-ASEAN-way

Heydarian, Richard J. 2015. "Face-Off: China vs. ASEAN in the South China Sea and Beyond." *National Interest*, January 9, 2015. https://nationalinterest.org/feature/face-china-vs-asean-the-south-china-sea-beyond-12000

Hirschmann, Raudhah. 2021. "Breakdown of Population by Ethnicity Malaysia 2019-2021." Statista, August 10. https://www.statista.com/statistics/1017372/malaysia-breakdown-of-population-by-ethnicity

Kaplan, Robert D. 2015. *Asia's Cauldron: The South China Sea and the End of a Stable Pacific*. New York: Random House Trade Paperbacks.

Krasner, Stephen D. 1982. "Structural Causes and Regime Consequences: Regimes as Intervening Variables." *International Organization* 36, no. 2: 185–205.

Mahadzir, Dzirham. 2014. "Malaysia's Maritime Claims in the South China Sea: Security and Military Dimensions." In *Entering Unchartered Waters? ASEAN and the South China Sea*, edited by Pavin Chachavalpongpun, 208–222. Singapore: ISEAS-Yusof Ishak Institute.

Roach, J. Ashley. 2014. *Malaysia and Brunei: An Analysis of Their Claims in the South China Sea*. Virginia: CNA Corporation.

Ruggie, John Gerard, Peter J. Katzenstein, Robert O. Keohane, and Philippe C. Schmitter. 2005. "Transformations in world politics: the intellectual contributions of Ernst B. Haas." *Annual Review of Political Science* 8, no. 1: 271–296.

Severino, Rodolfo C. 2014. "The Philippines and the South China Sea." In *Entering Unchartered Waters? ASEAN and the South China Sea*, edited by Pavin Chachavalpongpun, 166–207. Singapore: ISEAS-Yusof Ishak Institute.

Siphat Touch. 2015. "Patterns and Impacts of Chinese Assistance in Cambodia." In *Impact of China's Rise on the Mekong Region*, edited by Yos Santasombat, 195–225. London: Palgrave Macmillan.

Storey, Ian. 2005. "China's Thirst for Energy Fuels Improved Relations with Brunei." *China Brief* 5, no. 24: 8–10.

_____. 2017. "Assessing the ASEAN-China Framework for the Code of Conduct for the South China Sea." *Perspective*, no. 62: 1–7. https://www.iseas.edu.sg/images/pdf/ISEAS_Perspective_2017_62.pdf.

Thayer, Carlyle A. 2012. "ASEAN's Code of Conduct in the South China Sea: A Litmus Test for Community-Building?" *The Asia Pacific Journal* 10, no. 34, August.

The Guardian. 2014. "Tensions Rise in South China Sea as Vietnamese Boats Come Under Attack." May 7, 2014. https://www.theguardian.com/world/2014/may/07/chinese-vietnamese-vessels-clash-south-china-sea

Thuy, Tran Truong. 2009. "Compromise and Cooperation on the Sea: The Case of Signing the Declaration on the Conduct of Parties in the South China Sea." In *Proceedings of the International Workshop on 'The South China Sea: Cooperation for Regional Security and Development', co-organized by the Diplomatic Academy of Vietnam and the Vietnam Lawyers' Association*, Hanoi, November 26–27, 2009. http://www.cliostein.com/South%20China%20Sea/Conference/Special%20publication%20Hanoi%20scs%20workshop%202009.pdf

Tiezzi, Shannon. 2014. "China Woos Indonesia's New President." *The Diplomat*, November 5, 2014.

_____. 2018. "In Brunei, China Woos Rival South China Sea Claimant." *The Diplomat*, November 21, 2018.

Vuving, Alexander L. 2014. "Vietnam, the US, and Japan in the South China Sea." *The Diplomat*, November 26, 2014.

3

Understanding the Senkaku/ Diaoyu Islands Dispute: Diplomatic, Legal, and Strategic Contexts

YOICHIRO SATO AND ASTHA CHADHA

The Senkaku Islands, controlled by Japan, are also claimed by the People's Republic of China (PRC), which refers to them as the Diaoyu Dao, as well as the Republic of China (ROC) in Taiwan, which calls them the Diaoyutai Lieyu.[1] Japan's administrative control at present is facing a growing challenge from the PRC's Coast Guard and other naval assets. The tacit diplomatic stalemate, in which Beijing claims the islands but has neither brought an international legal case against Japan nor mounted a kinetic attempt to seize them that rises to the level of a casus belli, while Tokyo is refraining from enhancing its administrative control yet denies the existence of a dispute altogether, has continued to drift into competitive efforts over control of the islands in the post-Cold War period. This chapter discusses the Senkaku/ Diaoyu island dispute between Japan and China and analyses it using aspects of territorial and maritime sovereignty, international law, natural resource exploration, and the role of the United States, as well as the geopolitical implications of the same. The Chinese attempt to keep the United States on the sidelines as a neutral party outside the conflict, while Japan's lobbying of Washington attempts to clarify the US commitment to the defense of the islands through the bilateral alliance. The Sino-US rivalry that has been growing since the administration of US President Barack Obama has favoured Japan's desire for rhetorical US support, but Japan has concurrently

---

[1]   Hereafter, the Japanese name will be used for general references to the island group, but the Chinese name will be used in describing China's claims.

built its own maritime forces in order to balance against the increasingly assertive Chinese activities.

A Diplomatic Context on the Question of Sovereignty

Sino-Japanese relations have been severely affected by bilateral disputes, which range from their respective interpretation of history to national positions on maritime and territorial conflicts. However, the dispute concerning sovereignty over the Senkaku Islands has, over the past few decades, accelerated geopolitical tensions in the East China Sea (ECS). Presently administered by Japan, the uninhabited islands of the Senkaku chain comprise five islets – Uotsuri Island, Kuba Island, Taisho Island, Kitakojima Island, and Minamikojima Island – and three rocks – Tobise Island, Okinokitaiwa Island, and Okinominamiiwa Island (Hamakawa 2007).[2] Located 190 nautical miles away from the southwest coast of Okinawa, the Senkaku/Diaoyu islands are in close proximity to China's east coast (200 nautical miles) and Taiwan's northwest coast (120 nautical miles) (Pedrozo 2016).

These islands lie on the key sea lines of communication in the ECS, but only became part of an intense Sino-Japanese maritime conflict in the late 1960s after surveys by the United Nations Economic Commission for Asia and the Far East announced that there may be massive oil and hydrocarbon reserves off the Senkaku Islands (Chansoria 2018). Subsequently, in 1970–1971, the PRC government claimed that the Diaoyu (Senkaku) Islands are historically part of Taiwan, which China also claims as its own territory, making the islands sovereign Chinese territory. Japan, meanwhile, cited legal assertions based in international law as the basis for its sovereignty over the Senkaku Islands, which it has enjoyed de facto control over since 1895 without any complaints from China. The official position of the PRC is that 'Diaoyu Dao is China's inherent territory in all historical, geographical and legal terms,' according to historical evidence of the islands being administered as part of Taiwan since the Ming and Qing dynasties (MOFA of PRC 2012). But Chinese historical assertions are largely based on historical evidence, mainly under three broad categories – the use and naming of the islands by China, the jurisdiction of the islands during the Ming dynasty, and maps from the era illustrating the islands as Chinese territory.

To support its claims, Beijing makes reference to records from the Ming and Qing dynasties, including reports like Chen Kan's record, dating to 1534, of imperial Chinese envoys sent to Ryukyu for imperial-title conferring (*Shi Liu Qiu Lu*), which mentions the route from China to Ryukyu, passing by 'Diaoyu Dao, Huangmao Yu, Chi Yu' until the land of Ryukyu marked by Gumi

---

[2]   China calls these formations Diaoyu Dao, Huangwei Yu, Chiwei Yu, Nanxiao Dao, Beixiao Dao, Nan Yu, Bei Yu, Fei Yu, respectively (MOFA of PRC 2012).

Mountain (today's Kume Island). The Chinese claims hold that 'Diaoyu Dao and Chiwei Yu belong to China and Kume Island belongs to Ryukyu, and that the separating line lies in Hei Shui Gou (today's Okinawa Trough) between Chiwei Yu and Kume Island' (People's Daily 2012). The waters surrounding the Senkaku Islands were frequented by Chinese fishermen during that era. Furthermore, in published maps like Hu Zongxian's 1561 *An Illustrated Compendium on Maritime Security* (*Chou Hai Tu Bian*) China has stated that the Diaoyu Islands are illustrated in the Map of Coastal Mountains and Sands (*Yan Hai Shan Sha Tu*) and the foundation of a coastal defense zone by the Ming dynasty in the decade of the 1560s was a response to threats from Japanese pirates, which China claims included the Diaoyu Islands (Hamakawa 2007; MOFA of PRC 2012). The Qing court, according to the PRC government, placed the Diaoyu Islands under Taiwanese jurisdiction (as mentioned in A Tour of Duty in the Taiwan Strait or *Tai Hai Shi Cha Lu*) and Chen Shoqui's 1871 Volume 86 of Recompiled General Annals of Fujian (*Chong Zuan Fu Jian Tong Zhi*), held Diaoyu Dao among strategic coastal defense zones under the jurisdiction of Gamalan (present Yilan County) in Taiwan (Kerrigan 2012, 454–455). China has also referenced maps by foreigners such as the Japanese writer Hayashi Shihei in 1785, French cartographer Pierre Lapie in 1809, and the British Royal Navy in 1877 – which all coloured the Diaoyu islands the same as Taiwan (MOFA of PRC 2012).

While Japan has not raised any objections to the Chinese naming of the islands centuries earlier, it has cited international law, which dictates that the discovery of an island or geographical closeness are not sufficient conditions for asserting territorial sovereignty (Okinawa Peace Assistance Center 2016). Japan has also questioned the validity of maps such as Hayashi Shihei's 1785 Illustrated Outline of the Three Countries for lack of reason to believe that the author's intention was to draw the recognized territories of the era, since Taiwan on that map is inaccurately shown less than half the size of Okinawa's principal island (Hamakawa 2007). Tokyo considers these maps to be insufficient evidence, contending that the maps published during the era do not state that the Senkaku Islands to the west of Kume Island were affiliated with the Ming or Qing dynasties of China, and that their mere presence on a map does not instate them as Chinese territory (MOFA of Japan 2014). In a speech by then-Japanese Prime Minister Yoshihiko Noda in 2012, the Japanese stance was clarified: that the Senkaku Islands 'are clearly an inherent territory of Japan, in light of historical facts and based upon international law' (MOFA of Japan 2014; Noda 2012). Moreover, Japan denies any 'issue of territorial sovereignty to be resolved' in relation to the Senkaku Islands (MOFA of Japan 2016).

The Japanese Government, after incorporating the Ryukyu Islands into Okinawa Prefecture, placed the Senkaku Islands in the same prefecture after

1885 surveys (conducted according to the established methods of duly acquiring territorial sovereignty under international law) showed the islands as *terra nullius*, i.e., uninhabited with no sign of being under the control of any state (MOFA of Japan 2014). Japan has provided documents to argue that, indeed, the PRC recognised the Senkaku Islands as part of Japanese territory in the 1950s and 1960s, such as in a 1953 issue of the China's People's Daily (*Renmin Ribao*), which reports on the populace of the Ryukyu Islands (which includes the Senkaku/Diaoyu Islands) battling the US occupation (People's Daily 1953). This position is further evidenced by Beijing's silence on America's use of the Senkaku Islands (Taisho Island and Kuba Island) for firing drills, as well as a Chinese map publisher's atlas in 1958 illustrating the islands as the 'Senkaku Group of Islands' under Okinawa (MOFA of Japan 2010; Okinawa Peace Assistance Center 2016; Sakamoto 2016).

From the perspective of international law and mutual agreements, China claims it was unfairly forced to cede the islands of Formosa, Pescadores, and other islands under the Treaty of Shimonoseki in April 1895, and hence Japan had renounced all claim and authority over those territories including the Diaoyu Islands under the 1952 Sino-Japanese Peace Treaty (People's Daily 2012).[3] Japan, on the other hand, has pointed out the lack of evidence in the treaty or its Article 2 regarding the inclusion of Senkaku Islands in the ceded territories (Treaty of Peace 1895), since the Japanese Cabinet's decision to incorporate the Senkaku Islands into Okinawa Prefecture had been taken in January 1895, before the signing of the Treaty of Shimonoseki (MOFA of Japan 2014). Moreover, since Article 2 of the 1951 San Francisco Peace Treaty does not discuss sovereignty over the Senkaku Islands, Japan claims rights over those territories in the East China Sea (United Nations 1952). However, since Article 3 of the Treaty of San Francisco places the Senkaku Islands under US administration as part of the Nansei Shoto Islands, administrative rights over all these islands only reverted to Japan after the signing of the 17 June 1971 Agreement Between Japan and the United States of America Concerning the Ryukyu Islands and the Daito Islands (Agreement Between Japan and the United States of America 1971; United Nations 1952). Meanwhile, China never asserted sovereignty over these islands until 30 December 1971, after the discovery of petrochemical reserves, as

---

[3]   Japan renounced sovereignty over all territories it acquired in 'acts of aggression' under the San Francisco Peace Treaty of 1952. Neither the ROC government nor the PRC government was invited to the San Francisco Peace Treaty, and consideration to include the Senkaku Islands into the territories Japan must surrender was eventually dismissed by the US negotiators (Hara 2012). Japan subsequently signed a separate Sino-Japanese Peace Treaty in 1952 with the ROC government, but the Senkaku question was not addressed there either. The treaty was voided when Japan switched diplomatic recognition to the PRC government in Beijing in 1978.

revealed in a declassified US intelligence report which concludes that 'the Japanese claim to sovereignty over the Senkakus is strong, and the burden of proof of ownership would seem to fall on the Chinese' (Central Intelligence Agency 1971; MOFA of Japan 2013a; People's Daily 2012). Beijing deems Tokyo's arguments invalid and the 1971 treaty illegal, and claims that the United States 'arbitrarily expanded the scope of trusteeship' to include the Diaoyu islands (MOFA of PRC 2012).

Inactive ownership of the main island of the Senkakus in private hands has helped the Chinese and Japanese governments keep the issue low-profile, as long as that was what they both wanted. After the Meiji Government had allowed the placement of national landmarks on the Senkaku Islands in 1894 and incorporated them into Okinawa in 1895, the islands were leased to Japanese entrepreneur Tatsushiro Koga for his bonito fish business, which shut down three years later, and in 1978, the islands were sold to the Kurihara family (Hiraoka 2005). After China developed an interest in acquiring the islands, Beijing started testing Japanese resolve by sending quasi-private fishermen there to challenge Japanese control of the waters surrounding the islands. After about 100 Chinese fishing vessels congregated close to the Senkaku Islands, a Japanese nationalist group erected a lighthouse on Uotsuri island, followed by another lighthouse in 1996, which was protested by China and the ROC by raising their flags on the island. Japan responded with a diplomatic protest and removal of the planted flags by its Coast Guard. In 2002, the Japanese government leased the privately held Senkaku Islands, in order to enforce its ban on private landing (Japanese or foreign) on the islands in its effort to keep bilateral diplomacy under government control. Following a collision between a Chinese fishing trawler and two Japanese Coast Guard patrol boats inside the territorial waters of the Senkaku Islands in September 2010, the Japanese government under Prime Minister Yoshihiko Noda decided to nationalize the islands by purchasing them from the Kurihara family in September 2012.[4]

The 2012 announcement by the Japanese government to nationalize the Senkaku Islands incited violent protests in China outside Japanese diplomatic missions (Lee and Ming 2012). China's then-Premier Wen Jiabao stated that 'the Diaoyu Islands are an inalienable part of China's territory, and the Chinese government and its people will absolutely make no concession on issues concerning its sovereignty and territorial integrity' (China Daily 2012),

---

[4]   Noda's decision was prompted by an earlier decision by the then-governor of the Tokyo Metropolitan government Shintaro Ishihara to start a donation campaign to raise funds to purchase the islands. Ishihara's conservative leanings led to speculation that more provocative assertions of the sovereignty claim through activist landings and construction of permanent structures would be forthcoming.

and China deployed two maritime surveillance ships close to the Senkaku Islands (Pedrozo 2016). The nationalization by the Japanese government effectively put an end to a tacit bilateral management of the dispute. Ship incursions into both the territorial and contiguous waters jumped after September 2012, and they have remained high ever since (See Figure 1). Moreover, since 2020, the number of hours that Chinese ships have remained in the territorial waters has significantly increased (Yomiuri 2021), making the Chinese presence more regular than it was during the 2012–2019 period.

Broader Maritime Demarcation in the ECS

China and Japan have not demarcated their maritime boundary over the broad entirety of the East China Sea. The location of the Senkaku Islands within the overlapping zone between China's extended continental shelf claim and Japan's exclusive economic zone (EEZ) claim places a complex legal significance on the claims over the islands.

Article 121 (3) of the 1982 UN Convention on the Law of the Sea (UNCLOS) states that 'Rocks which cannot sustain human habitation or economic life of their own' cannot have an EEZ or a continental shelf (UNCLOS 1982, 66). While Japan argues that the Senkaku Islands are not just rocks and therefore do generate an EEZ and continental shelf, China has not stated an official position on the matter (Pedrozo 2016). Japan defines its boundary as the limit of its EEZ spreading to the west of the southern islands of Kyushu and Ryukyu, but not using the Senkaku Islands as the baseline of its EEZ claim. Meanwhile, China has defined its maritime boundary along its continental shelf's natural extension.

Article 57 of UNCLOS states that the boundary of an EEZ may be up to 200 nautical miles from the baseline or to the median line in case of claims of overlap from opposing coasts. Article 76 defines the extended continental shelf, permissible to the lesser of a continental shelf's end or 350 nautical miles from the baseline (Sato 2020; UNCLOS 1982). Japan cites the median line as the maritime boundary, while China cites the limitation of the extended continental shelf as the boundary. This implies an overlap in Japan-China claims of approximately 81,000 square miles in the ECS covering the Senkaku/Diaoyu islands. After 1990, the issue became politically contentious.

Natural Gas Deposits in Overlapping Claims

Several gas fields have been discovered along the edge of the continental shelf, and these fields have been a contentious issue between Japan and China. China has installed gas rigs close to (but outside) the Japan-claimed median line. From Beijing's perspective, the rigs are deep inside its own extended continental shelf boundary. In 2004, Japan and China held their first bilateral talks on the ECS disputes. Fearing that China would siphon off the gas in case the fields spread across the median line, Japan requested that China share its geological survey data. China refused, and instead dispatched guided-missile cruisers to the area in 2005. This led to a tense encounter with a Japanese patrol plane equipped with anti-ship missiles (Sato 2017).

Japan has continued to protest China's extraction operations on the contested Okinawa trough fields. Although in 2008, after the May summit meeting between then-Japanese Prime Minister Yasuo Fukuda and then-PRC President Hu Jintao, Tokyo and Beijing agreed to engage in joint gas exploration in four ECS gas fields. Japan had earlier refused China's proposals of joint resource exploration and development so close to the Senkaku/Diaoyu islands, previously made in 1990 and 2006 (Lee and Ming 2012), and it did so again in 2008. The 2008 agreement included one field on the Japanese side of the median line for joint exploration as well (Nikkei 2015). Further negotiations over details of the terms for joint development of the Shungyo/Chunxiao field dragged on, and while it halted production activities in other disputed regions, China began unilateral development of the Tianwaitian/Kashi gas field (Yoshida and Terada 2008). In 2010, after Japan's Coast Guard confronted a Chinese fishing trawler close to the Senkaku/Diaoyu islands, China cancelled joint energy exploration negotiations (France 24 2010). In a September 2011 White Paper titled *China's Peaceful Development*, the PRC government stated that it had 'made a constructive proposal to shelve disputes and seek joint development and done its utmost to uphold peace and stability in the South China Sea, East China Sea and the surrounding areas' (PRC 2011). That same year, Tokyo announced that the Japan Air Self-Defense Force (JASDF) had had to scramble fighter planes 156 times in response to Chinese military activity around the Ryukyu Islands (Japan Times 2012).

The dispute escalated in 2013 after China unilaterally established an air defense identification zone (ADIZ) over most of the ECS, compelling aircraft entering the zone to provide flight information to Chinese air traffic controllers (Sato 2013), which Japan diplomatically protested as a violation of international law and 'extremely dangerous as it could unilaterally escalate the situation surrounding the Senkaku Islands and lead to an unexpected occurrence of accidents in the airspace' (MOFA of Japan 2013b; Rinehart and Elias 2015). Under the Obama administration, then-Secretary of State John Kerry stated that the 'unilateral action constitutes an attempt to change the status quo in the East China Sea' (Kerry 2013). Washington issued a statement urging China to 'exercise caution and restraint,' and the then-

Secretary of Defense Chuck Hagel affirmed that Article 5 of the US-Japan Mutual Defense Treaty 'applies to the Senkaku Islands' (White 2013).

Meanwhile, Japan continued to protest China's placement of exploration platforms in the ECS – they had increased to 16 by 2012 – near Japan's proposed median line separating the EEZs, with then-Chief Cabinet Secretary Yoshihide Suga stating 'it is extremely regrettable that China is proceeding with unilateral development in the area while the boundary between Japan and China in the East China Sea is not yet fixed, despite (our) repeated protests' (Sayers and Kotani 2019, 4; Japan Times 2016). In its defense White Papers between 2013 and 2015, Japan under the Prime Minister Shinzo Abe's administration had expressed the need to increase the defense budget to JPY5.09 trillion (with a focus on strengthening protection of the Senkaku Islands) as well as a reinterpretation of Article 9 of the Japanese constitution that would enable collective self-defense by Japanese Self-Defense Forces (Ministry of Defense 2015).

One comforting factor is that China and Japan have agreed not to enforce their respective fishery rules in the overlapping part of their maritime claims against the other's fishing boats. The ongoing lawfare within the territorial waters of the Senkaku Islands notwithstanding, the two countries have largely abided by this agreement in the broader ECS.

Shifting Strategic Context

The dispute over the Senkaku/Diaoyu islands is being played out not only within the realms of history and law, but it is also entangled with the geopolitical strategic stances of Japan, China, and the United States. Tokyo and Beijing have taken differing approaches to the Senkaku Islands dispute in the East China Sea, and the US position on this dispute has been seemingly oscillating. Japanese policymakers have lobbied successive US administrations for explicit support for Japan's claim to sovereignty, but Washington has consistently stopped short of doing so by simply recognizing Japan's ongoing administrative control, without releasing an explicit statement on the applicability of the bilateral defense treaty to the defense of these islands. The Sino-Japanese conflict over the Senkaku/Diaoyu islands had continued to intensify politically, with the increased assertion of sovereignty from both sides. In the past, China and Japan have tacitly refrained from taking actions that the other may see as provocative and altering the status quo (Kaseda 2017).[5] Although the maritime and air-defense assertions in more recent years can also be viewed in terms of political rituals for domestic

---

[5]   The Chinese claim that then-Prime Minister Kakuei Tanaka admitted the existence of a dispute and agreed to shelve it during his visit to Beijing in 1972, however, this has not been substantiated by official diplomatic records of the Japanese government.

consumption within each country, the acts are increasingly regularized on both sides and more explicitly tied with logging the actual exercise of control. The grey-zone challenges posed by Chinese Coast Guard ships have been largely non-combative but grave enough to potentially spark conflict in the contested areas.[6] Japan fears that the Chinese Coast Guard ships may attempt to stop and board Japanese fishing vessels inside the territorial waters around the islands, presumably to register a record of law enforcement, but possibly also to draw out an overreaction from Japan in order to open a path to further escalation. Incidents of Chinese Coast Guard vessels chasing Japanese fishing boats in 2020 and 2021 have been met by a Japanese Coast Guard patrol boat placing itself between the Chinese ships and the fishing boat to deter any enforcement action by agents of the Chinese government (Japan Times 2020). In this context, the new Chinese Coast Guard Law of 2021 authorizing the country's patrol boats to fire upon foreign patrol boats and fishing vessels has elevated the risk of escalation and accidental clashes (Tan 2021).

Moreover, Chinese military vessels have been actively operating in the contiguous waters around the islands. For instance, in June 2016, a Jiangkai I-class frigate operating around the Senkaku Islands became the first People's Liberation Army Navy (PLAN) combatant vessel to enter the area, and in January 2018 Japan confirmed the submerged transit of a PLAN submarine around the Senkaku Islands, though Beijing did not acknowledge the latter (Ministry of Defense 2020). The lifting of the annual summer ban on the Chinese fleet's fishing in the East China Sea by the PRC in August 2020 raised tensions over its consequences for the Sino-Japanese Senkaku/ Diaoyu islands dispute, and was followed by a joint naval exercise by US and Japanese naval forces in the East China Sea (Sato 2020). The United States continues to have concerns about the Senkaku/Diaoyu islands dispute owing to the US-Japan Treaty of Mutual Cooperation and Security of 1960, according to which aggressive provocations by Beijing could compel American defense actions under Article 5 of that treaty. Japan is increasingly aware that it must shoulder the primary responsibility for the defense of the Senkaku Islands against all possible scenarios including a grey-zone attack, such as landing and occupation of the islands by disguised and armed Chinese fishermen (Eldridge 2020). It is when China accomplishes an occupation of the uninhabited Senkaku Islands before US forces can respond that the alliance commitment of the United States will be tested.

In February 2021, the PRC enacted the China Coast Guard Law, authorizing the use of weapons, inconsistent with the international law including geographical zones where Coast Guard rules are applicable (Ministry of

---

[6]   Grey-zone, in international relations, refers to the threats or operations of state or non-state actors towards another state that exceed acceptable peacetime behavior but fall short of attack or war, thus not qualifying for a traditional military response.

Defense 2021). Japan's defense White Paper confirmed the presence of China Coast Guard vessels around the Senkaku Islands between April and August 2020 for 111 consecutive days, totalling 333 days for 2020, during which cumulatively 1,161 Chinese Coast Guard vessels conducted activities in the East China Sea around the Senkaku Islands (Ministry of Defense 2021). UNCLOS Article 32 provides the right to conduct affairs without outside interference to warships and other government ships operated for non-commercial purposes. While a coastal state can demand that a foreign warship leave its territorial waters, international law is unclear over the degree of a coastal state's power to force a non-compliant warship to exit its territorial waters (UNCLOS 1982). Such legal ambiguity further complicates assessments of Beijing's actions in the East China Sea, while risking an escalation of the conflict. Moreover, with no efforts being made to diffuse the tensions or resolve the Senkaku/Diaoyu island claims, Japan would need to enhance its defensive capabilities, at least as long as China maintains such an active military and paramilitary presence in the East China Sea.

The growing tension in the East China Sea has kept pace with the disputes in the South China Sea to which it has been increasingly tied (Sato 2016). The rising US-China geopolitical rivalry and the efforts of the littoral states of the South China Sea to solicit stronger US commitments to regional maritime security have not only resembled the political dynamics in the East China Sea, but they have also activated Japanese maritime security assistance to Southeast Asian countries like the Philippines and Vietnam (Sato 2021). From the perspective of the Southeast Asian recipients of Japanese aid, Japan offered a means of diversified dependence in countries where domestic and external considerations render a hedging strategy more advantageous over bandwagoning on the United States (Tran and Sato 2018; Tran 2019).

Conclusion

The ambiguities of the three parties – Japan, China, and the United States – that masked the potentially explosive bilateral territorial and maritime boundary disputes are crumbling in the post-Cold War era, and the tension has been rising at an accelerated pace since the Japanese nationalization of the Senkaku Islands.

While neither the Chinese nor Japanese historical narrative can establish a strong claim of control over the islands, which were uninhabited for much of history, the Chinese emphasis on its dynastic records and the Japanese emphasis on contemporary international law mean that the two parties are not on the same page. While Japan frames its claim within the growing emphasis by the United States and its partners in the Quadrilateral Security Dialogue on a rules-based order (Hatakeyama 2021), China resorts to a combination of maritime force buildup and lawfare. International law has been of limited use on questions of sovereignty over the islands and maritime demarcation.

Japan's fear of abandonment by the United States (Atanassova-Cornelis and Sato, 2018) in the event of Chinese occupation of the Senkaku Islands has, to some degree, been eased by reassuring comments made by US officials, but it is Japan's own naval and Coast Guard buildup that will ultimately ensure both deterrence against China and a robust US commitment to the alliance. The perceived threat from China against the Senkaku Islands, not the US request for burden-sharing elsewhere, is indeed the most acceptable reason for the Japanese populace to support an increase in the defense budget.

Figure 3.1. China Coast Guard and Other Vessels in the Waters Surrounding the Senkaku Islands. Compiled with data from the Japan Coast Guard. https://www.kaiho.mlit.go.jp/mission/senkaku/senkaku.html

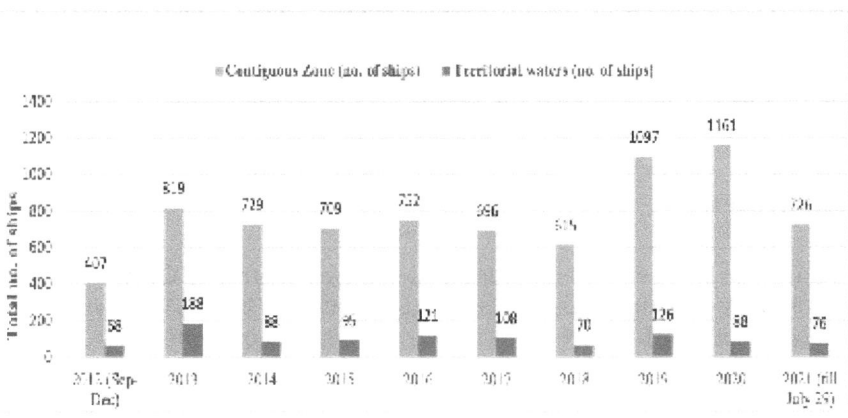

Note: Contiguous zone here refers to the maritime area adjoining the territorial sea up to 24 nautical miles from the baseline, from which the breadth of the territorial sea is calculated. A coastal state can exercise required control to prevent infringement of its laws and regulations (customs, immigration, etc.) on its territory and within its territorial sea, but the contiguous zone is subject to high seas freedom of navigation, overflight, military exercises, etc. (UNCLOS 1982, 35).

Figure 3.2 Overlapping Maritime Claims in the ECS. Source: Kenton Ngo/ Flickr. https://www.flickr.com/photos/kngo/3992534419/

References

Agreement between Japan and the United States of America Concerning the Ryukyu Islands and the Daito Islands. 1971. *Japan's Foreign Relations-Basic Documents* 3, 481–489. https://worldjpn.grips.ac.jp/documents/texts/ docs/19710617.T1E.html

Atanassova-Cornelis, Elena, and Yoichiro Sato. 2018. "The US-Japan Alliance Dilemma in the Asia-Pacific: Changing Rationales and Scope." *The International Spectator: Italian Journal of International Affairs* 54, no. 4: 78–93.

Central Intelligence Agency. 1971. *The Senkaku Islands Dispute: Oil Under Troubled Waters?* http://cryptome.org/2013/07/guccifer-cia-senkaku.pdf

Chansoria, Monika. 2018. "1969 Report by UN Economic Commission for Asia and the Far East: A Turning Point in the Historical Debate Over Senkaku Islands." *Japan Review* 2, no. 3: 36–47. www.pref.shimane.lg.jp/admin/pref/takeshima/web-takeshima/takeshima04/takeshima04-2/jitsuji-41

China Daily. 2012. "'Absolutely No Concession' on Diaoyu Islands: Wen." September 10, 2012. https://www.chinadaily.com.cn/china/201209/10/content_15748356.htm

Eldridge, Robert D. 2020. "It's Time for the U.S. to Re-Recognize Japan's Sovereignty Over the Senkaku Islands." *Japan Forward*, July 23, 2020. https://japan-forward.com/its-time-for-the-u-s-to-re-recognize-japans-sovereignty-over-the-senkaku-islands

France 24. 2010. "Japan Releases Chinese Fishing Vessel Crew but Holds Captain." September 13, 2010. https://www.france24.com/en/20100913-japan-releases-crew-seized-chinese-fishing-vessel-but-holds-captain

Hamakawa, Kyoko. 2007. "Issues on the Title of the Senkaku Islands: Analysis of the Viewpoints of Japan and China." *Issue Brief, National Diet Library*, No. 565: 1–10. https://www2.jiia.or.jp/en/pdf/digital_library/Hamakawa_senkaku.pdf

Hara, Kimie. 2012. *Cold War Frontiers in the Asia-Pacific*. New York: Routledge.

Hatakeyama, Kyoko. 2021. "Are We Ready for the Quad? Two Contradictory Goals." *Issues & Insights* 21, (SR 2), 28–33. https://pacforum.org/publication/are-we-ready-for-the-quad-two-contradictory-goals

Hiraoka, Akitoshi. 2005. "The Advancement of Japanese to the Senkaku Islands and Tatsushiro Koga in the Meiji Era." *Japanese Journal of Human Geography* 57, no. 5: 503–518. https://doi.org/https://doi.org/10.4200/jjhg1948.57.503.

Japan Times. 2012. "Fighters Launched 156 Times for China." April 27, 2012. https://www.japantimes.co.jp/news/2012/04/27/national/fighters-launched-156-times-for-china

_____. 2016. "China Brushes Off Japan's Protest Over Maritime Gas Exploration." October 13, 2016. https://www.japantimes.co.jp/news/2016/10/13/national/china-brushes-off-japans-protest-maritime-gas-exploration

_____. 2020. "Chinese Ships Chase Japanese Fishing Boat Near Senkaku Islands." May 9, 2020. https://www.japantimes.co.jp/news/2020/05/09/national/chinese-ships-chase-japanese-fishing-boat-senkaku

Kaseda, Yoshinori. 2017. "The Japan-China Gentlemen's Agreement Over the Senkaku Islands." In *Regional Institutions, Geopolitics and Economics in the Asia-Pacific: Evolving Interests and Strategies*, edited by Steven B. Rothman, Utpal Vyas and Yoichiro Sato, 93–112. New York: Routledge.

Kerrigan, Heather, ed. 2012. *Historic Documents of 2012*. London: SAGE Publications.

Kerry, John. 2013. "Statement on the East China Sea Air Defense Identification Zone." U.S. Secretary of State, November 23. https://2009-2017.state.gov/secretary/remarks/2013/11/218013.htm

Lee, Ivy, and Fang Ming. 2012. "Deconstructing Japan's Claim of Sovereignty Over the Diaoyu/Senkaku Islands." *The Asia-Pacific Journal* 10, no. 53: 1–48.

Ministry of Defense [Japan]. 2015. *Defense of Japan 2015*. https://warp.da.ndl.go.jp/info:ndljp/pid/11591426/www.mod.go.jp/e/publ/w_paper/2015.html

_____. 2020. *Defense of Japan 2020*. https://www.mod.go.jp/en/publ/w_paper/index.html

_____. 2021. *Defense of Japan 2021*. https://www.mod.go.jp/en/publ/w_paper/index.html

MOFA [Ministry of Foreign Affairs] of Japan. 2010. *The Basic View on the Sovereignty over the Senkaku Islands*. Ministry of Foreign Affairs of Japan. https://web.archive.org/web/20100930044112/http://www.mofa.go.jp/region/asia-paci/senkaku/senkaku.html

_____. 2013a. "The Senkaku Islands." Ministry of Foreign Affairs of Japan, March, 1–24. https://www.mofa.go.jp/a_o/c_m1/senkaku/page1we_000012.html

_____. 2013b. "China's Establishment of an Air Defense Identification Zone in the East China Sea (Protest by Mr. Junichi Ihara, Director-General of the Asian and Oceanian Affairs Bureau, MOFA, to Mr. Han Zhigiang, Minister of the Chinese Embassy in Japan)." Ministry of Foreign Affairs of Japan, November 23. https://www.mofa.go.jp/press/release/press4e_000100.html

_____. 2014. *The Senkaku: Islands Seeking Maritime Peace based on the Rule of Law, not force or coercion*. https://www.mofa.go.jp/region/asia-paci/senkaku/pdfs/senkaku_pamphlet.pdf

_____. 2016. "Senkaku Islands." Ministry of Foreign Affairs of Japan, April 13. https://www.mofa.go.jp/region/asia-paci/senkaku/qa_1010.html

MOFA [Ministry of Foreign Affairs] of PRC [People's Republic of China]. 2012. "Diaoyu Dao, an Inherent Territory of China." Ministry of Foreign Affairs of the People's Republic of China, September 26. https://www.fmprc.gov.cn/mfa_eng/topics_665678/diaodao_665718/t973774.shtml

Nikkei. 2015. "Nihon Keizai Shimbun." July 23, 2015. https://www.nikkei.com/article/DGXZZO76056900T20C14A8000048

Noda, Yoshihiko. 2012. "Press Conference by Prime Minister Yoshihiko Noda on the Occasion of the 67th Session of the United Nations General Assembly (Speeches and Statements by Prime Minister)." September 26. https://japan.kantei.go.jp/noda/statement/201209/26naigai_kaiken_e.html

Okinawa Peace Assistance Center. 2016. "Commissioned Research Report on the Senkaku Islands-related Documents." https://www.cas.go.jp/jp/ryodo_eg/img/data/archives-senkaku02.pdf

Pedrozo, Raul. 2016. "International Law and Japan's Territorial Disputes." *International Law Studies* 92, no. 1. https://digital-commons.usnwc.edu/ils/vol92/iss1/4.

People's Daily. 1953. "Battle of People in the Ryukyu Islands Against the U.S. Occupation." January 8, 1953. https://www.mod.go.jp/js/Press/press2019/press_pdf/p20190726_02.pdf

_____. 2012. "Full Text: Diaoyu Dao, an Inherent Territory of China." September 25, 2012. http://en.people.cn/102774/7960441.html

PRC [People's Republic of China]. 2011. "China's Peaceful Development." Information Office of the State Council. http://english.www.gov.cn/archive/white_paper/2014/09/09/content_281474986284646.htm

Rinehart, Ian E., and Bart Elias. 2015. "China's Air Defense Identification Zone (ADIZ)." CRS Report. https://sgp.fas.org/crs/row/R43894.pdf

Sakamoto, Shigeki. 2016. "The Senkaku Islands as Viewed through Chinese Law." *Review of Island Studies*, 1–24.

Sato, Yoichiro. 2013. "Chinese Announcement of the Air Defense Identification Zone - What Follows." *PacNet Newsletter* 87. https://www.files.ethz.ch/isn/176660/Pac1387_0.pdf

_____. 2016. "Japan and the South China Sea Dispute: A Stakeholder's Perspective." In *The South China Sea Dispute: Navigating Diplomatic and Strategic Tensions*, edited by Ian Storey and Cheng-yi Lin, 272–290. Singapore: Institute of Southeast Asian Studies.

_____. 2017. "Japan's Maritime Security: Continuity and Post-Cold War Evolution." In *Maritime Security in East and Southeast Asia: Political Challenges in Asian Waters*, edited by Nicholas Tarling and Xin Chen, 125–144. New York: Routledge.

_____. 2020. "The Sino-Japanese Maritime Disputes in the East China Sea." Center for International Maritime Security. https://cimsec.org/the-sino-japanese-maritime-disputes-in-the-east-china-sea

_____. 2021. "Japan's Strategic Indo-Pacific Vision." In *The Rise of Global Strategies: Free and Open Indo-Pacific Concept*, edited by Csaba Moldicz and Gabriella Kovács, 167–185. Budapest: Budapest Business School.

Sayers, Eric, and Tetsuo Kotani. 2019. "An Alliance Strategy for the East China Sea." The Sasakawa Peace Foundation, *Policy Mamorandum #2*, 1–6. https://www.spf.org/jpus-j/spf-asia-initiative/spf-asia-initiative003.html

Tan, Jia Ning. 2021. "China's Coast Guard Law Could Jolt Region Into Action, Experts Say." *Straits Times*, March 9, 2021. https://www.straitstimes.com/asia/east-asia/chinas-coast-guard-law-could-jolt-region-into-action-experts-say

Tran, Bich Thi. 2019. "Presidential Turnover and Discontinuity in the Philippines' China Policy. *Asian Perspective* 43, no. 4: 621–646.

Tran, Bich Thi, and Yoichiro Sato. 2018. "Vietnam's Post-Cold War Hedging Strategy: A Changing Mix of Realist and Liberal Ingredients." *Asian Politics & Policy* 10, no. 1: 73–99.

Treaty of Peace. 1895. *Treaty of Peace between the Empire of Japan and the Empire of China, Treaty of Shimonoseki*, Nihongaikoubunsyo, Dai 28 ken, April 17. https://worldjpn.grips.ac.jp/documents/texts/pw/18950417.T1E.html

UNCLOS [UN Convention on the Law of the Sea]. 1982. "United Nations Convention on the Law of the Sea of 10 December 1982." United Nations, 7–208.

United Nations. 1952. *Treaty of Peace with Japan.* United Nations 136 (1832), 45–164. https://treaties.un.org/pages/showDetails.aspx?objid=08000002801528c2

White, Harry. 2013. "The ADIZ and Rebalancing on the Run." *The Strategist*, November 28, 2013. https://www.aspistrategist.org.au/the-adiz-and-rebalancing-on-the-run

Yomiuri Shimbun. 2021. "中国海警船、尖閣沖領海に４７時間６分滞在…過去２番目の長さ." July 12, 2021. https://www.yomiuri.co.jp/politics/20210712-OYT1T50148

Yoshida, Reiji, and Shinichi Terada. 2008. "Japan, China Strike Deal on Gas Fields." *Japan Times*, June 19, 2008. https://www.japantimes.co.jp/news/2008/06/19/national/japan-china-strike-deal-on-gas-fields

4

China's Strategic Thinking on the Diaoyu/Senkaku Island Dispute

DUAN XIAOLIN

In January 2021, the government of the People's Republic of China (PRC) enacted the China Coast Guard Law. In Article 22, the law states that 'when the national sovereignty, sovereign rights, or jurisdiction is being illegally violated at sea by a foreign organization or individual, or is in imminent danger of illegal violation, a coast guard agency shall have the power to take all necessary measures including the use of weapons to stop the violation and eliminate the danger.' It also allows Chinese Coast Guard personnel to forcibly board noncompliant foreign vessels that they deem are 'illegally' engaged in economic activities in Chinese-claimed waters (Standing Committee of the National People's Congress 2021). In response, Japanese government officials reinterpreted the existing laws on maritime rights enforcement, which granted the Japanese Coast Guard the authority to fire when foreign vessels aim to land personnel on the Diaoyu/Senkaku Islands (DSI). Before this, the Japanese Coast Guard was only allowed to use force in case of self-defence and emergency, subject to the defence-oriented provisions inherent in the pacifist constitution of Japan (Kaneko 2021). This regulatory escalation, with the potential to spur kinetic conflict, illustrates why the international community expressed concerns that China's new law could be invoked to assert territorial claims in the East China Sea and the South China Sea, and the spiral of distrust and rivalry among competing claimants could generate catastrophic impacts and continue the destabilisation of the region (Asia Maritime Transparency Initiative 2021).

The DSI dispute also creates strategic impacts beyond itself. Considering America's security commitment to defend territories administered by the

Japanese government, including the DSI, and given recent Sino-US competition, both sides (the United States and China) tend to stand firm in the dispute to avoid showing any signs of weakness, making rational dialogue and crisis management even more challenging.

Will the DSI dispute be a flash point in East Asia that triggers a great-power war? Rather than examining China's specific policies in the DSI dispute, this chapter will attempt to decode the general behavioural patterns of Chinese leaders in their quest for territorial integrity, and then explore the implications for the DSI dispute. The relative-gains concept and the instrumental value of disputed territories both fail to provide coherent explanations for China's territorial strategies. Instead, what matters most are the political meanings of disputed territories within the context of China's grand strategy.

In the DSI disputes, the possible energy reserves and other maritime rights are not China's primary concerns. Rather, DSI claims are embedded within China's policies on Taiwan and Hong Kong, its strategic concerns over domestic stability and economic development, and Beijing's desire to maintain a friendly international environment that it has deemed necessary for domestic development. China was mostly trying to muddle through and balance among competing domestic and international, economic and political interests in the dispute, rather than implementing a well-crafted strategy aimed at restoring its control over the islands. China's new thinking of Japan and East Asian integration will continue to hinder Beijing's incentives to invoke foreign policy and military adventurism in the dispute. The author thus predicts that the DSI dispute will not trigger a major crisis and the issue will, in all likelihood, continue to be shelved for the foreseeable future.

In the first section of this chapter, an explanation is provided for why relative gains and the instrumental value of disputed territories do not provide a coherent explanation for China's strategic behaviours. The second section proposes to shift the analytical focus to the political meanings of disputed territories in China's grand strategy, elaborating upon the DSI issue. In the third section, China's strategic calculus over the islands is examined and how this creates instability, but until the promulgation of the aforementioned law, has prevented the use of force. The author concludes that China's DSI policy has been to balance competing domestic and international, economic and political interests. Despite the rise in Chinese nationalism and the strongman-style leadership exhibited by China's Paramount Leader Xi Jinping, China has no intention of engaging in military adventurism in this dispute. In the fourth and final section, the author examines the reasons for cautious optimism amid the current Sino-US rivalry and then discusses policy implications.

Getting China Wrong

It is common practice for scholars of international relations to utilize the rational choice approach to understand the strategic behaviours of nation-states. Empirical studies of states' actions in territorial disputes – including dispute onset and escalation, the use of force, and peaceful resolution – examine the importance of relative power asymmetries (economic and military strengths), economic, ethnic, and religious values, the locations of disputed territories, domestic politics, and international audience costs (Carter 2010; Heldt 1999; Huth 1996).

In recent years, the media, pundits, and scholars have paid close attention to China's territorial behaviours, particularly since 2010. According to the popular narrative, China is more and more war-prone in dealing with maritime disputes and is trying to flex its military muscle to elbow other competing claimants out. In June 2020, China and India were on the brink of war due to a brawl in the Galwan River Valley. The international community became worried that, with the rise of China's economic and military strength, it would be ready, willing, and able to take control over these territories using military force. However, the media and many pundits usually misunderstand China's strategic motives in maritime disputes, and they particularly overestimate the importance of relative gains and the instrumental value of disputed territories.

The concept of relative gains is a valuable paradigm to explain states' strategic behaviours, particularly in the realist tradition. The popular narrative tends to attribute China's assertiveness since 2010 to its rising economic and military strength and predicts an even more aggressive China with the modernization of Chinese naval forces. The merits of the relative-gains argument are evident. For example, China used to lack sufficient means to strengthen its control over remote disputed waters and features such as the Spratly Islands, the DSI, and Aksai Chin along the China-India border. A weak China in the 1980s–1990s was more willing to de-escalate territorial crises. Since 2010, however, Beijing has tended to view such crises as windows of opportunity, responding in a deliberately escalatory manner in an effort to create a new *status quo* in its favour (Swaine 2013). However, a systematic review of China's strategic behaviours reveals the weaknesses inherent in casually linking power and assertiveness.

For example, China has historically been more likely to confront powerful rivals over territorial issues (including India, the Soviet Union, Vietnam and the United States – the latter on the Taiwan issue during the Cold War), but has peacefully resolved disputes with its weak neighbours, and made significant concessions to the latter in the territorial negotiations (Fravel 2008; Nie and Li 2008). On the matter of Taiwan, China's response was more aggressive and war-prone during the tenure of Republic of China (ROC) President Lee Teng-hui, to the point of firing missiles into the area during the island's 1996 presidential elections. In contrast, China's countermeasures against President Chen Shui-bian's pro-localization moves in the middle 2000s were harsh but mostly rhetorical, despite China's military and economic strengths having made significant progress since the 1995–1996 Taiwan Strait Crisis (Bush 2013; Ross 2000).

In the South China Sea, China has not exploited the weaknesses of its small neighbours in Southeast Asia. China's territorial claims have been consistent with its long-term policies; indeed, sometimes, Chinese assertiveness is a reaction to the provocative moves of other claimants, and of the United States.[1] Beijing also has no intention to escalate or resort to the use of force despite the occasional diplomatic standoff or confrontation in disputed waters. In the recent China-India border disputes, for example, Beijing did not adopt economic retaliatory measures the way New Delhi did; China acknowledged four deaths of officers and soldiers in February 2021, albeit eight months after the incident, to avoid fuelling domestic nationalism amid the high-intensity military standoff. All this suggests that the relative-gains explanation oversimplifies China's strategic calculation and thus provides an ill-informed understanding of Beijing's moves.

Fravel (2010) points out the importance of the United States in deterring Chinese aggression. Washington claims to be neutral on the sovereignty of the islands, but *de facto* takes Tokyo's side and reiterates its security commitment to defend territories administered by Japan, including the DSI (Blanchard 2000). The Korean war might serve as a typical case to illustrate how China will dare to fight a powerful enemy, in this case the combined international forces operating under the United Nations Command, for the sake of strategic and ideological reasons (Shen 2012). When Beijing shifted its focus to economic development instead of ideology-oriented domestic and foreign policies, its foreign policies turned to serve the needs of domestic development, and thus there was a tendency for Beijing to restrain itself from such diplomatic and military adventurism.

---

[1] For example, since the middle 2000s Vietnam has made significant progress in offshore petroleum exploitation in waters also claimed by China, while China remained reluctant in do similar things, though it did disrupt Vietnam's efforts. Vietnam and Malaysia's submission to the Commission on the Limits of the Continental Shelf (CLCS) claimed that the outer limits of their continental shelf in the South China Sea went beyond 200 nautical miles, so China submitted counter-claims to prevent the CLCS from qualifying these claims, which triggered new tensions at that time. When the United States expanded its commitment and interests in the South China Sea, this made China feel insecure and thus Beijing began acting assertively (Fravel 2011; Lind, 2017; Johnston 2013).

Energy reserves, fishing rights, and other maritime rights are also frequently used to explain China's recent assertiveness in its maritime disputes. As highlighted by the Japanese government in its official claim over the DSI, 'it is only since the 1970s that the Government of China and the Taiwanese Authorities began making their own assertions about the Senkaku Islands, which was after a survey conducted by an agency of the United Nations in autumn of 1968 had indicated the possibility of the existence of petroleum resources on the East China Sea, and attention was focused on the Senkaku Islands,' adding, 'until then, they had never expressed any objections' (MOFA of Japan 2016). However, the role of energy in China's overall calculus should not be overestimated for several reasons. Whether it is economically feasible to exploit the energy resources in disputed waters still needs further investigation; the market mechanism is a more efficient way for China to acquire resources instead of conquering and utilizing disputed territories. It is also questionable whether the DSI and islets in the South China Sea will be acknowledged as islands and generate entitlement to an exclusive economic zone according to international law, thereby undermining the value of these disputed territories and waters to a large extent. Beijing also declared that its territorial claims over the DSI have nothing to do with the petroleum stores believed to be there (People's Daily 2012).

Overall, the tendency to seek a linear causal mechanism that would simply attribute China's strategic behaviour to either a relative-gains calculation in China's favour, or one focusing on the instrumental value of disputed territories and waters, is misleading. The analytical focus herein will therefore shift to the political meanings of the disputed territories in China's grand strategy.

The Political Meanings of Disputed Territories

A historical review highlights the political meanings of disputed territories in China's grand strategy and policy-making. Whether territorial disputes are peacefully resolved or lead to military conflict usually serves the needs of China's grand strategy.

China's use of force in territorial issues usually involves more strategic concerns. The China-India border disputes are partly an outgrowth of India's ambitions to defend its traditional interests in Tibet in the 1950s. The PRC largely inherited its sovereignty claims over the South China Sea islands from the ROC, which lost the Chinese Civil War and fled to Taiwan in 1949. During the Cold War, the ROC used its superior naval forces to threaten the communist regime's survival. From this perspective, Beijing certainly had no incentive to back down from previous claims, and it tried to strengthen its control over the disputed waters, as the dispute involved regime survival and long-term competition with the ROC as to which was the sole representative of the nation's territorial interests (Jiang 2006, 130–131). The China-Soviet border dispute that led to the Zhenbao/Damansky Island clash in 1969 was part of Mao Zedong's struggle over ideological rightness and leadership in the global Communist Camp, as well as in domestic affairs (Shen and Xia 2011). The Sino-Vietnam border conflict in 1979 was not simply a response to 'the Vietnamese government killing local Chinese, sending others to labour camps and expelling many to become "boat people," and to a dispute over the Spratly Islands in the South China Sea' (Copper 2009), but were rooted in domestic and structural concerns including China's relations with the Soviet Union and the United States, as well as a power struggle among political elites in China.

Compared with these disputes that involved military conflicts, more of China's territorial disputes were resolved peacefully, and China made significant concessions to its competing claimants. Beijing's concessions were mostly to strengthen its control over China's periphery, inhabited mainly by ethnic minorities, by resolving border issues with its weak neighbours. It also wanted to build friendly relations with these weak neighbours, either among Third World countries or those in the Communist Camp, both of which were perceived to be ideologically close to the Chinese Communist Party (CCP). Chinese leaders would like to trade territorial concessions for periphery stability, international recognition, and friendship with these small neighbours (Fravel 2008). The DSI dispute is a case in point to explain how the political meanings of disputed territories shape China's strategic behaviour.

China did not make its first territorial claim over the DSI in 1970, when Beijing noticed the rise of the *Baodiao* (protecting the Diaoyu Islands) movement in Taiwan, Hong Kong and particularly in the overseas Chinese community in the United States. By waiting until 1971, Beijing was able to exploit the ROC's weak position on the island dispute and de-legitimise the ROC's claim to be the representative government of the Chinese nation, while winning the hearts and minds of overseas Chinese communities. Since then, the DSI dispute has continued to disrupt the Sino-Japan bilateral relationship. On the China side, the dispute was closely connected to China's strategic interest in annexing Taiwan, controlling Hong Kong, and the CCP's need to accommodate domestic nationalism, which occasionally provides Beijing both the motivation and the pretence to escalate its claims and act assertively. Meanwhile, China's territorial interests and their political importance were subordinated to serve more strategic needs to improve its relations with Japan and the West and to create a friendly environment for domestic reform and opening-up (Chung 2001; Duan 2019).

Since the 1970s, an essential factor defining China's DSI policy has been Taiwan and Beijing's 'One-China principle.' Granted, the importance of these factors is in decline as the DSI dispute is basically marginalized in Taiwan's political discourse, and had been reduced to a scuffle over fishing rights between Taipei and Tokyo until the signing of their 2013 fishery agreement. From Beijing's perspective, Taipei's weak stance on its DSI claims is a disappointment to those ROC citizens that claim a Chinese identity, as well as fishermen in southern Taiwan whose fishing activities around the DSI have been curtailed and whose fishing boats risk being detained by the Japanese Coast Guard. By criticizing Taipei's lack of action against Tokyo, Beijing has been able to exploit the weaknesses of Taipei's political system, and win the hearts and minds of some of the people living in Taiwan.

In the 1990s, Hong Kong was the centre of the *Baodiao* movement, as Taiwan repressed such social movements which, Taipei worried, could be easily exploited by Beijing to destabilize society. The dispute was probably the only issue that could unite different political groups within Hong Kong. Both the pro-China and pro-democracy parties had their affiliated *Baodiao* factions and lobbied Beijing for a hard-line policy on the dispute. Beijing had more substantial incentives to accommodate their demands, because it wanted to cultivate Chinese patriotism among Hong Kong citizens and elites, to pave the way for a peaceful handover of Hong Kong in 1997. According to an editorial in *The South China Morning Post* (1996), 'For the first time since the rift between them started seven years ago [referring to the Tiananmen Square massacre in 1989], political activists in HK and the mainland government are united in a common cause against a common adversary.' However, since the handover of Hong Kong to China, patriotism in the former British colony has waned, and the DSI dispute was no longer a politically salient issue. These days, few activists attempt to organize *Baodiao* movements or to land on the islands.

Since the 1990s, the DSI dispute and other irritants to the Sino-Japanese relationship have continued to arouse nationalistic sentiment in China, constraining the flexibility of the PRC government's policy response. However, Beijing has come to realize that nationalism is a double-edged sword. The CCP worries that anti-foreign sentiment may destabilize society, disrupt its grand strategy to develop the economy, and, more importantly, turn into an anti-government movement (Reilly 2014; Zhao 2005).

While many factors continue to pressure leaders in Beijing to escalate the territorial claims over the islands, a more defining and pacifying factor that could de-escalate the dispute is the shared commercial interests between China and Japan, two of the world's major economies that are both integrated into the global value chain. In the early stages of China's reform and opening-up, commercial transactions with Japan, official development assistance, and private investment from Japan were critical for China. As China further integrates itself into the global economy, the two countries are deeply interdependent. Although political tensions occasionally disrupt the commercial relationship, and Japanese companies have recently tried to reduce their dependence on Chinese resources and markets by diversifying their global investments, no Japanese companies want to leave the Chinese market entirely (Dreyer 2014; Iida, 2017, 138–162).

China: Mudding Through

Michael Pillsbury's famous albeit controversial book *The Hundred-year Marathon: China's Secret Strategy to Replace America As the Global Superpower* elaborates how China has carefully drafted its strategies, exploited the weaknesses of the United States, and ultimately turned itself into the only peer competitor that could challenge the United States in all aspects (Pillsbury 2015). From this perspective, does China have a well-drafted strategy to seize control over the islands? In other words, how can we understand China's DSI strategy (if indeed Beijing has one)? Close observation reveals that China was mostly muddling through the territorial contingencies rather than implementing a well-crafted strategy aimed at taking control of the islands.

Firstly, China's territorial claims were opportunistically aimed at weakening the ROC's legitimacy as the government of all of China in the early 1970s. Still, Beijing did not take substantive action to exercise sovereignty over the islands. At critical moments of the normalization of the Sino-Japanese relationship in the 1970s, Chinese leaders suggested that the dispute should be secondary to the relationship normalization, and then proposed that the disputes be shelved and left to future generations to effect a possible peaceful resolution.

Secondly, China's DSI policies were mostly reactive, designed to deal with contingencies created by *Baodiao* activists in the Chinese-speaking world and provocations from among the right-wing in Japan in the 1990s and early 2000s. In China, the *Baodiao* social groups and activists were unwelcome. The Chinese government's responses during most of the 1990s and 2000s were aimed at de-escalation and crisis management (Downs and Saunders 1998).

Thirdly, the dispute has led to a series of diplomatic standoffs and paramilitary confrontations since 2010. The Chinese government believes that the boat collision incident that year, and the Japanese government's purchase of three of the islands from their private owner in 2012, constituted unilateral changes to the *status quo* and damaged China's territorial interests, so it had to take firm action, including instituting routine patrols in the surrounding waters, to restore its losses from the dispute. After a series of assertive moves, including diplomatic standoffs, propaganda warfare, and increased frequency of patrols by Chinese vessels, the PRC government has satisfied hard-line Chinese nationalists, publicized the dispute in the international community, and expanded its presence in the waters surrounding the DSI. Still, Beijing surprisingly claims that it has no intention of retaking the islands, which it perceives to be very risky at the moment. To avoid miscalculation, Chinese ships exert a regular presence around the islands.

Nationalist pressure may yet force the PRC government to act aggressively sooner or later (Cairns and Carlson 2016; Weiss 2014). Although the government has tried its best to censor sensitive information and repress online anti-Japanese sentiment, and to redirect people's attention to economic developments in times of crisis, the rapid development of information technology and the growth of social media make it difficult for the CCP regime to steer society away from such online discussions. Given the efficiency with which the regime is able to censor other sensitive topics, however, it has been suggested that the Chinese government is, in fact, leveraging this nationalism and anti-Japanese sentiment to rally popular support and fuel the CCP's legitimacy to rule (Zhao 2013). In times of domestic instability and economic crises, Chinese leaders tend to engage in foreign-policy adventurism as a means of diverting the Chinese people's attention from the government's domestic failures. For several reasons, the author doubts the logic inherent in such claims.

Firstly, whether the Chinese government is fuelling anti-Japanese sentiment at home remains open to intellectual debate. For example, scholars have found that elites' manipulation of domestic nationalism is constrained by the existing cultural and historical givens and 'had to adhere to the cultural parameters of the traditions of the people, politicizing their sense of ethnic community, and reinterpreting those traditions as deep cultural resources for a political struggle for national self-determination' (Smith 2001, 119). Japan's historical revisionism angered people in China and the Republic of Korea (ROK), both of which suffered from Tokyo's war crimes. That means that anti-Japanese sentiment in China is not simply a result of the CCP's political use of history, but has historical origins and deep cultural roots. Secondly, how strong Chinese nationalism is and how influential it is over foreign policy-making is still unclear (Duan 2017; Johnston 2016). To what extent individuals are willing to sacrifice their interests for the sake of a nationalist course of action remains unclear, as many Chinese are fine with traveling to Japan and purchasing Japanese products. Thirdly, we cannot assume that the nationalistic pressure only accumulates to a higher level. As official and social exchanges between China and Japan return to normal after territorial contingencies, there is the possibility that such pressure will ease, which can terminate or even reverse the downward spiral of rivalry between the two countries.

China observers have expressed worries that Xi's consolidation of personal power and China's new practice of 'Great Power Diplomacy with Chinese Characteristics' will create new sources of instability. They believe that China has edged away from its traditional diplomatic doctrines of 'Keeping a low profile' and 'shelving disputes' in dealing with unsolved territorial issues (Chen and Wang 2011; Yan 2014). Rather, under Xi, China has been more willing to leverage its economic and military strengths to advance its territorial interests – in ways subtle and not – to create a new *status quo* in its favour without going so far as to resort to the use of force. However, this does not mean that Xi has embraced hard, realpolitik doctrines (Wang 2019). As long as China still adheres to the grand strategy of reform and opening-up and prioritizes economic development, Beijing would be foolhardy to jeopardize the stable international environment so necessary for its own domestic development by engaging in foreign-policy and military adventurism over its territorial disputes.

The author does not believe that China will seize the islands by force in the foreseeable future. As this chapter attempts to highlight, China's strategies in the territorial disputes in general (and the DSI in particular) are part of its grand strategy, which involves tradeoffs among short- and long-term interests, territorial and economic interests, and domestic and international interests. Mostly, China was steering a middle course and balancing its competing interests among domestic stability and economic development. It is therefore a strategic necessity for China to create a friendly international environment not only to safeguard its territorial interests in the dispute, but to avoid irritants to its relations with Japan and the United States, and to uphold its prestige as the world's second largest economy. In addition, a weak stance in the DSI dispute may encourage provocative moves by competing claimants in other territorial disputes throughout Southeast Asia and India. Beijing's DSI policy is a combined product of these factors and reactions to contingencies as a sign of political representativeness and responsiveness. The multiple layers of China's strategic interests, the rationality of Chinese leadership and bureaucrats, and the tight political control over the army precludes the possibility of military adventurism.

Reasons for Cautious Optimism amid Sino-US Rivalry

With the rise of China's economic and military strength, the Sino-US relationship is increasingly characterized by tense great-power rivalry. Power transition theorists, or 'Thucydides Trap' advocates, argue that a rising power and an established power are destined to engage in a military conflict over global leadership and the associated benefits (Allison 2017; Lemke and Tammen 2003; Kugler and Organski, 1989). War could happen either when the rising power acts as a revisionist actor and tries to build a new world order, or when the established power is trapped by a better-now-than-later logic and starts a preventive war to eliminate the threat from the rising power before it loses the strategic advantage (Levy 1987).

The rancour between China and the United States is worsening in a number of fields – trade, technology, media, diplomacy, propaganda and political and economic systems. Under the administration of President Barack Obama, American policymakers noticed the necessity of managing the challenge of a rising China and increased the US diplomatic, military, and economic involvement in the Asia-Pacific Region. However, Obama still valued Sino-US cooperation on many global and regional issues, including climate change, nuclear non-proliferation, and global economic recovery. After Donald Trump was elected president, friction between the two powers evolved into full-scale competition and confrontation in geopolitics, trade, technology, media, and diplomacy. The COVID-19 pandemic only accelerated this downward spiral of rivalry. A new Cold War seemed to have emerged between the two great powers (Landler 2018).

DSI is a flashpoint in the Sino-US relationship, considering that America has been deeply involved in the dispute since the 1970s. Although it claims to be neutral on sovereignty issues, the United States clearly 'favored in both word and deed Japanese claims to the islands' (Blanchard 2000, 97). A series of territorial contingencies and strategic action-reaction intensified the great power competition.

Firstly, American strategists usually see Chinese assertiveness in the dispute as a test of America's security commitment to its Asian allies, and any signs of weakness or reluctance will only attract further aggression from China. America therefore needs to stand firm and sometimes act decisively to show its resolve. Secondly, the Japanese government keeps lobbying for a more active role for the United States in the dispute. Japan has become the tail that wags the American dog to check China's behaviour, even though the United States sometimes prefers to act with caution. For example, in 2012, then-US Assistant Secretary for East Asian and Pacific Affairs Kurt Campbell believed that the nationalization of the DSI islands would surely antagonize Beijing and thus urged his Japanese counterparts to 'consult and advise Beijing on their plans' (Japan Times 2016). Even if senior officials believed that Japan's purchasing decision was reckless, America chose to stand firm with Japan and deterred China's countermeasures after the nationalization took place. Thirdly, Japan felt directly threatened by China partly due to its assertiveness in the dispute and thus attempted to enhance security linkages with regional powers such as India and Australia, which is likely to facilitate the formation of a balancing coalition to check China's moves (Kliman and Twining 2014, 14–16; Koga 2016).

However, we still have strong reasons for cautious optimism that the dispute could de-escalate. Tactically, both the Chinese and Japanese governments have enhanced their control over the islands, and *de facto* barred either Chinese *Baodiao* activists or Japanese nationalists' from landing on the islands and raising tensions; America's firm and clear commitment to defend the islands leaves no room for Beijing to drive a wedge between Tokyo and Washington on the dispute and thus minimizes the strategic uncertainties. Moreover, bilateral relations between China and Japan, and China's strategic needs in a post-pandemic world, continue to disincentivise China from invoking foreign-policy adventurism in the DSI dispute.

The economic cooperation and integration between China and Japan will be more intensive in the foreseeable future. Firstly, thanks to the Trump presidency, the world has witnessed the other side of the United States, that is liable to promote protectionism-oriented trade policies, abandon its commitment to global governance, and retrench from its security commitment to European and Asian allies. China, Japan, and Korea suffered from President Trump's solutions to America's trade imbalance problems, including a tariff war and renegotiating new trade agreements in America's favour. Amid the trade war, the three countries revived the delayed agenda of East Asian integration. On January 21, 2021, the PRC Ministry of Commerce announced that 'the country [China] will boost China-Japan-South Korea FTA talks and free trade talks with Gulf Cooperation Council, Israel and Norway, while actively considering joining the Comprehensive and Progressive Agreement for Trans-Pacific Partnership' (Global Times 2021). Secondly, the successful conclusion of the Regional Comprehensive Economic Partnership (RCEP) will also further integrate the two countries' supply chains in automobile manufacturing, steel, textiles, and other sectors. What's more, Asia continues to develop into the world's economic centre. China and Japan are important engines and beneficiaries of Asia's growth, and they share more common interests in regional affairs. Thirdly, the COVID-19 pandemic may also have enhanced their shared interest in economic cooperation. The Chinese government was very effective in controlling the pandemic and restoring social order and the Chinese economy, even as other major economies were still struggling with the virus. Along with other measures to improve the business environment, China remains an attractive place for foreign investors, including Japanese companies. Last but not least, as the United

States since Trump administration began engaging in a high-tech decoupling from China, Japan became an important country for China to access high-technology components.

Although their bilateral relationship has not improved significantly since its historical low in 2012, foreign policymakers in both China and Japan have met on various occasions. They agree that a stable bilateral relationship is very important, and have been trying to normalize high-level dialogue and cooperation. Since 2014, Chinese President Xi and Premier Li Keqiang have met with Japanese Prime Minister Shinzo Abe 14 times, including Abe's official visit to Beijing in 2018, and a second visit in December 2019 to attend the Eighth Japan-China-ROK Trilateral Summit. In 2019, Abe invited Xi to visit Japan in Spring 2020 and Xi accepted the invitation 'in principle,' although Xi's trip to Japan was delayed largely due to the COVID-19 pandemic. Both countries are motivated and ready to improve their relations and expand Sino-Japan cooperation in trade and investment, tourism, culture and sports, communication, and coordination on regional affairs (MOFA of PRC 2019).

Conclusion: How China's Strategic Calculus Creates Instability but Prevents War

In this chapter, the author has reviewed the important factors that shape China's strategic behaviours in the territorial disputes. While the notion of relative gains and the instrumental value of disputed territories both fail to provide a coherent explanation for China's strategy in dealing with territorial issues, this chapter highlights how the political meanings of disputed territories take effect. The DSI issue was closely related to China's regime competition with the ROC during the Cold War, and Beijing's efforts to press its 'One China' paradigm; appeasing the patriotism of Hong Kong's pro-China elements to facilitate a stable handover of the former British colony in 1997; and more recently, its concerns over social order and the strategic need to accommodate domestic nationalist sentiment. When the *Baodiao* movement was largely being marginalized in Taiwan and Hong Kong's popular discourse, the nationalism in China was rising, and played a more prominent role in shaping China's Japan policy and its DSI strategies.

Since the nationalization of three DSI features by the Japanese government in 2012, multiple factors have created new sources of instability, as well as the reason for cautious optimism. On one hand, China's strategic need to defend its territorial interests and to accommodate domestic nationalism, the practice of 'Great Power Diplomacy with Chinese Characteristics' launched during the Xi presidency, and frequent patrols by Chinese vessels in waters surrounding the DSI have served to create new sources of instability and increase the risk of conflict due to miscalculation. On the other hand, there are reasons for cautious optimism. By strengthening their control over the islands and surrounding waters, China and Japan are limiting the possibility that nationalistic elements might land on the islands and drag Beijing and Tokyo into a military confrontation, or even just another diplomatic crisis. America has reiterated its security commitment to defend the DSI as Japanese territory, which could deter military adventurism on the part of Xi. The most pacifying factor is the increasing shared interests in interdependent economic relations and regional integration.

The author believes that China still prioritizes the strategic interests of economic development and a friendly relationship with Japan over its territorial interests in the DSI. At this stage, China has no incentive to escalate the dispute because its routine patrols have advanced its territorial interests in the DSI and appeased Chinese nationalists. The worst scenario would be if Japan made any further proactive moves in the dispute, or if an incident should occur during a Chinese patrol of the surrounding waters, either of which would arouse popular anti-Japanese sentiment in China and compel Beijing leaders to respond harshly. Overall, the author believes that the DSI dispute will continue to be shelved, and will not trigger any significant crises in the foreseeable future.

References

Allison, Graham. 2017. *Destined for War: Can America and China Escape Thucydides's Trap?* New York: Houghton Mifflin Harcourt.

Asia Maritime Transparency Initiative. 2021. "Force Majeure: China's Coast Guard Law in Context." March 30. https://amti.csis.org/force-majeure-chinas-coast-guard-law-in-context

Blanchard, Jean-Marc F. 2000. "The U. S. Role in the Sino-Japanese Dispute Over the Diaoyu (Senkaku) Islands, 1945-1971." *The China Quarterly* 161, 95–123.

Bush, Richard C. 2013. *Uncharted Strait: The Future of China-Taiwan Relations*. Washington: Brookings Institution Press.

Cairns, Christopher, and Allen Carlson. 2016. "Real-World Islands in a Social Media Sea: Nationalism and Censorship on Weibo During the 2012 Diaoyu/Senkaku Crisis." *The China Quarterly* 225, 23–49. https://doi.org/10.1017/S0305741015001708.

Carter, David B. 2010. "The Strategy of Territorial Conflict." *American Journal of Political Science* 54, no. 4: 969–987. https://doi.org/10.1111/j.1540-5907.2010.00471.x.

Chen, Dingding, and Jianwei Wang. 2011. "Lying Low No More?: China's New Thinking on the Tao Guang Yang Hui Strategy." *China: An International Journal 9*, no. 2: 195–216.

Global Times. 2021. "China Plans to Expand Free Trade Network, Accelerate FTA Talks." January 21, 2021. https://www.globaltimes.cn/page/202101/1213551.shtml

Chung, Chien-Peng. 2001. *Domestic Politics, International Bargaining and China's Territorial Disputes*. New York: Routledge.

Copper, John F. 2009. "The Sino-Vietnam War's Thirtieth Anniversary." *American Journal of Chinese Studies* 16, no. 1: 71–74.

Downs, Erica S., and Phillip C. Saunders. 1998. "Legitimacy and the Limits of Nationalism: China and the Diaoyu Islands." *International Security* 23, no. 3: 114–146.

Dreyer, June T. 2014. "China and Japan: 'Hot Economics, Cold Politics.'" *Orbis* 58, no. 3: 326–341. https://doi.org/10.1016/j.orbis.2014.05.002.

Duan, Xiaolin. 2017. "Unanswered Questions: Why We may be Wrong about Chinese Nationalism and its Foreign Policy Implications." *Journal of Contemporary China* 26, no. 108: 886–900.

_____. 2019. "Think Territory Politically: The Making and Escalation of Beijing's Commitment to Sovereignize Diaoyu/Senkaku Islands." *The Pacific Review* 32, no. 3: 419–445. https://doi.org/10.1080/09512748.2018.1490805.

Fravel, Taylor. 2008. *Strong Borders, Secure Nation: Cooperation and Conflict in China's Territorial Disputes: Cooperation and Conflict in China's Territorial Disputes*. Princeton: Princeton University Press.

_____. 2010. "Explaining Stability in the Senkaku (Diaoyu) Dispute." In *Getting the Triangle Straight: Managing China-Japan-US Relations*, edited by Gerald Curtis, Ryosei Kokubun and Wang Jisi, 144–164. Washington: The Brookings Institution Press.

_____. 2011. "China's Strategy in the South China Sea." *Contemporary Southeast Asia* 33, no. 3: 292–319. https://doi.org/10.1355/cs33-3b.

Global Times. 2021. "China Plans to Expand Free Trade Network, Accelerate FTA Talks." January 21, 2021. https://www.globaltimes.cn/page/202101/1213551.shtml

Heldt, Berger. 1999. "Domestic Politics, Absolute Deprivation, and Use of Armed Force in Interstate Territorial Disputes, 1950-1990." *The Journal of Conflict Resolution* 43, no. 4: 451–478.

Huth, Paul. 1996. *Standing Your Ground: Territorial Disputes and International Conflict*. Ann Arbor: University of Michigan Press.

Iida, Keisuke. 2017. *Japan's Security and Economic Dependence on China and the United States: Cool Politics, Lukewarm Economics*. New York: Routledge. https://doi.org/10.4324/9781315651897.

Kugler, Jacek, and A.F.K. Organski. 1989. "The Power Transition: A Retrospective and Prospective Evaluation." In *Handbook of War Studies*, edited by Manus Midlarsky, 171–194. Boston: Unwin Hyman.

Japan Times. 2016. "US Urged Japan to Consult with China Before 2012 Senkakus Purchase." January 31, 2016. https://www.japantimes.co.jp/news/2016/01/31/national/u-s-urged-japan-consult-china-2012-senkakus-purchase/#.Vq4vH7IrKUk

Jiang, Zemin. 2006. *Selected Works of Jiang Zemin Volume 2*. Beijing: Renmin Chubanshe.

Johnston, Alastair I. 2013. "How New and Assertive is China's New Assertiveness." *International Security* 37, no. 4: 7–48.

_____. 2016. "Is Chinese Nationalism Rising? Evidence from Beijing." *International Security* 41, no. 3: 7–43.

Kaneko, Reito. 2021. "Japan Can Shoot at Foreign Government Vessels Attempting to Land on Senkakus, LDP Official Says." *Japan Times*, February 25, 2021. https://www.japantimes.co.jp/news/2021/02/25/national/senkakus-east-china-sea-japan-coast-guard-defense.

Kliman, Daniel M., and Daniel Twining. 2014. *Japan's Democracy Diplomacy*. Washington: The German Marshall Fund of the United States.

Koga, Kei. 2016. "The Rise of China and Japan's Balancing Strategy: Critical Junctures and Policy Shifts in the 2010s." *Journal of Contemporary China* 25, no. 101: 777–791. https://doi.org/10.1080/10670564.2016.1160520.

Landler, Mark. 2018. "Trump Has Put the U.S. and China on the Cusp of a New Cold War." *New York Times*, September 19, 2018. https://www.nytimes.com/2018/09/19/us/politics/trump-china-trade-war.html.

Lemke, Douglas, and Ronald L. Tammen. 2003. "Power Transition Theory and the Rise of China." *International Interactions* 29, no. 4: 269–271.

Levy, Jack S. 1987. "Declining Power and the Preventive Motivation for War." *World Politics* 40, no. 1: 82–107. https://doi.org/10.2307/2010195.

Lind, Jennifer. 2017. "Asia's Other Revisionist Power: Why U.S. Grand Strategy Unnerves China." *Foreign Affairs* 96, no. 2: 74–82.

MOFA [Ministry of Foreign Affairs] of Japan. 2016. "Recent Developments in Japan-China Relations: Basic Facts on the Senkaku Islands and the Recent Incident." http://www.mofa.go.jp/region/asia-paci/senkaku/index.html

MOFA [Ministry of Foreign Affairs] of PRC [People's Republic of China]. 2019. "Xi Jinping Meets with Prime Minister Shinzo Abe of Japan." December 23. https://www.fmprc.gov.cn/mfa_eng/zxxx_662805/t1727654.shtml

Nie, Hongyi, and Bin Li. 2008. "China's Policy Choices in the Territorial Disputes" (中国在领土争端中的政策选择). *Quarterly Journal of International Politics* 16 (国际政治科学), 1–34.

People's Daily. 2012. "China's Sovereignty Claim Has Nothing to Do with Resources." October 17, 2012, 3.

Pillsbury, Michael. 2015. *The Hundred-Year Marathon: China's Secret Strategy to Replace America as the Global Superpower*. New York: Henry Holt and Company.

Reilly, James. 2014. "A Wave to Worry About? Public Opinion, Foreign Policy and China's Anti-Japan Protests." *Journal of Contemporary China* 23, no. 86: 197–215. https://doi.org/10.1080/10670564.2013.832519.

Ross, Robert S. 2000. "The 1995-96 Taiwan Strait Confrontation: Coercion, Credibility, and the Use of Force." *International Security* 25, no. 2: 87–123.

Shen, Zhihua. 2012. *Mao, Stalin and the Korean War: Trilateral Communist Relations in the 1950s*. New York: Routledge.

Shen, Zhihua, and Yafeng Xia. 2011. "The Great Leap Forward, the People's Commune and the Sino-Soviet Split." *Journal of Contemporary China* 20, no. 72: 861–880. https://doi.org/10.1080/10670564.2011.604505.

Smith, Anthony D. 2001. *Nationalism: Theory, Ideology, History*. Cambridge: Polity Press.

South China Morning Post. 1996. "Rivals United by Islands Dispute." September 17, 1996. http://archive.today/1ygb0.

Standing Committee of the National People's Congress. 2021. "Coast Guard Law of the People's Republic of China." Lawinformationchina.Com, February 1. https://www.lawinfochina.com/display.aspx?lib=law&id=34610

Swaine, Michael D. 2013. "China's Maritime Disputes in the East and South China Seas." Carnegie Endowment for International Peace, April 4. https://carnegieendowment.org/2013/04/04/china-s-maritime-disputes-in-east-and-south-china-seas-pub-51417

Wang, Jianwei. 2019. "Xi Jinping's 'Major Country Diplomacy:' A Paradigm Shift?" *Journal of Contemporary China* 28, no. 115: 15–30. https://doi.org/10.1080/10670564.2018.1497907.

Weiss, Jessica C. 2014. "The Flame of Chinese Nationalism." *Foreign Policy*, September 17. http://www.jessicachenweiss.com/uploads/3/0/6/3/30636001/2014.11.02--ft_review_of_powerful_patriots.pdf

Yan, Xuetong. 2014. "From Keeping a Low Profile to Striving for Achievement." *The Chinese Journal of International Politics* 7, no. 2: 153–184. https://doi.org/10.1093/cjip/pou027.

Zhao, Suisheng. 2005. "China's Pragmatic Nationalism: Is It Manageable?" *The Washington Quarterly* 29, no. 1: 131–144.

_____. 2013. "Foreign Policy Implications of Chinese Nationalism Revisited: The Strident Turn." *Journal of Contemporary China* 22, no. 82: 535–553. https://doi.org/10.1080/10670564.2013.766379.

5

The Dokdo and Kuril Islands: Japan's Twin Disputes

SERAFETTIN YILMAZ

Whereas there is considerable scholarship on the maritime territorial disputes in the South China Sea (SCS), the long-lingering conflicts in the North Pacific Ocean (NPO) have received much less attention. The disagreements in these two adjacent regions have similarities: First, both are based on claims of historical title such as first discovery, first utilization, status as *terra nullius*, etc. Second, conflicts in both have geopolitical rationale such as control over key passages or access to a wider region. Third, both involve economic benefits such as exploitation of minerals, fish stocks and energy resources. Fourth, the disagreements are a legacy of colonialism and the post-WW2 arrangements of formerly colonized areas. There exists a critical difference, however: Whereas territorial conflicts in the SCS are largely between China and its neighbours, in the Northeast Asian sub-region (NEA), Japan is the country in territorial disputes with its neighbours. These disagreements have proven to be sticky and protracted due to security and economic interests. This chapter offers an account of the origins, development, and dynamics of the territorial conflicts Japan has with South Korea and Russia in the Dokdo and Kuril Islands.

The Dokdo/Takeshima Islands Question

The Dokdo Islands (Takeshima, in Japanese) are a group of sea features located in the Sea of Japan (also known as East Sea). The features are controlled by South Korea and disputed by Japan. Composed of two islands and 89 surrounding islets, the total area of the group is approximately 187,000 square meters. The two main islands, Seodo (West Islet) and Dongdo (East Islet), host a number of structures such as a docking facility, a heliport, and living facilities. Dokdo is located over 87 kilometres southeast of the nearest Korean island, Ulleungdo, whereas the nearest Japanese island (Oki) is located more than 157 kilometres to the southeast. Designated as state-owned land, Dokdo and its surrounding waters are patrolled by the Dokdo Coast Guard and Korea Coast Guard vessels. Other than the Coast Guard, several lighthouse staff and local government officers, Dokdo is also home to a number of civilian residents.

Korean claims of ownership to Dokdo date back to the sixth century (AD 512). Over the centuries, the islands were referred to by different names, but Korean sovereignty and administrative control continued uninterrupted even after the adoption of a 'vacant island policy' from the early 15th to the late 19th centuries, which prohibited settlement on islands considered too remote from the Korean mainland (Shin 1997). Successive administrations promulgated policies to manage offshore islands, such as sending survey teams to the islands and the near waters, and updating their administrative status. Japan, it should be noted, contends that what is depicted as Dokdo in the earliest Korean text sounds more like Utsuryo Island. Nevertheless, Korea dismisses the Japanese interpretation, and officially rejects the existence of a dispute at all.

Japanese historical documents on Dokdo are relatively recent, with the earliest records dating back to the late 1700s, which is a report of a trip to Oki Island. The report has been presented by Japan as proof of sovereignty ever since the territorial question first emerged in the early post-War years. However, Korean researchers argue that the document weakens Japan's position since it mentions the proximity of Dokdo to the Korean mainland (Ji 2010). In addition to this document, Tokyo relies on a host of historical texts such as field reports, maps, and administrative proclamations. Thus, Japan claims that both historically and from the point of view of international law, a valid dispute does indeed exist over the ownership of Dokdo.

Colonial Legacies

The Korean and Japanese contest for control over Dokdo spans over 300 years. As early as the 1600s, conflict over fishing rights off the shores of several islands, including Dokdo, led to early negotiations between the two sides. Contentions intensified with the Meiji Restoration and the opening up of Korea to Japan in the 1870s. Japanese expansionism eventually led to the First Sino-Japanese War of 1894-1895 and the Russo-Japanese War of 1904–1905, involving, among others, competition for domination over Korea. With the Treaty of Shimonoseki (1895) that ended the First Sino-Japanese War, Japan ensured the recognition of Korea as an independent state by the Qing dynasty. Likewise, the wording of the peace treaty signed at the end of the Russo-Japanese War guaranteed Russia's recognition of Japanese interests in Korea.

Japan extended its *de facto* domination over Korea through a series of treaties and on-the-ground actions, including negotiating with Russia for a greater presence in Korea in return for recognizing Russia's interests in Manchuria, setting alliances with Great Britain and the United States to ensure their consent for an eventual incorporation of Korea, and forcing Korea to sign the Korean-Japanese Protocol Agreement in 1904 (which paved the way for the deployment of Japanese troops in the country). By 1905, Korea had already fallen under full Japanese control. Eventually, the second and third Korean-Japanese Agreements (November 1905 and 1907, respectively) ended Korean sovereignty and made it a Japanese protectorate. This included the Dokdo Islands. Although Japan formally annexed Korea in 1910, the question remains whether Tokyo treated Dokdo as a Japanese territory, or as part of an occupied Korea.

Post-War Complications

Dokdo was incorporated in 1905 as *terra nullius* (no man's land), and in spite of Korean protestations, it was placed under the jurisdiction of the Shimane Prefectural government, a prefecture located in the northern region of west Japan. The backlash by Korean officials and intellectuals was of little significance since Korea had already become a protectorate of Japan by this time. Japan's recognition of Dokdo as a no man's land implied that by the time they were consolidated as a Japanese territory, the islands had 'no traces of ownership by any country,' thus legitimizing the Japanese action. The *terra nullius* argument was rejected by a number of Korean experts, however (Ch'oe 2015). In any case, Japanese assertion of control over Dokdo was only a continuation of its policy of territorial expansion. Dokdo was significant not only as a fishing grounds, but also as a naval base that became important in the major sea battles of the Russo-Japanese War.

After more than 40 years, Japan's *de facto* control over Dokdo Islands ended when it signed the Treaty of Peace with Japan (also known as the Treaty of San Francisco) in 1951. However, much as wartime declarations had, the post-war peace treaty, too, failed to provide an effective solution, instead leaving the issue in perpetual limbo. In both the Cairo Declaration (1943) and the Potsdam Declaration (1945), the status of Dokdo remained unclear even though these documents demanded the relinquishment of the territories occupied by Japan. Furthermore, geopolitical and ideological rivalries among the victorious nations became manifest during the negotiations over a peace treaty with Japan. Reflecting internal disagreements among the Allied powers, the Dokdo islands were included in some of the early drafts of the treaty and were missing in others, including the final draft, as desired by the US side (Emmers 2010, 10).

This vagueness caused the disagreement between Japan and Korea to linger on into the post-War era: The former holds that Dokdo was not specifically mentioned in the text and therefore remained outside the scope of the treaty, since it was an inherent territory of Japan when annexed. The latter, conversely, argues that Article 2(a) of the Treaty implied that Dokdo as being included in the 'all right, title and claim' to be renounced by Japan. Thus, goes the Korean argument, the islands' lack of mention did not mean that Dokdo was not included, as more than 3,000 other offshore territories were likewise not mentioned in the text (Emmers 2010, 9; Schrijver and Prislan 2015, 290–291).[1]

The US refusal to allow the peace treaty to clearly refer to the status of the Dokdo Islands was an outcome of the emerging Cold War geopolitics. Indeed, by 1945, the Korean Peninsula has already been divided into two zones of influence, with the north and south occupied by troops from the Soviet Union and the United States, respectively. By 1951, the United Nations was well into the war in Korea. On the one hand, Washington did not want to completely alienate its southern ally on the Korean Peninsula by explicitly ruling out Korean control over the offshore islands, including Dokdo, while, on the other, it did not want to specify the islands in the text of the treaty lest they fall in the hands of the Communists in the event that the North prevailed. Eventually, upon the US rejection of Korean requests to include several more offshore islands in the peace treaty, in January 1952, Korean president Syngman Rhee proclaimed the unilateral imposition of jurisdiction over waters off the Korean coast, circumscribing Dokdo within the affected territory (Bukh 2015, 50).[2]

The two sides signed the Treaty on Basic Relations between Japan and the Republic of Korea in 1965. As part of the agreement, a joint regulation zone was established, allowing fishermen from the two countries to operate in the region. Diplomatic normalization, however, did not prevent sporadic flare ups in the decades that followed. In the 1970s, bilateral relations deteriorated upon the establishment of Exclusive Economic Zones (EEZ) by both countries with overlapping claims – the conclusion of a series of agreements on the

---

[1]   In fact, the Peace Treaty annulled the MacArthur Line, which demarcated the waters in the area and kept Japanese fishing boats away from the region, leading to numerous confrontations over fishing activities.

[2]   Up until the repeal of Rhee's proclamation in 1965, thousands of Japanese fishermen were arrested in the waters defined by the line.

management of the northern and southern parts of the continental shelf in the Yellow Sea notwithstanding (Zhang 2015, 377–378).

Post-Cold War Optimism and Rising Tensions

In the early post-Cold War era, there were several reasons to be optimistic about Korea-Japan relations in general, and the Dokdo question in particular. First, in both Japan and Korea, domestic political developments suggested a likely shift in attitude: In Japan, the dominant political party, the Liberal Democratic Party, lost power for the first time in 1993. In the same year, the first freely-elected civilian leader assumed the presidency in South Korea. Also, the end of the Cold War heralded a normalization of politics in East Asia, allowing the two countries to participate in the emerging regional security regimes.

Furthermore, in 1996, South Korea and Japan signed the United Nations Convention on the Law of the Sea (UNCLOS), which paved the way for the two sides to determine their EEZ and agree on overlapping claims. Later, in 1998, Korea and Japan signed a new fisheries agreement to replace the 1965 accord, which created intermediate zones which fishing vessels could enter (Xue 2005). Finally, on the economic plane, the impact of the Asian financial crisis of 1996 led the two countries to participate in regional frameworks such as the Chiang Mai Initiative and the ASEAN+3.

Such optimism was short lived, however. Domestically, the two governments' official positions on maritime claims followed those of their predecessors even though, theoretically, both countries now shared similar democratic values and adhered to basic international norms. Also, the wave of regionalism in East Asia did not lead to any meaningful change in attitude toward sovereignty-related issues. Participation in the UNCLOS or growing bilateral trade and people-to-people communication – positive as these developments were – did not preclude contentions over overlapping maritime claims (Bong 2013, 194–195).

In fact, a series of developments in the 2000s brought the Dokdo question to the fore. In 2004, Korea issued postage stamps depicting Dokdo, leading to protests in Japan. A year later, Shimane Prefecture ordained 22 February as Takeshima Day. In the same year, Tokyo announced a maritime surveillance mission in the vicinity of Dokdo Islands, which prompted Korea to send gunboats to the area (Bukh 2015, 56; YNA 2020). Bilateral relations were further strained when the Japanese government asked textbook publishers to describe Dokdo as Japanese territory.

Tensions over the contested territories continued throughout the second decade of the new millennium as well. In 2012, Lee Myung-bak paid a visit to Dokdo, becoming the first Korean president to do so. In reaction, members of the Japanese cabinet and the ruling party participated in Takeshima Day celebrations (Ismail 2017, 86–87). South Korean military drills aimed at defending Dokdo as part of the country's new defense concept 'with a focus on responding to potential threats by neighbouring countries, particularly Japan' generated backlash in Tokyo several times over the past decade (Jeong 2018). More recently, Japan's reopening of the National Museum of Territory and Sovereignty, where the Dokdo islands are presented as national territory, elicited criticism from Korea.

Dokdo Islands: Political and Economic Significance

The claim to sovereign control based on historical entitlement has been a strong rationale in contests over territory, especially in East Asia. In the case of the Dokdo Islands, nationalism on both sides has been a critical impediment to a negotiated solution (Wiegand and Choi 2017). However, even though the utility of nationalist sentiment in generating a rally effect in domestic politics has been demonstrated (Hwang, Cho, and Wiegand 2018; Fearon 1994), beneath those sentiments of national pride lie other geopolitical and economic rationales (Pereslavtsev 2018, 76).

Among the factors complicating the territorial claims is the geographic location of the islands as a forward base for the observation and monitoring of military activities.[3] Dokdo can help enhance sea and air situational awareness, especially if it is further enlarged using island-building techniques. Dokdo also holds significant economic value in the form of marine and hydrocarbon resources. In terms of marine wealth, the waters surrounding the islands have been traditional fishing areas for centuries. The islands also provide shelter for fishing boats as a resting area in peace time and a safe harbour during storms. According to the Korean Website K-Dokdo, the region is also believed to contain large amounts of gas hydrate deposits.

Strategies for Dokdo

As a historical issue, Dokdo conjures different meanings in Korea and Japan. From a Korean perspective, Dokdo is as much a question about its past as its present. For Japan, on the other hand, the question is a modern one detached from any emotional attachment to the past. Herein lies the problem

---

[3]   During the Russo-Japanese War of 1905, Japan monitored the Russian Navy using an observation tower on the island.

of closure: For Japan, the treaty of 1965 normalizing ties with Korea ended a chapter in its history, including its pre-war efforts bent on territorial expansion. Japan's attitude of letting bygones be bygones, however, does not find an audience in Korea, for which Dokdo is considered historical territory.

Japan presents Dokdo as a contemporary dispute waiting for a practical resolution. Part of this strategy involves internationalization of the question as a legal debate, which explains why Japan has attempted to take the Dokdo issue to the International Court of Justice several times in the past (Park and Chubb 2011). For Korea, the Japanese 'proposal … is not even worthy of consideration' since 'there is no territorial dispute over [Dokdo]' (MOFA of the ROK 2012). Accordingly, the question of whether earlier cases might constitute a legal precedent for the present conflict is moot. First and foremost, Korea officially rejects the existence of a dispute. Second, since each territorial conflict has its own characteristics, citing precedent is rather difficult (Schrijver and Prislan 2015).

The Kuril Islands/Northern Territories Question

The Kuril Islands (Kurilskiye Ostrova, in Russian, and known as Northern Territories/Southern Chishima in Japan, or Chishima-rettō) form a natural barrier between the Sea of Okhotsk and North Pacific Ocean. Extending 1,200 kilometres between the southern tip of the Kamchatka Peninsula and the Japanese island of Hokkaido, it consists of 56 islands that cover 15,600 square kilometres. The four islands (the Southern Kurils) at the heart of the dispute are Iturup (Etorofu), Kunashir (Kunashiri), Shikotan, and Habomai. The islands are currently administered by Sakhalin Oblast as South Kuril District. Tectonically and volcanically active, the Kuril archipelago is inhabited by over 10,000 people from various ethnic groups, as well as several thousand Russian troops (Kaczynski 2007; Elleman, Nichols, and Ouimet 1999, 490).

Officially, Japan considers Russia's control over 'four islands located off the northeast coast of the Nemuro Peninsula of Hokkaido' an 'occupation.' Japan's claims are historical and based on first discovery and continuous settlement. It calls for a 'flexible' negotiated solution with Russia eventually ceding control, reiterating that it would not subject the 'Russian current residents on the islands' to any sort of forced relocation or deportation (MOFA of Japan 2011).

Russia stresses that its sovereignty over the islands is not to be discussed, holding that its possession of the South Kurils is legal, thus, especially in view of the amendments to the Russian Constitution which bars any transfer of national territory, 'no changes are possible in this position' (Zakharova 2020). The Russian government also rejects the argument that the islands would be returned to Tokyo upon the completion of a peace treaty with Japan (MOFA of the Russian Federation 2020).

Kuril Islands Conflict: Historical Development

Originally settled by Ainu people, the Kuril Islands saw a number of expeditions carried out by Dutch, Japanese, and Russian explorers. Czarist Russia incorporated the islands into the empire in 1786. Japan exerted effective control over the islands by the early 19th century. In the Treaty of Shimoda (1855), the two sides partitioned the island chain, with Japan retaining the southern Kuril Islands of Iturup, Kunashir, Shikotan, and Habomai. However, since the treaty left the question of the ownership of Sakhalin unanswered, conflicts continued until the Treaty of St. Petersburg (1875) in which Russia ceded control over all of the Kuril Islands in exchange for keeping Sakhalin (Hasegawa 1998, 8). The Russo-Japanese War of 1904–1905 resulted in the defeat of the Russian Navy and led to the Portsmouth Peace Treaty (1905), in which Japan took the southern part of Sakhalin below the 50th parallel (Martin 1967; Keene 2002, 628). From 1875 to 1945, the entire Kuril Islands chain remained under Japanese control.

The Kuril question resurfaced at the Yalta (Crimea) Conference in February 1945 in which, in an effort to enlist Russia in the war against Japan, the allied powers promised to give the Kurils and Sakhalin to the Soviet Union upon Japan's defeat. This led to the USSR's withdrawal from the Soviet-Japanese Neutrality Pact of 1941, which was to have been in effect for five years. Japan argues that the Yalta Accords were contrary to the language of both the Atlantic Charter (1941), to which the Soviet Union pledged allegiance, and the Cairo Declaration (1943), which stressed the USSR's acquiescence to the Atlantic Charter. It further holds that, as per the Cairo Declaration, 'it is clear that the Northern Territories do not constitute territories that Japan seized "by violence and greed"' (MOFA of Japan, n.d.).

The USSR took control of Southern Sakhalin and four Kuril islands between 18 August and 1 September 1945 without any resistance from what was left of the Japanese military (Elleman, Nichols, and Ouimet 1999, 492–494). On 2 September 1945, Japanese Foreign Minister Mamoru Shigemitsu and General Yoshijiro Umezu signed the Instrument of Surrender on the deck of the USS Missouri. As stipulated by the terms of the Potsdam Declaration of July 1945, Japan's sovereignty was limited to the four main islands (Honshu, Hokkaido, Kyushu, and Shikoku) as well as minor islands to be determined by the allies. The Soviets incorporated the Kuril Islands in February 1946 and, over the following three years, deported most of the Japanese-speaking residents to Hokkaido.

The Treaty of Peace was designed to bring an effective end to the war and settle all questions related to territories occupied by Japan during its period of military expansion. Along the lines of the Yalta agreement, Article 11(c) of the treaty stated that 'Japan renounces all right, title and claim to the Kuril Islands, and to that portion of Sakhalin and the islands adjacent to it' (Treaty of peace with Japan 1952). The Soviet Union participated in the conference, however it did not sign the Treaty because, among other reasons, the Treaty did not promulgate to which states these territories were going to be transferred. Japan stresses the USSR's non-participation in the treaty and argues that the four southern islands were not included in the Kuril chain.

During the decades leading up to the end of the Cold War and the dissolution of the Soviet Union, the Kurils remained a major impediment of a conclusive peace treaty between Japan and the USSR. The two sides agreed on a joint declaration on ending the state of war and normalized diplomatic relationship in 1956. Historical records show that Japanese negotiations over a peace treaty with Russia were strongly influenced by ideological considerations and the Washington's own geopolitical interests. At the outset of the talks held in London in June 1955, Japan asked for a two-island solution, namely, the return of Habomai and Shikotan – a proposal that was initially rejected by the Soviets. However, as the talks proceeded, the Russian side acceded to the Japanese request on the condition that Tokyo would keep the islands demilitarized and promise that its security alliance with the United States would not target a third state. The US delegation objected to the Russian conditions, especially those related to naval access to the Sea of Japan, which brought the negotiations to a standstill (Elleman, Nichols, and Ouimet 1999, 497). Furthermore, when in mid-1956 Japan seemed to eventually agree on the terms of a peace treaty with Russia in return for the retention of two of the four southern islands, the US government notified the Japanese side that if Japan did not reclaim all four islands, the United States would not return Okinawa (Schoenbaum 2008, 121; Clark 2005, 3). As a result, although the two sides restored diplomatic relations in 1956, the territorial disagreement remained unsettled.

It is stated in the Soviet-Japanese Joint Declaration that the USSR 'agrees to hand over to Japan the Habomai Islands and the island of Shikotan ... the actual handing over these islands to Japan shall take place after the conclusion of a peace treaty' (MOFA of Japan 2001). Drawing on this, Japan argues that, as a legally binding document, the treaty established Japan's sovereignty over the islands. Russia, however, argues that 'following Japan's signing a security treaty with the United States in 1960, the former Soviet Union revoked its liabilities concerning the transfer of the islands' (TASS 2019).

Post-Cold War: Japan's Monetization Attempt

Whereas during the years preceding diplomatic normalization Japan mostly maintained a hawkish strategy of 'politics first, economy second,' by conditioning cooperation in trade to the solution of the Kurils question, its diplomatic efforts, especially in the first decade of the post-Cold War era, evolved to one in which it sought to retain the islands by offering economic assistance in return (Chang 1998, 176).

Although the two countries officially ended the war and normalized relations, Cold War divisions and geopolitics forestalled any meaningful solution. Up until the 1970s, the Soviet Union rejected the existence of a dispute, and peace treaty negotiations came to a standstill. Diplomatic dialogue over the islands started only when General Secretary of the Communist Party of the Soviet Union Mikhail Gorbachev paid a state visit to Japan in 1991 when the two sides signed the Japan-Soviet Joint Communiqué and acknowledged the existence of a territorial issue (MOFA of Japan 2001).

Russia officially recognized the Kuril dispute in 1993. Confirming the 1956 Joint Declaration, the Tokyo Declaration on Russian-Japanese Relations expressed that the two parties 'have undertaken serious negotiations on the issue of where Etorofu, Kunashiri, Shikotan and the Habomai Islands belong' (MOFA of Japan 1993). Throughout the 1990s, well aware of the political and economic challenges the Russian Federation faced, Japan embarked on an ambitious course of money diplomacy to take back the claimed territories. However, in spite of several high-profile exchanges between the two parties throughout the 1990s, the territorial problem remained unsolved (Tarlow 2000, 127–128; Chang 1998, 189).

Thus, in the first two decades of 2000, the debate gradually shifted from the return of the islands to Japan to the management and development of the region. Improving domestic conditions was a key factor in this shift: better political and economic stability in Russia revived a stronger sense of territorial control. The policy of semi-acknowledgement of a dispute evolved into a complete rejection of the existence of a territorial issue. In Japan, nationalist sentiment grew against the backdrop of disputes with China and South Korea. Gradually, therefore, a Japanese solution to the Kurils issue became a distant likelihood (TASS 2020).

The Kuril Islands are significant, both economically and geopolitically. In terms of resources, 'the four islands are believed to be rich in minerals...' (Chang 1998, 182). They are also 'surrounded by rich fishing areas, where a third of the amount of fish caught in the Far East seas is caught' (Hamzah, Esmael, and Abbas 2020). The islands' geographic location is crucial in view of the opening up of the Russian Arctic coastline (the Northeast Passage) as an alternative sea route for East Asian trade, especially that from China via the Sea of Japan and the Sea of Okhotsk (Yilmaz 2017, 65–66). Furthermore, considering the extensive and growing level of energy cooperation between China and Russia in the Arctic region, the Kuril Islands are of strategic importance for the sea-based energy trade (Chun 2020).

Militarily, too, the Kuril Islands are important. They serve as a practical outpost overlooking the North Pacific Ocean. The Russian military objects to any sort of transfer of the South Kurils, given that they are instrumental 'to prevent American submarines to pass through the straights around the island' and 'to protect the Far East coastline against potential threats from the US, China and Japan' (Chang 1998, 181). The islands 'control the movements of the Russian fleet in the Pacific located in Vladivostok,' and therefore foreign ownership of the islands would pose a potential threat to Russia's naval presence in the Pacific (Hamzah, Esmael, and Abbas 2020; AP News 2020).

Japan's Twin Disputes: Comparison and Prospects

It should be understood that Japan's two territorial conflicts have some commonalities and differences. First, the parties that enjoy *de facto* control over the islands decline to acknowledge that a dispute even exists. This is especially true in the case of South Korea. As for Russia, over the past two decades, the country's strategy has shifted from considering a monetized or two-island solution to a policy of rejecting the existence of a dispute. Japan's position vis-à-vis the Kuril Islands is therefore weaker now than it was in the late 1980s and early 1990s.

Second, in both cases, practical considerations appear to be more pronounced even though the presence of strong nationalist sentiments cannot be ignored. Both Dokdo and the Kuril Islands are of economic and geopolitical importance to the countries claiming them. Economically, the islands and their surrounding waters are destinations for marine tourism, mineral resource extraction, and fishing activities. The location of both island groups offers advantages in terms of naval outreach, as well as, in the case of the Kurils, control over the sea routes in the Arctic-bound trade between East Asia and Western Europe.

Moreover, as the disputing party in both cases, Japan's strategy provides insights into the pragmatism of the country's foreign policy. One such instance was Tokyo's attempt to use check book diplomacy in the 1990s to assume control over the Kurils against the backdrop of the crisis Russia was undergoing. Finally, in both instances, Japan has actively sought internationalization. This is especially true in the case of Dokdo, in which Japan has attempted several times to bring the dispute to international arbitration. For its part, South Korea has firmly ruled out any third-party arbitration and instead seeks to highlight Dokdo by promoting its nature, culture, and folklore. Tokyo's attempts reflect its capacity to devise flexible diplomatic solutions, since the government objects any sort of internationalization of the dispute over the Senkaku/Diaoyu Islands by denying the existence of a dispute over these East China Sea features. Meanwhile, unlike Korea, Russia seems less concerned about Japan's internationalization attempts vis-à-vis the Kuril Islands.

Obviously, to fully account for the two territorial questions, one needs to factor in the ideological and geopolitical considerations of the United States in the years immediately after WW2 and the ensuing Cold War. US opposition to any explicit reference to the Dokdo Islands during the drafting of the Peace Treaty out of concern that Korea might fall to the Communists no doubt contributed to the present-day dilemma. Similarly, in the years leading up to the normalization of Japan-Russia relations, Washington objected to a two-island solution. It is also worth noting that, at present, the United States maintains a more-or-less neutral position on the Dokdo question between Japan and South Korea, whereas on the issue of the Kurils, it has publicly endorsed the Japanese position (Japan Times 2014).

It follows that, in the post-war era, political and economic normalization has failed to lead to a solution in either of the territorial conflicts. In fact, Japan today has much less room to manoeuvre on its territorial claims than before (much like the rest of the territorial disputes in the East and South China Seas). Deepening economic ties, ideological affinity, and the all-encompassing US security umbrella involving both Japan and South Korea have all failed to facilitate a negotiated solution on the Dokdo Islands. In the same way, diplomatic normalization and huge economic potential has fallen short of providing a basis for constructive communication between Russia and Japan over the Kuril Islands. Furthermore, while international law is theoretically applicable through the voluntary employment of dispute-resolution mechanisms, this has proven ineffective since both South Korea and Russia refuse to entertain such an idea. This intransigence is unlikely to change in the foreseeable future.

In both cases, perhaps the strategy with the highest chance of success is a realistic one: one that best manages the differences between the relevant parties and having the aim of promoting stable relations, rather than continuing to try to bring those disagreements to an amicable end. Such a shelving of disagreements may lead to a protracted situation, further solidifying mutually exclusive positions. Management of the differences in the interpretations of territorial title, therefore, needs to focus on finding mechanisms for communication and information-sharing to avoid misunderstandings, and making sure that disagreements do not impede cooperation in other issue areas.

Figure 5.1: Dokdo (Korean)/ Takeshima (Japanese) Islands. Source: Ksiom/ Wikimedia commons.
https://commons.wikimedia.org/w/index.php?curid=4696039

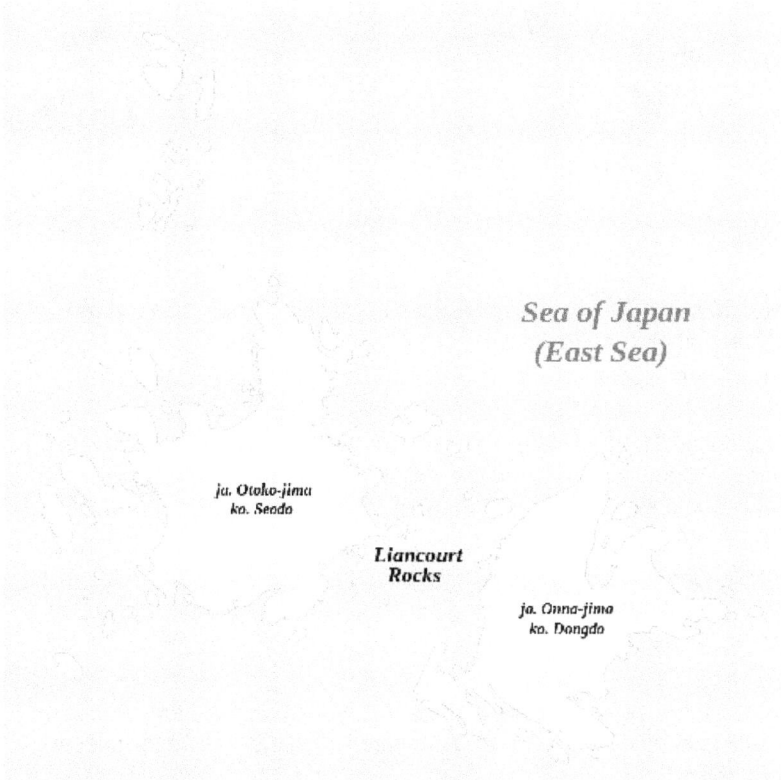

Sea of Japan
(East Sea)

ja. *Otoko-jima*
ko. *Seodo*

Liancourt Rocks

ja. *Onna-jima*
ko. *Dongdo*

Figure 5.2. Kuril Islands. Source: Hardscarf/Wikimedia commons.
https://commons.wikimedia.org/w/index.php?curid=1396806

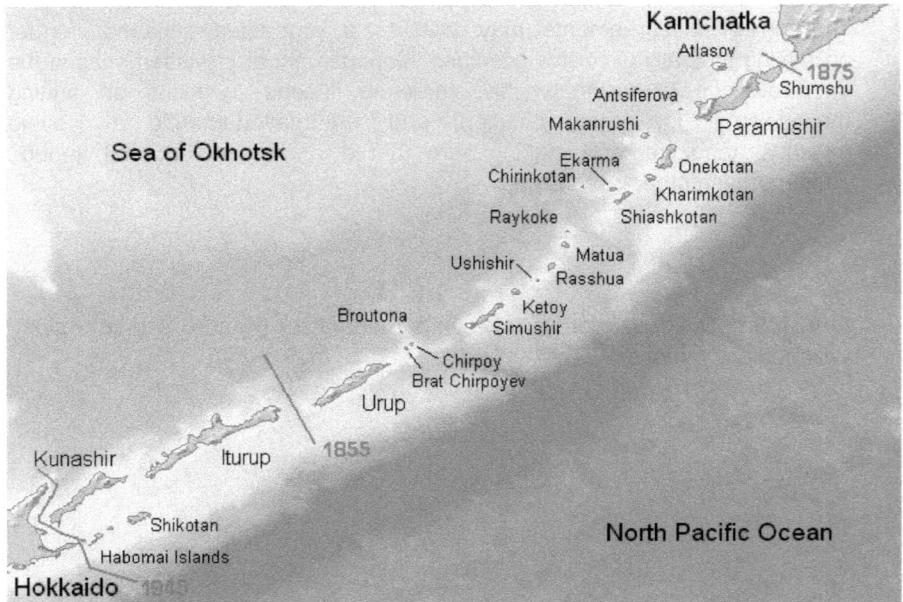

References

AP News. 2020. "Russia Deploys Missiles to Pacific Islands Claimed by Japan." December 1, 2020. https://apnews.com/article/international-news-world-war-ii-kuril-islands-japan-russia-15dbd41dba12496daaeb1b59e5244681

Bong, Youngshik D. 2013. "Built to Last: The Dokdo Territorial Controversy. The Baseline Conditions in Domestic Politics and International Security of Japan and South Korea." *Memory Studies* 6, no. 2: 191–203.

Bukh, Alexander. 2015. "Shimane Prefecture, Tokyo and the Territorial Dispute Over Dokdo/Takeshima: Regional and National Identities in Japan." *The Pacific Review* 28, no. 1: 47–70.

Chang, Duckjoon. 1998. "Breaking Through a Stalemate? A Study Focusing on the Kuril Islands Issue in Russo-Japanese Relations." *Asian Perspective* 22, no. 3: 169–206.

Ch'oe, Yong-Ho. 2015. "Japan's 1905 Incorporation of Dokdo/Takeshima: A Historical Perspective." *The Asia-Pacific Journal* 13-9, no. 3: 1–27.

Chun, Zhang. 2020. "China's 'Arctic Silk Road'." *The Maritime Executive*, 10 January, 2020. https://www.maritime-executive.com/editorials/china-s-arctic-silk-road

Clark, Gregory. 2005. "Japan-Russia Dispute Over Northern Territories Highlights Flawed Diplomacy." *The Asia-Pacific Journal* 3, no. 4: 1–5.

Elleman, Bruce A, Michael R. Nichols, and Matthew J. Ouimet. 1999. "A Historical Reevaluation of America's Role in the Kuril Islands Dispute." *Pacific Affairs* 71, no. 4: 489–504.

Emmers, Ralf. 2010. "Japan-Korea Relations and the Tokdo/Takeshima Dispute: The Interplay of Nationalism and Natural Resources." *RSIS Working Paper* 212, 1–43.

Fearon, James D. 1994. "Domestic Political Audiences and the Escalation of International Disputes." *American Political Science Review* 88, no. 3: 577–592.

Hamzah, Majeed Kamil, Ahmed Abid Esmael, and Faisal Shallal Abbas. 2020. "The Future of Russian-Japanese Relations in Light of the Crisis in the Kuril Islands." *Utopía y Praxis Latinoamericana* 25, no. 1: 291–304.

Hasegawa, Tsuyoshi. 1998. *The Northern Territories Dispute and Russo-Japanese Relations: Between War and Peace, 1697-1985*. Berkeley: University of California.

Hwang, Wonjae, Wonbin Cho, and Krista Wiegand. 2018. "Do Korean-Japanese Historical Disputes Generate Rally Effects?" *The Journal of Asian Studies* 77, no. 3: 693–711.

Ismail, Azlie Bin. 2017. "The Dokdo/Takeshima Dispute: Responses and Approaches." *International Journal of East Asian Studies* 6, no. 1: 82–99.

Japan Times. 2014. "U.S. Recognizes Japan's Sovereignty Over Russian-Held Isles: Official." August 14, 2014. https://www.japantimes.co.jp/news/2014/08/14/national/u-s-recognizes-japans-sovereignty-over-russian-held-isles-official

Jeong, Jeff. 2018. "Is 'Radar Feud' Sign of Future Military Confrontation Between South Korea and Japan?" *Defence News*, 26 December, 2018 https://www.defensenews.com/global/asia-pacific/2018/12/26/is-radar-feud-sign-of-future-military-confrontation-between-south-korea-and-japan

Ji, Guoxing. 2010. "Dokdo and Sino-Japanese Diaoyudao Disputes." *Korea Herald*, April 4, 2010. http://www.koreaherald.com/view.php?ud=20081124000068

Kaczynski, Vlad M. 2007. "The Kuril Islands Dispute Between Russia and Japan: Perspectives of Three Ocean Powers." *Russian Analytical Digest* 20. https://css.ethz.ch/content/dam/ethz/special-interest/gess/cis/center-for-securities-studies/pdfs/RAD-20-6-8.pdf

Keene, Donald. 2002. *Emperor of Japan: Meiji and His World, 1852-1912*. New York: Columbia University Press.

Martin, Christopher. 1967. *The Russo-Japanese War*. London: Abelard-Schuman.

MOFA [Ministry of Foreign Affairs] of Japan. 1993. "Tokyo Declaration on Japan-Russia Relations – Provisional Translation." October 13. https://www.mofa.go.jp/region/n-america/us/q&a/declaration.html

———. 2001. "Joint Compendium of Documents on the History of Territorial Issue between Japan and Russia." March 1. https://www.mofa.go.jp/region/europe/russia/territory/edition92/period5.html

———. 2011. "Northern Territories Issue." March 1. https://www.mofa.go.jp/region/europe/russia/territory/overview.html

———. (n.d.). "Japan's Northern Territories: For a Relationship of Genuine Trust." https://www.mofa.go.jp/region/europe/russia/territory/pamphlet.pdf

MOFA [Ministry of Foreign Affairs] of ROK [Republic of Korea]. 2012. "MOFAT Spokesperson's Commentary on the Japanese Government's Announcement on Dokdo." August 17. https://dokdo.mofa.go.kr/m/eng/dokdo/government_announce_list.jsp?pagenumber=7&sn=1&st=&sn02=&st02=&sc=&sdate=&edate=&orderby=&sort=&status=&at=view&idx=2036&category=us

MOFA [Ministry of Foreign Affairs] of the Russian Federation. 2020. "Comment by the Information and Press Department on the May 6 Article in the Japanese Newspaper Asahi." May 8. https://www.mid.ru/en/web/guest/kommentarii_predstavitelya//asset_publisher/MCZ7HQuMdqBY/content/id/4116799.

Park, Dong-Joon, and Danielle Chubb. 2011. "South Korea and Japan: Disputes Over the Dokdo/Takeshima Islands." *East Asia Forum*, 17 August, 2011. https://www.eastasiaforum.org/2011/08/17/south-korea-and-japan-disputes-over-the-dokdotakeshima-islands

Pereslavtsev, Nikolai I. 2018. "Korean-Japanese Dispute Concerning Liancourt Islands and the Position of Russia." *Asia-Pacific Journal of Marine Science & Education* 8, no. 1: 75–81.

Schoenbaum, Thomas J. 2008. *Peace in Northeast Asia: Resolving Japan's Territorial and Maritime Disputed with China, Korea and the Russian Federation*. Cheltenham: Edward Elgar Publishing.

Shin, Yong-Ha. 1997. "A Historical Study of Korea's Title to Tokdo." *Korean Observer* 28.

Schrijver, Nico J., and Vid Prislan. 2015. "Cases Concerning Sovereignty Over Islands Before the International Court of Justice and the Dokdo/Takeshima Issue." *Ocean Development and International Law* 46, 281–314.

Tarlow, Lisbeth L. 2000. "Russian Decision-Making on Japan in the Gorbachev Era." In *Japan and Russia: The Tortuous Path to Normalization, 1949-1994*, edited by Gilbert Rozman. London: Palgrave Macmillan.

TASS. 2019. "How the Kuril Islands Dispute Arose, and the Story Behind Russian-Japanese Peace Efforts." January 21, 2019. https://tass.com/world/1041010

_____. 2020. "New Japanese PM Plans to Finalize Talks on Kuril Islands." October 26, 2020. https://tass.com/world/1216253

Treaty of peace with Japan: Signed San Francisco Sept. 8, 1951, with related documents. 1952. Washington.

Wiegand, Krista, and Ajin Choi. 2017. "Nationalism, Public Opinion, and Dispute Resolution: The Dokdo/Takeshima Dispute." *Journal of Asian Pacific Communication* 27, no. 2: 232–245.

Xue, Guifang. 2005. "Bilateral Fisheries Agreements for the Cooperative Management of the Shared Resources of the China Seas: A Note." *Ocean Development & International Law* 36, no. 4: 363–374.

Yilmaz, Serafettin. 2017. "Exploring China's Arctic Strategy: Opportunities and Challenges." *China Quarterly of International Strategic Studies* 3, no. 1: 57–78.

YNA. 2020. "IHO's Decision on Name of Seas Between Korea, Japan." 17 November, 2020. https://en.yna.co.kr/view/PYH20201117162600325

Zakharova, Maria. 2020. "Briefing by Foreign Ministry Spokesperson [Press briefing]." July 16. https://www.mid.ru/en/web/guest/foreign_policy/news/-/asset_publisher/cKNonkJE02Bw/content/id/4234569

Zhang, Weiqiang. 2015. "A Study on the Delimitation of the Sea of Japan." *China Oceans Law Review* 2, 345–369.

6

US Policy in the South China Sea Across Three Administrations: Pivot, Transactionalism, and Strength Through Alliances

ADAM GERVAL AND MARK HENDERSON

Territorial disputes in the South China Sea (SCS) have shifted the narrative of security studies of   the region. As the People's Republic of China (PRC) has grown more assertive, the role of the United States to safeguard free navigation has been challenged. Across administrations, traditional allegiances have been in flux, while under the administration of US President Joe Biden, they appear to have become more dynamic. US air and naval superiority are currently being maintained, but the growing PRC defense budget and rapid increases in the quality and quantity of force has begun to change international perceptions. Finally, western assumptions about social and political developments in China have missed the mark. Why has the PRC not begun to liberalize political control as a result of economic development? Where is China's civil society? How has the PRC become a great power while continuing to violate human rights and bend international rules? During the Obama administration, chief US strategists claimed that, as the PRC developed, so too would its sense of international responsibility. So far, Beijing has been showing us the exact opposite. The PRC has been playing games in international organizations, placing their experts in key roles and backing sympathetic candidates for leadership positions. Unambiguous human rights violations are being broadcasted to the world in Xinjiang and Hong Kong. Relations across the Taiwan Strait have returned to a level of tensions not seen in recent memory. China's Paramount Leader Xi Jinping has removed political opposition and will begin an unprecedented third term at the top of the PRC political structure.

The sum of these trends shows an increasingly aggressive and authoritarian government in the PRC, which runs counter to the world's aspirations for China. Recognition of this fact may have begun long before the administration of former President Donald Trump, but US policy on China changed most dramatically in the Trump years. Interestingly, US actions in the South China Sea have been relatively constant. There has been no equivalent to a trade war, as we have seen with economic disputes. In maritime policy, the US position remains largely unchanged: to maintain open shipping lanes and ensure freedom of navigation. Instead, the changes have largely been a means to that end. With the singular exception of reference to the 2016 China-Philippines arbitration, much of the change in US policy has been in the reliance on traditional alliances, frequency of operations, and public messaging on maritime disputes.

Priority Number One: Navigation

Freedom of navigation has continued to be priority No. 1 for the United States, regardless of who is in office. It is worth mentioning that the beneficiaries of that policy are not only US citizens: a South China Sea that is free for all has allowed economies, even those not physically in the region, to be able to consistently rely on steady shipping costs. Volatility in international commerce undermines the function of liberalized capital markets. Economic growth in the Indo-Pacific has been no exception to that rule, as we can see in the ever-growing transit of goods through the South China Sea. More than US$3 trillion in goods moved through the SCS in 2016, including more than 30% of the world's crude oil trade (CSIS 2021).

US maintenance of unobstructed transport for commercial, civilian, and innocent-passage military vessels is quite simple. Complications largely arise in jurisdiction over economic activity and enforcement of national maritime rules. As a result, the United States adheres to many provisions of the United Nations Convention on the Law of the Sea (UNCLOS), despite never having formally ratified it into US law. Nevertheless, legal distinctions made within UNCLOS are important when trying to understand the largely neutral position of the United States in disputes between claimants over what constitutes a territorial sea, a contiguous zone, and an exclusive economic zone (EEZ). Under the provisions of UNCLOS, rocks and low-tide elevations, for example, do not generate exclusive economic zones, but can extend overlapping territorial sea and contiguous zones from land or naturally formed islands. These distinctions are important for determining what a nation can and cannot do in a particular maritime area: they also represent the fundamental pieces that academics in security studies and international relations have come to wrestle with in creating a larger strategic analysis of the Indo-Pacific region (Fruend 2017).

With that in mind, navigation, mining activities, and research and exploration endeavours are affected differently through the three zone types afforded by land, islands, rocks, and low-tide elevations. In the case of territorial waters, commercial and military vessels may conduct innocent passage through another country's 12-mile zone so long as they do not carry out certain activities while in transit, such as surveillance, fishing, and military exercises. This is not true of contiguous zones, where governments may only conduct punitive operations on vessels that have infringed on regulations inside their territorial waters. The wider EEZ is, for navigation purposes, considered international waters. Any claim which inappropriately widens the range of territorial waters beyond 12 miles, draws improper straight-baselines (only afforded to archipelagic states), labels a rock or low-tide elevation as an island, or restricts navigation (in maritime and aviation) are considered excessive maritime claims. This is where so many of the disputes are generated.

To combat excessive maritime claims, the United States works multilaterally through strategic consultations and diplomatic demarches, as well as through operational assertions called freedom of navigation operations (FONOPS). Such operations and consultations ensure open shipping lanes and access to waters where the United States has vital trade and security interests. The program of FON operations 'includes both planned FON assertions (i.e., operations that have the primary purpose of challenging excessive maritime claims) and other FON-related activities (i.e., operations that have some other primary purpose, but have a secondary effect of challenging excessive maritime claims)' (US Department of Defense 2017). For example, the United States may send a naval vessel through territorial waters (within 12 miles of a naturally occurring island or continental land formation) without giving prior notification. In doing so, the US vessel has conducted an action which is within the legal rights conferred by UNCLOS but conflicts with the demands of a claimant making excessive maritime claims, such as purporting to require prior notification. In another scenario, a US military vessel may linger or conduct a training exercise in an area which is improperly labelled as territorial waters, thus illustrating that the claim is excessive by conducting activities that would otherwise be unacceptable within the 12-mile zone.

It is important to note that the United States does not side with claimants over matters of sovereignty. Rather, the primary strategy has been to ensure that UNCLOS navigation norms are followed, regardless of the origin of the excessive maritime claims. This means that the United States conducts

FONOPS in response to excessive claims of its allies and partners as well. It is also worth stating that FONOPS are not exclusively used to delegitimize excessive maritime claims in the SCS, and may be wielded by partners and allies with a varying subset of strategic goals in mind.

Free and unimpeded navigation in the South China Sea is of crucial importance to the United States and others with a vested economic and security interest in the Indo-Pacific. The trillions of dollars in trade that pass through the region annually would be significantly impeded if commercial travel was diverted around contested waters. Additionally, limited navigation would allow an increasingly assertive China to further threaten longstanding US security concerns with partners like Japan, the Philippines, and Taiwan.

The Obama Years: Pivot to Asia

Conflicting political claims in the South China Sea began after the Sino-Japanese War. They continued after World War II, maintaining relevance following the Treaty of San Francisco, largely concerning the intersection of Japanese, Kuomintang (KMT)[1], and PRC interests. In the late 1960s, the discovery of underwater oil deposits and the conflict between China and Vietnam led the United Nations to establish UNCLOS. Following years of tension, the PRC entered into agreements with the United States (the Military Maritime Consultative Agreement), the Association of Southeast Asian Nations, or ASEAN (the Declaration on the Conduct of Parties in the South China Sea), and Japan (the Joint Energy Accord). Whether it was due to China's growing regional predominance, a shrinking US presence in the Indo-Pacific, or a combination of external factors, stability in the South China Sea did not last. Beijing's three policy goals became regional integration, resource control, and enhanced security (Dutton 2011). This approach would ultimately conflict with longstanding US policy in the region aimed at maintaining free navigation. As a result, the US position in the South China Sea was forced into the limelight in 2010 when the SCS disputes began to heat up.

In July 2010, then-Secretary of State Hillary Clinton clarified the US position in the SCS, which would ultimately merge with President Barack Obama's Pivot to Asia. In front of the UN General Assembly, Clinton unambiguously unveiled a policy dedicated to freedom of navigation and began a long-held precedent of neutrality in maritime disputes. Shortly thereafter, President Obama gave a landmark speech in the Australian Parliament in 2011 in which he cemented the policy objectives of the United States in the South China Sea (CFR 2021).

---

[1]   The Kuomingtang was the most influential political party in China from 1928 to 1949 and a common term to refer to the military forces of the Republic of China (ROC), founded by Sun Yat-sen in 1912 and led from 1925 to 1975 by Chiang Kai-shek.

The tenets of that policy are as follows:

1. Freedom of Navigation and Unimpeded Trade (Air and Sea): UNCLOS freedoms were paramount. The PRC policy (Law of the Sea) of required notification before military transit through EEZs was rejected and viewed as a minority opinion. The establishment of Air Defense Identification Zones (ADIZ) in the South China Sea by the PRC and others is problematic and destabilizing, despite an often inadequate ability to enforce their integrity. Although unrealistic ADIZ claims proliferated, a growing People's Liberation Army (PLA) Air Force (PLAAF) alone was in a position to challenge long-established aviation routes, including for civilian and commercial transport.

2. Peaceful Dispute Resolution: US policy here may have been ambitious, but it has thus-far been upheld, with a few notable exceptions. This is where the misrepresentation of China's 'peaceful rise' came into play. The expectation that the growing global power would refrain from coercive diplomacy and bullying was incorrect. Instead, grey zone tactics largely carried out by civilian fishing boats, sand dredgers, oil prospectors, and the PRC Coast Guard has agitated regional claimants and raised anxieties in the region.

3. UN Convention on the Law of the Sea (UNCLOS) as a Foundation: The United States encourages regional claimants to adhere to the tenets of UNCLOS, despite not having ratified it. The most substantial challenge to the UNCLOS system, aside from island-building and military buildup, is the nine-dash line. The line encircles nearly all of the SCS and is accompanied by ambiguous claims to certain rights based on historical arguments.

4. Diplomatic Partnership: Until the Trump administration took power, the playbook encouraged regional or multilateral negotiation over maritime disputes. During the Obama years, this approach contradicted Beijing's preference for bilateral negotiation, largely as a tactic to isolate and intimidate counter-claimants. US diplomatic capital was underutilized from 2016–2020, ironically turning the established strategy on its head.

5. A Consensus on the Code of Conduct: ASEAN claimants and Beijing agreed to the Declaration on the Conduct of Parties in the South China Sea in 2002. Although the declaration is non-binding, the thought was that such a framework would decrease the likelihood of conflict while disputes were slowly negotiated, likely over many years (Bader and McDevitt 2014).

This framework was largely what the United States implemented in the region from 2008 to 2016 in order to meet its strategic goals. Taylor (2016) explains that, beginning in 2009, the policy began to evolve. First, policy was altered in accordance with the level of tension engendered by the disputes. Second is the US policy of neutrality and not taking sides in the disputes. Third, as its involvement in managing tensions has grown, Washington has been careful to emphasize the process over the product: in other words, that the process for managing conflicting claims be peaceful. To this end it has supported the conclusion of a binding code of conduct between China and ASEAN. Fourth, US policy 'has sought to shape China's behaviour in the South China Sea by highlighting the costs of coercion and the pursuit of claims that are inconsistent with customary international law' (Fravel 2016).

These goals were largely projected onto the PRC and other regional claimants. In 2021, the Congressional Research Service outlined specific and general goals in the context of US-PRC competition. By viewing it from such a perspective, academics and policymakers are able to refocus the lens through which we view the SCS conflicts. Instead of understanding the maritime disputes as stand-alone interests, we are able to view the South China Sea in its proper light, in the context of competition between Washington and Beijing. Washington's general interests in this effort include: (1) nurturing lasting security partnerships in the Indo-Pacific region with long-term partners such as Japan, the Philippines, and Taiwan; (2) rejecting the position that 'might makes right' in dealing with territorial disputes (Stewart and Pearson 2019); (3) maintaining the US security architecture; (4) ensuring continued US leadership in the region; and (5) protecting freedom of navigation.

According to O'Rourke (2021), specific US interests include halting China's ongoing island construction, military buildup, and excessive maritime and ADIZ claims near Vietnam and the Philippines; (2) encouraging Beijing to cease its coercive actions near the Senkaku Islands, Spratly Island, and Scarborough Shoal; and (3) and convincing the PRC to rein in its non-military assets that are conducting illegal sand dredging and invasive fishing.

It was not until 2016 that the United States signalled a potential change from its position of absolute neutrality. Leading up to that point, the Obama administration conducted several FONOPS in order to assert UNCLOS conventions, even if that meant little headway on resolving individual disputes (Werner 2019). Ultimately the operations were safeguarding the primary US interest in freedom of navigation. Below is a table tallying the FONOPS from 2012–2020, which allows us to contrast tangible operations among the three administrations.

As mentioned above, the position of the United States changed after the UN 2016 tribunal ruling for Manila and against Beijing over the Spratly Islands and Scarborough Shoal. The Permanent Council of Arbitration, headquartered in The Hague, ruled in favour of the Philippines on several designations of maritime objects and against the excessive maritime claims being made by the PRC (PCA 2013). Specifically, the ruling found that Beijing had no basis to assert historic rights, nullifying many of the subsequent claims predicated on the nine-dash line (Poling 2020).

At the East Asia Summit in 2016, then-Secretary of State John Kerry commented that the arbitration was 'final and legally binding on both China and the Philippines.' However, he added, 'we are still studying the decision and have no comment on the merits of the case' (Hindustan Times 2016). Despite the firm US stance on sovereignty, Kerry encouraged both parties to comply with the ruling. His comments were precedent-setting, as no previous US government official had endorsed a particular position on maritime disputes in the South China Sea. The previous US position, originating in 2009, was that Beijing had offered no coherent legal basis to its nine-dash line claims (US Department of State 2019).[2] The subtle difference between the two was to connect UNCLOS norms directly to claimants while falling short of enforcing the specific ruling of the arbitration (countries could still disagree on the judgement) by abstaining from calling PRC claims 'illegal.' Instead, by calling the claims 'destabilizing' or 'aggressive,' the administration was able to support the ruling, avoid pushing Beijing into a corner, and maintain the primary goal of supporting free commercial transit and navigation.

For the duration of the Obama presidency, policy was rational and comprehensive in its approach. It maintained ultimate neutrality on specific disputes, even after the 2016 arbitration, while protecting navigation and commercial activity. Although conflicts did not escalate during those years, Obama's approach was, however, incapable of preventing the PRC from building bases on disputed SCS islands, flexing its military muscle, and engaging in bilateral diplomatic coercion (McDevitt 2015).

The Trump Years: Transactionalism and Assertive Messaging

By the time Trump took office in 2017, Xi had been in power for nearly four years, and the PRC had effectively transformed its approach, jettisoning the rhetoric of the 'peaceful rise' and 'good neighbour' diplomacy in favour of the 'Chinese Dream' and promoting 'Xi thought.' As a result, the Trump administration transformed US policy in recognition of increasing PRC

---

[2]   The term nine-dash line refers to the PRC demarcation for claims over large swathes of maritime areas in the South China Sea. Based as they are on a 1947 map, the United Nations Convention on the Law of the Sea has rejected those claims as excessive.

assertiveness and military buildup. For the American public, trade policies were front and center, but strategic options in the South China Sea seemed consequential.

In retrospect, the Trump administration pulled from several options from 2017–2021, with a heavy emphasis on rollback-style public messaging and tangible actions aimed at containment, especially in the latter years. Trump's transactional style of policy provided minimal assistance in the way of tangible commitments to countries in the region. There were, however, voices calling for an increase in US landpower in the South China Sea to deter the PRC and buttress allies' military positions. Bouchat (2017) argued that 'US landpower gives pause to states with aggressive intentions, creates networks that enhance abilities synergistically, and may also break down barriers to misunderstanding – all of which should result in a stabilizing role for US landpower through its proper application in the South China Sea region' (Bouchat 2017).

President Trump began to heavily employ economic sanctions and ramped up public and diplomatic messaging. Opponents of the policy claim that sanctions under the International Emergency Powers Act were not adequately justified during this time and were instead viewed as rhetorical attempts to counter PRC claims. In any case, such statements certainly supported countries like Malaysia, Vietnam, and Indonesia. Relying too heavily on rhetoric of support for non-PRC claimants called into question the US commitment to its partners, particularly in the absence of military action (Williams 2020). The US Department of State is no stranger to such rhetoric. In the words of then-Secretary of State Mike Pompeo, 'America stands with our Southeast Asian allies and partners in protecting their sovereign rights to offshore resources … and [we] reject any push to impose "might makes right" in the South China Sea or the wider region.' Moreover, then-Assistant Secretary of State David Stillwell stated, 'there is room for [sanctions],' pointing out that 'nothing is off the table' (Pamuk and Brunnstrom 2020).

Coupling public statements with sanctions may have been the Trump administration's way of avoiding concrete ramifications while stopping short of provoking armed conflict. Ultimately, the United States has been frequently thrust into a position where action must be taken vis-à-vis increased PLA Navy and Air Force operations. Claimants look to the United States to take that action, ideally before the South China Sea becomes 'a Chinese lake' (Brands and Cooper 2018).

Nguyen (2016) sums up the shift from a hopeful Obama administration to that of an assertive and recalcitrant Trump policy in the South China Sea by recognizing PRC 'buildup in the southern reaches of the South China Sea to establish greater control of its near seas, in the process diminishing US access to the waters and airspace of the world's most critical waterways.' In response, US policymakers assured the PRC that they would suffer the 'net effect' of aggressive and provocative actions (Nguyen 2016).

James (2017) asserts that the ramping up of assertive language under Trump was to some degree due to congressional voices. 'Signals by a president's own party members are generally more powerful, while signals from members of Congress from the opposite party are less so,' he writes. Despite less support from across the aisle, the South China Sea has been viewed as a battlefield for supremacy in the Indo-Pacific. In the words of Scott (2017), 'the nature of the challenge and its broader stakes, along with the array of economic interests and global concerns that connect the US and China, as well as the interests of various factions of the US political system, worked to establish competing interests and priorities that muted partisanship and generated more cooperative efforts.'

In 2020, Trump's Indo-Pacific Strategy – calling for a Free and Open Indo-Pacific (FOIP) – was declassified, revealing specific components of its competitive strategy with China in the South China Sea and elsewhere (Chang 2020). Tenets of the strategy included: (1) 'naming and shaming' the PRC for its actions in the SCS (He and Ramasamy 2020); (2) the imposition of economic sanctions on PRC officials linked to such actions; (3) carrying out FONOPS and overflights in the SCS and the Taiwan Strait (Zhen 2019); (4) strengthening the US military presence and countering the PRC buildup in the Indo-Pacific (O'Rourke 2021a); and (5) encouraging allies and partners to do more individually and in coordination with one another to defend their interests in the SCS region (Ng 2019).

The report made conclusions about Beijing's strategy as well, citing a desire to utilize weakened US partnerships. The overall policy picture began to coalesce by late 2018 and grew in intensity until the transfer of power in January 2021. In an effort to connect specific actions under Trump to a mosaic of policy goals, the table below shows a timeline of major diplomatic and policy actions, short of military operations.

As the Trump administration faced losing re-election in 2020, longstanding US ambiguity towards legal claims in the SCS began to shift. Statements by the Department of Defense and the State Department were representative of that shift, especially concerning Vietnam, the Philippines, and Indonesia. For example, US Ambassador to the United Nations Kelly Craft sent a note to the UN Secretary General which read, 'the United States again urges China to conform its maritime claims to international law as reflected in the

Convention; to comply with the Tribunal's 12 July 2016 decision; and to cease its provocative activities in the South China Sea' (Gertz 2020).

Secretary Pompeo went as far as to break from with the previous administration's precedent by edging further into the Beijing-Manila dispute in the Spratly Islands and Scarborough Shoal, stating that, 'Beijing's claims to offshore resources across most of the South China Sea are completely unlawful, as is its campaign of bullying to control them.' Regarding the rights afforded to the land formations, specifically, Poling (2020) shows that the shift explicitly declared, 'it is illegal for China to engage in fishing, oil and gas exploration, or other economic activities in those areas, or to interfere with its neighbours' rights to do so' (Poling 2020).

By labelling PRC claims as illegal, the United States took a definitive position on the dispute, rather than defaulting to UNCLOS norms or a specific code of conduct. In doing so, the Trump administration may have been hoping to corner its successor into a specific policy towards Beijing (Quinn 2020). Some scholars argue that once Trump ramped up anti-PRC efforts, components of his aligned more with the Obama administration's efforts. The policy aimed to; (1) increase the military presence in the East and Southeast Asia regions; (2) collect international support against the PRC; and (3) propagate the PRC's global image as a villain (Hu 2021). Regardless of the similarities in method, the goal has remained the same from Obama to Trump and into the Biden administration: to maintain freedom of navigation in the Indo-Pacific.

The Biden Administration: Strength Through Alliances

Scholars and insiders alike speculated on the Biden administration's approach to Beijing, especially in the early days of 2021. Campaign rhetoric leading up to the 2020 US presidential election was critical of Beijing on both sides of the aisle, but there was still little clarity as to how that would translate into policy. If the wider policy was unclear, a path forward in the South China Sea was completely indiscernible, especially due to pressing concerns on the economy and public health (due to the COVID-19 pandemic). Area specialists like Glaser and Poling of the Center for Strategic and International Studies had been encouraging cooperation with partners like the Philippines to tamp down coercion from Beijing while working with other Southeast Asian partners to ensure that US absenteeism would cease under a new administration.

At the very least, there is consensus that the PRC is a growing threat to democratic principles, as well as sustained trepidation over an ever-increasing PRC military budget, which has grown from roughly US$120 billion in 2009 to nearly US$250 billion in 2019 (SIPRI 2021). A report by the US Chief of Naval Operations, Admiral Michael Gilday, reiterated the need to offset Beijing's naval build-up: 'To defend our Nation and interests around the globe, we must be prepared to flawlessly execute our Navy's timeless roles of sea control and power projection,' the report reads, adding 'there is no time to waste; our actions in this decade will set the maritime balance of power for the rest of the century' (CNO 2021).

Language in the early days answered the call for a return to historic alliances. During his confirmation hearing and in statements following his appointment, Secretary of State Anthony Blinken alluded to Beijing as an opponent, a challenge, and a potential partner, simultaneously. The United States, moving forward, would approach the PRC from a position of strength, derived from US partners and allies. Regarding the Philippines, Blinken reaffirmed that Washington considers the US-Philippine Mutual Defense Treaty applicable in the event of armed attacks against the Philippine forces, public vessels, and aircraft in the Pacific, as well as in the South China Sea. According to a State Department press release, the United States rejects any of China's maritime claims in the South China Sea that exceed what is permitted by UNCLOS (US Department of State 2021a). The appointment of Kurt Campbell, an Obama-era China hand, to the Biden administration has sent signals to allies in the region. The United States seems to be returning to Asia with an expanding roster of partners who are weary of PRC bullying and coercion.

The positions expressed over the dispute between Manila and Beijing have been similar to the sentiments in other regional disputes, like those the PRC has with Vietnam, Indonesia, Japan, and Taiwan. For example, a visit to Japan and South Korea by Secretary Blinken and Department of Defense Secretary Austin reaffirmed the US commitment to long-time allies in the Indo-Pacific. Statements from the Department of State are representative of the shift back towards reliance on existing security alliances, such as reiterating America's 'unwavering commitment to the defense of Japan under Article V of our security treaty, which includes the Senkaku Islands' (US Department of State 2021b).

During Blinken's discussions with then-Japanese Prime Minister Yoshihide Suga, support from Japan was unexpectedly given to joint defense of Taiwan in the case of a PRC attack. A subsequent high-level trip to Europe further demonstrated a longing for partnerships over key issues (like human rights and freedom of navigation) among Western nations that operate in the Indo-Pacific (Bennan 2021). This is especially apparent with partners like the United Kingdom, the Czech Republic, and members of the 16+1 (a term used to describe a forum for cooperation between Beijing and Eastern European countries) that are reluctant to allow PRC leadership to take hold globally. Developments like the new PRC Coast Guard law in January 2021 has led US partners in the Quadrilateral Security Dialogue (India, Australia, and

Japan) to coalesce around a welcome US return to the South China Sea. Growing concerns in Europe over Chinese expansionism saw the HMS Queen Elizabeth aircraft carrier deployed to the SCS, and even Germany dispatched a frigate to traverse the SCS for the first time since 2002, to support freedom of navigation (Aljazeera 2021).

Perhaps most telling in the early days of the Biden administration was the outcome of the US-China meetings in Anchorage, Alaska. From the outside, analysts have seen a continuation of PRC grandstanding for domestic audiences, while the private meetings were likely less confrontational (Politico 2021). How else can one explain the willingness of PRC Foreign Minister Yang Jiechi to meet after the US placed powerful sanctions over Chinese actions in Hong Kong and Xinjiang? Much of the Trump-era toughness on key issues has seemingly remained, as well as the mechanisms to deal with them. The legislative provisions of the National Defense Authorization Act (2019–2020) remain in place to counter PRC military and technological prowess. Regional fora like ASEAN and the Asia-Pacific Economic Cooperation (APEC), as well as the G7, may serve a largely unchanged strategy under Biden. The Department of State has endeavoured to design a regionally focused policy while reporting on PRC activities, including in the South China Sea (Heydarian 2021).

Moving forward, the Biden administration will have to consider the role of Congress in maritime disputes, especially related to mutual defense agreements and a potential, but unlikely, ratification of UNCLOS in the United States. Campbell and Wyne (2020) claim that, 'increased risks caused by ramped up military activity in the South China Sea is becoming cause for concern for experts who believe that the traffic is inevitably going to lead to an accident or escalate into a crisis scenario.' First, US policy makers will have to ask tough questions about bilateral security treaties. For example, what level of strategic clarity or ambiguity is appropriate to deter PRC conflict with the Philippines and Japan? Also, what contingency planning has the Department of Defense put in place to deal with such an eventuality? Finally, has diplomatic messaging been effective in reaching an understanding on a path forward with America's Japanese and Filipino counterparts?

Congress may also raise the question again (last discussed in June 2012) of whether the United States should become a signatory to UNCLOS. In 2012, hearings in the Senate Foreign Relations Committee revealed arguments for and against its adoption under US law. Proponents pointed to navigational rights, increased legitimacy in citing provisions of the treaty (including those related to foreign military activities in exclusive economic zones), and a move away from reliance on non-binding international norms alone (Browne 2019). Opponents have argued that Beijing has, thus far, been able to cite international law to defend activities in their EEZs. Similarly, UNCLOS has not been able to resolve maritime disputes along the PRC's nine-dash line, which leaves little incentive to enshrine such justification in US law, especially from a policy perspective (Dutton 2011). Instead, the United States could better serve regional stability and the interests of US partners by continuing the FONOPS program and bilateral defense support (Bromund and Schaefer 2018). Given the current status quo, a change in the US relationship with UNCLOS is unlikely.

It is important to add a caveat to our current understanding of US policy in the South China Sea, and that is recognition of the larger foreign policy concerns of the Biden administration. For the greater part of 2021, the number one priority was to tackle the Covid-19 challenge. Beyond that, Biden pushed for a new energy policy aimed at decarbonisation, energy security, and energy development. Much of those objectives will rely on cooperation with the PRC, and they may take precedence over the long-standing irritants in the South China Sea.

US maritime policy in the South China Sea across the Obama, Trump, and Biden administrations has certainly taken on different forms and varying degrees of intensity. The primary objective, however, has remained constant: maintenance of free navigation.

Table 6.1. Reported FON Operations in the SCS by year since 2012 (CRS 2021)

Year	SCS FONOPs	Taiwan Strait Transits
2012	5	9
2013	2	12
2014	3	4
2015	2	1
2016	3	12
2017	6	3
2018	5	3
2019	7	9
2020	8	13

Table 6.2. Major SCS Diplomatic, Policy, and Legislative Actions during the Trump Administration. Sources: Author's compilation based on a variety of public sources.

Date	Policy Action or Legislation
December 2018	US Congress passes the Asia Reassurance Initiative Act to 'promote United States values as well as economic and security interests in the Indo-Pacific region' (US Congress 2018).
May 2018	The Department of Defense rescinds China's invitation to the Rim of the Pacific Exercise (RIMPAC) (Lubold and Page 2018).
November 2018	US National Security Advisor Bolton publicly opposes agreements with the PRC in the SCS that would limit freedom of navigation (Watts 2018).
January 2019	US Admiral John Richardson warned the PLAN that PRC militia and coast guard vessels would be treated as navy ships (Panda 2019).
March 2019	Secretary Mike Pompeo asserts that an attack on Filipino forces or vessels would activate provisions of the US-Philippine Mutual Defense Treaty (Kraska 2020).
December 2019	US Congress passes the Global Fragility Act (2019) to support weakened states that would be of US national security interest (US Congress 2020).
December 2019	The US Strategy to Prevent Conflict and Promote Stability is submitted with the Global Fragility Act (2019) to provide a framework for moving countries from fragility to stability, and from conflict to peace (US Department of State 2021c).
May 2020	A presidential proclamation restricts visas for PRC students and researchers connected to Military-Civil Fusion institutions, specifically in the STEM fields (Federal Register 2020).
July 2020	The Pacific Deterrence Initiative was introduced to the National Defense Authorization Act for Fiscal Year 2021, aimed at transparently allocating resources to defend US interests in the region (Reed and Inhofe 2020).
July 2020	Secretary Pompeo releases a statement rejecting PRC Codes of Conduct on working with 3rd parties in maritime disputes (Pamuk and Brunnstrom 2020).
August 2020	The United States begins imposing visa restrictions on PRC officials related to SCS coercion (US Department of State 2020).
January 2021	The Department of Defense published its Freedom of Navigation (FON) Report for fiscal year 2020, listing China's remaining excessive maritime claims.
January 2021	Secretary Pompeo announces additional sanctions on Chinese state-owned enterprises (SOEs) that were responsible for militarisation or construction of disputed outposts designed to access offshore resources (Lee 2021).
January 2021	The Department of Commerce begins to add several SOEs to the Entity List which restricts US exports to foreign companies. Principle among them was the Chinese National Offshore Oil Corporation (CNOOC) (Lefebvre 2021).

References

Aljazeera. 2021. "German Warship to Cross South China Sea for First Time Since 2002." March 4, 2021.

Bader, Jeffrey, Kenneth Lieberthal, and Michael McDevitt. 2014. "Keeping the South China Sea in Perspective." The Foreign Policy Brief, Brookings, August.

Bouchat, Clarence. 2017. "US Landpower in the South China Sea." Strategic Studies Institute, United States Army War College, July.

Brands, Hal, and Zach Cooper. 2018. "Getting Serious About Strategy in the South China Sea." *Naval War College Review* 71, no. 1, Article 3.

Bennan, David. 2021. "Antony Blinken Calls Out China in First Foreign Trip to Japan, South Korea." *Newsweek*, March 16, 2021.

Bromund, Ted R., James J. Carafano, and Brett D. Schaefer. 2018. "7 Reasons US Should Not Ratify UN Convention on the Law of the Sea." *Daily Signal*, June 2, 2018.

Browne, Andrew. 2019. "A Hole in the US Approach to Beijing." *Wall Street Journal*, May 20, 2014.

Campbell, Kurt, and Ali Wyne. 2020. "The Growing Risk of Inadvertent Escalation Between Washington and Beijing." Lawfare, August 16, 2020.

CFR [Council on Foreign Relations]. 2021. "China's Maritime Disputes: Timeline." Accessed March, 2021. https://www.cfr.org/timeline/chinas-maritime-disputes

Chang, Felix K. 2020. "From Pivot to Defiance: American Policy Shift in the South China Sea." Foreign Policy Research Institute, August 24, 2020.

CNO [Chief of Naval Operations] 2021. "CNO Releases Navigation Plan 2021." United States Navy Press Office, January 11, 2021.

CRS [Congressional Research Service]. 2021. "Taiwan Strait Transit (TST) passages and Freedom of Navigation Operations (FONOPS) conducted by CPF (Commander, US Pacific Fleet) forces in the South China Sea (SCS) from CY 2012 through 17 Feb 2021." US Navy Information Paper.

CSIS [Center for Strategic and International Studies]. 2021. "How Much Trade Transits the South China Sea?" Accessed May, 2021. https://chinapower.csis.org/much-trade-transits-south-china-sea

Dutton, Peter. 2011. "Three Disputes and Three Objectives." *Naval War College Review*, 54–55.

Federal Register. 2020. "Suspension of Entry as Nonimmigrants of Certain Students and Researchers From the People's Republic of China." Presidential Proclamation 10043. May 29, 2020.

Fravel, Taylor. 2016. "U.S. Policy Towards the Disputes in the South China Sea Since 1995." In P*ower Politics in Asia's Contested Waters*, edited by Enrico Fels and Truong-Minh Vu, 389–402. Heidelberg: Springer.

Fruend, Eleanor. 2017. "Freedom of Navigation in the South China Sea: A Practical Guide." Belfer Center for Science and International Affairs, Harvard Kennedy School, June.

Gertz, Bill. 2020. "US Protests Beijing Illegal Sea Claim." *Washington Times*, June 3, 2020.

He, Wendy, and Haridas Ramasamy, Haridas. 2020. "Namingand Shaming China: America's Strategy of Rhetorical Coercion in the South China Sea." *Contemporary Southeast Asia* 42, no. 3: 317–345.

Heydarian, Richard. 2021. "QUAD Summit Next Step Towards an Asian NATO." *Asia Times*, March 13, 2021.

Hindustan Times. 2016. "US' Kerry Says No Military Solution to South China Sea Dispute." August 31, 2016.

Hu, Bo. 2021. "Sino-US Competition in the South China Sea: Power, Rules and Legitimacy." *Journal of Chinese Political Science*.

Kraska, James. 2021. "China's Maritime Militia Vessels May Be Military Objectives During Armed Conflict." *The Diplomat*, July 7, 2020.

Lee, Matthew. 2021. "US Imposes New Sanction on Beijing over South China Sea." *Associated Press*, January 14, 2021.

Lefebvre, Ben. 2021. "US Bans Exports to China's State-Owned Oil Company CNOOC." *Politico*, January 14, 2021.

Lubold, Gordon, and Jeremy Page. 2018. "US Retracts Invitation to China to Participate in Military Exercise." *Wall Street Journal*, May 23, 2018.

McDevitt, Michael. 2015. "The South China Sea: Assessing US Policy." *American Foreign Policy Interests* 37, no. 1: 23–30.

Ng, Eileen. 2019. "US Official Urges ASEAN to Stand Up to Chine in Sea Row." *Associated Press,* October 31, 2019.

Nguyen, Phuong. 2016. "Deciphering the Shift in America's South China Sea Policy." *Contemporary Southeast Asia* 38, no. 3: 389–421.

O'Rourke, Ronald. 2021. "US-China Strategic Competition in South and East China Seas: Background and Issues for Congress." Congressional Research Service Report. R42784. March 18, 2021.

_____. 2021. "Renewed Great Power Competition: Implications for Defense – Issues for Congress." Congressional Research Service Report. R43838. March 4, 2021.

Pamuk, Humeyra, and David Brunnstrom. 2020. "US Says Room for Sanctions in Response to China in South China Sea." *Reuters*, July 14, 2020.

Panda, Ankit. 2019. "The US Navy's Shifting View of China's Coast Guard and 'Maritime Militia'." *The Diplomat*, April 30, 2019.

PCA [Permanent Council of Arbitration]. 2013. "The South China Sea Arbitration (The Republic of Philippines v. The People's Republic of China)." Accessed March, 2021. https://pca-cpa.org/cases

Poling, Gregory. 2020. "How Significant is the New US South China Sea Policy?" Center for Strategic and International Studies, July 14, 2020.

Politico. 2021. "China and US Open Alaska Meeting with Undiplomatic War of Words." March 18, 2021. https://www.politico.com/news/2021/03/18/china-us-alaska-meeting-undiplomatic-477118

Quinn, Colm. 2020. "The US Declared China's South China Sea Claims 'Unlawful.' Now What?" *Foreign Policy*, July 14, 2020.

Reed, Jack, and Jim Inhofe. 2020. "The Pacific Deterrence Initiative: Peace Through Strength in the Indo-Pacific." War on the Rocks, May 28, 2020.

Scott, James. 2017. "The Challenge of the South China Sea: Congressional Engagement and the US Policy Response." *All Azimuth: A Journal of Foreign Policy and Peace* 7, no. 2: 1–26.

SIPRI [Stockholm International Peace Research Institute]. 2021."Chinese Military Expenditure 2009-2019." Military Expenditure Database. Accessed May, 2021.

Stewart, Phil, and James Pearson. 2019. "US to Provide Ship to Vietnam to Boost South China Sea Patrols." *Reuters*, November 20, 2019.

US Department of Defense. 2017. "Annual Freedom of Navigation Report: Fiscal Year 2017." Report to Congress, December 31, 2017.

US Congress. 2018. "S.2736 - Asia Reassurance Initiative Act of 2018." 116th Congress (2017-2018). https://www.congress.gov/bill/115th-congress/senate-bill/2736

US Department of State. 2019. "A Free and Open Indo-Pacific, Advancing a Shared Vision." Media Note, November 4, 2019.

US Department of State.2020. "H.R.2116 - Global Fragility Act." 116th Congress (2019-2020). https://www.congress.gov/bill/116th-congress/house-bill/2116

_____. 2020. "US Imposes Restrictions on Certain PRC State-Owned Enterprises and Executives for Malign Activities in the South China Sea." Press statement. Michael R. Pompeo, Secretary of State, August 26, 2020.

US Department of State. 2021. "Protecting and Preserving a Free and Open South China Sea." Media Note, January 14, 2021.

_____. 2021. "Secretary Blinken's Call with Philippine Secretary of Foreign Affairs Locsin." Media Note. January 27, 2021.

_____. 2021. "US-Japan Joint Press Statement." Media Note, March 16, 2021.

_____. 2021. "United States Strategy to Prevent Conflict and Promote Stability." Global Publishing Solutions (A/GIS/GPS). Accessed March, 2021.

Watts, Jake Maxwell. 2018. "Bolton Warns China Against Limiting Free Passage in South China Sea." *Wall Street Journal*, November 13, 2018.

Werner, Ben. 2019. "Beijing Irked at Twin US South China Sea FONOPS." *USNI News*, November 22, 2019.

Williams, Robert. 2020. "What did the US Accomplish With its South China Sea Legal Statement?" Brookings Institution, July 22, 2020.

Zhen, Liu. 2019. "US War planes on Beijing's Radar in South China Sea, American Air Force Chiefs Say." *South China Morning Post*, December 9, 2019.

7

Assessing Neutrality: The United States' Role in the Diaoyu Islands Dispute

ALANA CAMOÇA GONÇALVES DE OLIVEIRA

On 21 April 2014, then-US President Barack Obama declared in a joint press conference that the Diaoyu Islands (referred to as the Senkaku in Japan, and Diaoyutai in Taiwan) are subject to Article 5 of the Treaty of Mutual Cooperation and Security between the United States and Japan – the article that commits the United States to defend Japan if it is attacked by a third party (Obama 2014). This was the first time that a sitting US president made this statement publicly, and openly challenged the traditional US position of not taking sides in territorial disputes. In fact, Obama continued to argue that the US does not take a position on the sovereignty of the Diaoyu islands, though it does take a position in ensuring that all countries follows basic international procedures in resolving their disputes peacefully. Nevertheless, the speech clearly identified China as a threat to international order, and that Washington would stand beside Tokyo to protect the islands, since Beijing was not acting in accordance with international rules and norms.

Even though the tensions over the Diaoyu Islands took centre stage in the international arena after the episodes of escalation in 2010–2012 – indeed, these tensions have been growing due to the increase of the Chinese presence in Japan's territorial waters over the years – the origins of the disagreement can be better understood if one take into account not only their historical roots but how other major players have helped to shape the dispute. The origins of the dispute can be traced back to Japan's imperialism in Asia in the late 19th century and the Japanese incorporation of the Ryukyu Kingdom, known today as Okinawa (Chen 2014; Shogo 2009). As for US involvement in the history of the dispute, it is possible to highlight three major events: (i) the Allied Forces' occupation of Japan after the end of World War II and the 1951 Treaty of San Francisco, (ii) the reversion of Okinawa to Japan in 1971–1972 and (iii) the US' Pivot to Asia strategy.

In order to better understand the current status of the Diaoyu Islands issue, this chapter will present an analysis of the role of the US in the dispute. Then, it will show how US neutrality on the sovereignty dispute between China and Japan – and the fine line it walks regarding this stance – were shaped by US policy strategies and choices. In other words, the ambiguity of its neutrality has been serving US strategic interests in East Asia and increasing the legitimacy for the US to act in the region. It will also show that, due to the on-going balance-of-power transformations taking place in the region, the neutrality discourse is dwindling. The chapter is divided in two parts. Firstly, it will briefly review each claim over the Diaoyu islands and describe the US' official stance in regard to the dispute. Secondly, it will analyse the role of the US in regard to the Diaoyu Islands, presenting how US neutrality has served Washington's strategic interests in East Asia.

Diaoyu Islands Dispute, the Claimants, and the US Neutrality Stance

In recent years, we have seen a growing amount of attention paid to this dispute over a group of small islands nestled between Japan, Taiwan and China in the East China Sea (ECS). The dispute is catalysing a deterioration of the East Asia security environment and is closely affecting the security and foreign policies of countries in the region. The disputed islands are located in the ECS, about 170 km northwest of Ishigakijima, 170 km from Taiwan, and 330 km from the Chinese coast. Japan, China, and the ROC support their claims based on international treaties signed during the 19th and 20th centuries.

Japan asserts that the islands were incorporated into its territory through the Okinawa Prefecture in 1895 during the Sino-Japanese War (1894–1895). The Japanese government points out that the territory was only incorporated after provincial authorities recognized that there had been no previous occupation of these islands by any other country – the *terra nullius* principle. Post-World War II, Japan points out that the islands were under US control as per the Treaty of San Francisco, but the islands were returned to Japan in 1972 as part of the Japan-US Okinawa Reversion Agreement (Suganuma 1996; Eldridge 2014).

Differently, China claims that the islands were not *terra nullius* because of their discovery during the Ming dynasty (1368–1644), and because Chinese fishermen have exploited the islands and their adjacent waters for generations. The People's Republic of China (PRC) authorities also argue that the islands were used as a navigation demarcation in the waters between Ryukyu and China. Moreover, the Chinese government also claims that, at the end of the 19th century, after the Japanese victory in the First Sino-Japanese War (1894–1895), the Diaoyu islands were among the territories that China ceded to Japan in the 1895 Treaty of Shimonoseki.

According to China's claims, because the Qing dynasty (1644–1912) ceded the islands to Japan in the Treaty of Shimonoseki, they should have been handed over to the ROC as stipulated in the Cairo Declaration (1943), the Potsdam Declaration (1945) and the San Francisco Treaty (1951), given that Japan was obliged to return Formosa, the Pescadores, and 'the islands appertaining to Formosa.' Thus, Beijing asserts that the United States should have not held control over the Diaoyu Islands at the end of the war. The Chinese government argues that Japan should have been stripped of all the islands in the Pacific which it had seized or occupied during its imperial period of colonial expansion. Although none of the aforementioned documents explicitly mentions the Diaoyu Islands, the Cairo Declaration does state that 'Japan will also be expelled from all other territories which she has taken by violence and greed.' Since about the 1970s, the PRC has interpreted this phrase to include the Diaoyu Islands. Officially, the Republic of China's (ROC) stance is the same as that of the PRC, though the government in Taipei is nowadays less active in pressing these claims.

Although territorial disputes are usually followed by conflicts between the countries that claim sovereignty over specific territories, other countries can play an important role in those disputes. Other countries can serve as mediators or provide military, economic, and even discursive support for one of the countries before, during, and after the dispute. Thus, in order to better understand the Diaoyu islands dispute it is important to highlight the US' role.

Even though the US government does not claim sovereignty over the islands, the Diaoyu group was under US control between 1951 and 1972. In addition, the United States has been an important player in the East Asia security theatre since the end of World War II. The US government's position is one of neutrality and opposition to the use of force to resolve issues of sovereignty (Oliveira 2021). Washington has constantly reiterated this stance since the beginning of the dispute in the late 1960s and early 1970s. With the reversion of Okinawa in 1972, for example, the United States placed the islands under Japanese administration. At the time, US Secretary of State William Rogers stated that the Okinawa reversion treaty did not affect the return of administrative rights over the islands to Japan, from which the rights were received, and 'can in no way prejudice any underlying claims. The US cannot add to the legal rights Japan possessed before it transferred administration of the islands to us, nor can the United States, by giving back what it received, diminish the rights of other claimants' (US Congress 1971).

However, the US position on the dispute cannot simply be regarded as one of neutrality. Washington has constantly been concerned with its own strategic, security, and foreign policy interests in dealing with the islands. In recent years, the growing US concern about China's rise has shifted Washington's foreign policy in East Asia since the Obama administration, and its discourse on neutrality has been fading.

Neutrality vs. US Strategic Interests

The US Administration of Ryukyu and its Strategic Position in East Asia

The United States occupied Japan at the end of World War II, and at the time Washington's interests in Okinawa increased due to its geopolitical location. Eldridge (2001) argues that a top secret report, designated NSC 13/3, by the US National Security Council (NSC) in 1949, before the signing of the San Francisco Treaty, already noted that 'the United States intends to retain on a long-term basis the facilities at Okinawa and such other facilities as are deemed by the Joint Chiefs of Staff to be necessary in the Ryukyu Islands south of 29° N, Marcus Island and the Nanpo Shoto south of Sofu Gan,' which is the northern end of the Ryukyu Islands (NSC, 1949).

Nonetheless, in the 1951 San Francisco Peace Treaty, the US administration pursued a strategy of maintaining its access and presence in East Asia through its control over the Okinawa islands. The treaty not only officially effected the surrender of Japan and ended the US occupation of Japanese territory, but also granted control over Okinawa and the surrounding islands to the United States. The latter is achieved through Article 3 of the international treaty, which presents the Nansei Shoto south of 29 degrees north latitude (including the Ryukyu Islands and the Daito Islands), as a territory where the US would have sole administrative authority. It is noteworthy that the San Francisco treaty did not name the Diaoyu explicitly as being among the islands that were ceded to the United States.

The vagueness of the San Francisco Treaty became one of the major problems involving territorial claims, not only in the Sino-Japanese territorial disputes, affecting other territorial disputes in the region. As Kimie Hara (2007) observes, disputes over the Takeshima/Dokdo Islands, the Sakhalin Islands, and the Spratly Islands are also inherited from the Treaty of San

Francisco, which was neither signed by the ROC nor the PRC – to say nothing of the USSR or either of the Koreas (Hara 2007).

During the Cold War, as the US administered the Ryukyu Islands (including the Diaoyus), it was careful to characterize its governance there as temporary in nature. Even though the US had gained control over the islands, it never really severed relations between Okinawa and Japan. The Tokyo government was granted 'residual sovereignty' over the Ryukyu Islands. According to Smith (2013, 3–4), the rationale for this policy of residual sovereignty rested on at least three major considerations: (a) the US sought to cultivate Japan as a key Cold War ally in the Asia-Pacific, (b) it offered the Japanese government an incentive to allow the US military to use bases in Okinawa, and (c) residual sovereignty was, in part, meant to reduce anti-American sentiment in Japan. The idea of Japanese residual authority over the islands of Okinawa allowed the Ryukyu Islands to somehow remain united to Japanese territory, facilitating US control and discourse as a benevolent promoter of the international system.

On 29 February 1952 and 25 December 1953, the United States Civil Administration of the Ryukyu Islands (USCAR) issued two documents, respectively titled Ordinance No. 68 on the Government Provisions of the Ryukyu, and Proclamation No. 27 on the Geographical Boundaries of the Ryukyu Islands. Both documents defined the territorial limits that had not been outlined in the San Francisco Peace Treaty. Considering the geographical coordinates, the Diaoyu Islands were clearly part of the territories administered by USCAR (Eldridge 2001; Oliveira 2019).

As the Cold War intensified and containment policies were strengthened, US administrations, beginning with that of President Dwight D. Eisenhower (1953–1961), believed that it was strategically and militarily important to maintain control of the islands of Okinawa as a means of safeguarding US interests and power in the Asian theatre. In a National Security Council (NSC) report, for example, the US government acknowledged that Japan desired to recover the Ryukyu territory, but due to the 'critical strategic importance of these islands, the United States must continue to impress upon the Japanese its intention to retain control over them pending the establishment of enduring conditions of peace and stability in the Far East' (NSC 1954).

As early as the 1940s, an American administration of Ryukyu was not only in the interests of the United States, but of the ROC as well, as evidenced by conversations about the situation in the region between US President Franklin D. Roosevelt (1933–1945) and Chiang Kai-shek, head of the Nationalist government in China from 1928 to 1949, and from then until his death in 1975 head of the Chinese Nationalist government in exile on Taiwan (Zhai 2015). During the Cairo Conference in late November 1943, Roosevelt and Chiang discussed the possibility of Okinawa becoming a territory to be under shared administrative authority between the United States and the ROC. However, this vision did not make it into the final wording of the San Francisco Peace Treaty.[1]

The deterioration in international stability that took place soon after World War II pressured Washington to secure a strategic ally in the region. In the late 1940s and early 1950s, the United States created and strengthened a policy of containment[2], which would be the guide and central reference for US foreign policy between the years 1947 and 1989[3]. The incorporation of Asia into the containment scheme was the first important expansion of America's area of operation and occurred as it was on its way to becoming a country with a global projection capacity. During this period, the dispute over the Diaoyu Islands had not yet been triggered, but amid US strategies during the Cold War, the Ryukyu Islands together with the San Francisco Treaty established dubious boundaries that would later be one of the main problems of the sovereignty claims over the disputed islands.

The Reversion of Okinawa and the Beginning of the Diaoyu Islands Dispute

In 1965, US President Lyndon Johnson (1963–1969) presented his Okinawa policy in a joint communiqué with Japanese Prime Minister Eisaku Sato (1964–1972). The statement reveals Japan's eagerness to recover administrative authority over the islands, asking the American president to

---

[1]   During conversations prior to the signing of the Cairo Declaration, Roosevelt asked more than once if the Republic of China would want the Ryukyu territory. Chiang Kai-shek answered that China would agree to a joint occupation of Ryukyu by the ROC and the US and, eventually, a joint administration of both countries but under the trusteeship of an international organization (Zhai 2015).

[2]   The policy of containment was to contain the threat posed by the USSR at that time and was inspired by George Kennan's ideas, a career US Foreign Service Officer. This idea inspired the Truman administration's foreign policy. The first time that containment was presented was in the form of an anonymous contribution to the journal *Foreign Affairs*. In this article Kennan, under the pseudonym Mr. X, writes that the main element of any US policy toward the Soviet Union must be that of a long-term, patient, but firm and vigilant containment of Russian expansive tendencies. https://history.state.gov/milestones/1945-1952/kennan

[3]   This is one of the reasons why the United States started to have an interest in stabilizing the economies affected by the war as soon as possible, as in the case of Japan. Nonetheless, Washington signed the Mutual Security Treaty with Japan in 1951, and this treaty was revised in 1960.

understand the feelings of the people of Okinawa and Japan on this matter. Sato also offered his thoughts on the East Asia geopolitical scenario while the US government argued that they looked forward to the moment when the islands could be returned to Japan. It was clear back then that, with military bases on Okinawa supporting US operations in Vietnam, providing a strategic location for the US presence in East Asia, and safeguarding Japanese interests, it was impossible to predict when reversion would be possible (Ryukyu Archive 1965).

In the ensuing years, the Japanese government and US authorities continued negotiations over the islands. On 14 and 15 November 1967, during meetings in Washington between Sato and Johnson, the process began to take shape. Both US and Japanese leaders shared their interest in returning administrative rights over the Ryukyu Islands to Japan at the earliest possible date (Worldjpn 1967). An agreement over the reversion of the islands would not occur until the administration of US President Richard Nixon (1969–1974), however. In November 1969, Nixon met with Sato in Washington to establish the terms of reversion and issued a joint statement reporting that the two governments had agreed to immediately enter into consultations regarding specific arrangements for accomplishing an early reversion of Okinawa, and declaring that this would occur in 1972 (Smith 2013).

During the Nixon administration, the reversion of Okinawa was a priority in order to enhance the Japan-US alliance and diminish the problems that the United States was facing in regard to the discontentment of the Okinawan population over the US presence in the region. However, the return of negotiations over Okinawa were impacted by energy surveys conducted by the Committee for the Coordination of Joint Prospecting for Mineral Resources in Asian Offshore Areas, under the authority of the United Nations Economic Commission for Asia and the Far East in 1968 and 1969. The report revealed that the ECS might contain substantial energy deposits (Drifte 2013; 2016; Smith 2013).

The studies did not show the exact amount of resources that existed in the Diaoyu Islands' surroundings, but almost immediately after the announcement, several Western companies expressed an interest in exploring the region (Park 1973). Soon after the exploration intentions began to arise, the Chinese government took a position claiming sovereignty over the islands but demonstrated the willingness to negotiate the continental shelf and its exploration with other claimants of territorial waters in the ECS, namely the ROC, South Korea, and Japan (Park 1973). On 21 December 1970, the Japan-Korea Cooperation Committee, as well as the Japan-Taiwan Cooperation Committee, convened to establish an offshore development and research liaison committee (Park 1973; Suganuma 1996; Friedheim 2019). The PRC condemned the move, releasing a critical note on 3 December 1970, through the State-run Xinhua News Agency. In this note, China criticized this cooperation and the joint development in the vicinity of the Diaoyu Islands. The following day, the PRC regime announced in a radio broadcast that the Diaoyu Islands were not, in fact, part of Ryukyu territory, but belonged to the continental shelf of China.

All this took place as other important events were developing that would shift the Cold War balance of power. The necessities of Cold War geopolitics directly involved the United States in negotiations over the disputed islands. In the late 1960s and early 1970s changes in the balance of power during the Cold War were becoming evident: the US rapprochement with China; negotiations over Okinawa; and the consequent return of the Diaoyu Islands to Japan, all brought difficulties for the US strategy in the region. Nixon and Henry Kissinger – the latter serving concurrently as Secretary of State and National Security Adviser – had planned to make their approach to China while maintaining friendly relations with Taiwan and Japan. During the Okinawa resolution process, and due to the emergence of the dispute over the Diaoyu Islands, the US government was pressured by PRC and ROC leaders to intercede on their behalf, but in the end Washington opted for a position of neutrality (Eldridge 2001; Eldridge 2014). The discourse of neutrality at the moment can be explained by two important US interests: (a) maintenance of the Japan-US relationship and a strong US presence in East Asia, and (b) rapprochement with China while maintaining good relations with Taiwan.

In maintaining the Japan-US relationship, during the mid-1960s, the United States had started to review its policy on Okinawa, since US officials were increasingly concerned with the anti-US sentiment among citizens in Japan and Okinawa (Komine 2013). Even though this pressured Washington to rush the reversion of Okinawa, the US military maintained its bases on the islands after their return to Japan. In fact, this territory still remains a vital cornerstone of US forces in Asia due to its strategic location. During the reversion negotiations, it is noteworthy that Nixon's government had some demands. One of them was related to textile trade policies in favour of the United States, and the other had to do with transit and entry of nuclear weapons into Okinawa in emergency situations.

On the latter issue, Wakaizumi Kei (2002) revealed in his memoir that, at the moment of the elaboration of the 21 November 1969 Joint Statement by Japanese Prime Minister Sato and US President Nixon which states that both the United States and Japan have an interest in returning Okinawa, the two leaders moved into a private office following a procedure prearranged by Kissinger and Wakaizumi, Sato's secret emissary. The officials elaborated the confidential 'Agreed Minute' between Nixon and Sato regarding the possibility for entry of nuclear weapons into Okinawa during emergencies (Wakaizumi 2002; Komine 2013). The Agreed Minute states that 'in time of great emergency the United States Government will require the re-entry of nuclear weapons and transit rights in Okinawa with prior consultation with the Government of Japan' (Ryukyu Archives 1969). According to Komine (2013), without a confidential written assurance for the emergency re-entry of nuclear weapons, the reversion of Okinawa itself could have been opposed by the US government. This issue is related to the dispute insofar as the US interest in maintaining relations with Japan and getting its agenda done made it hard for Washington to follow, for example, the ROC request for the non-reversion of the Diaoyu Islands to Japan. At the time, 'the deal [had] gone too far and too many commitments [had been] made to back off now (Smith 2013, 34).

Regarding the rapprochement with China, secret talks between Washington and Beijing were being conducted in the early 1970s. Initially, negotiations took place through indirect channels. The first tentative steps toward overt rapprochement came only after an April 1971 ping-pong tournament held in Japan, when the American team received an invitation to play in China. Later, the incident would become known as ping-pong diplomacy. In July 1971, Kissinger secretly travelled to China after an invitation from Zhou Enlai and, on the 15th of that month, Nixon publicly announced his trip to China.

During the July 1971 meeting, Kissinger and Zhou debated Beijing's interest in a 'One China' policy, discussed the principle of reciprocity between countries, and presented their concerns regarding the regional environment, including the issue of Japanese militarism. It should also be noted that Nixon and Kissinger both played the so-called Japan Card; raising the conceptual possibility of a militaristic and expansionist Japan to exploit fears, long held by the Chinese, of a revival of Japanese militarism, in order to justify the US-Japan Security Treaty and to legitimize the stationing of US troops in the region (NSA 1971). The territorial dispute between China and Japan, especially regarding the islands near Okinawa, made the American military presence more acceptable to the countries of the region and the world (Hara 2015). While emphasizing the China threat and prioritising Japan's defense, Nixon managed to secure tacit approval from the Chinese for a US presence in Okinawa for Japan's defense, thus exploiting China's fear of a revival of Japanese militarism.

Also, it is important to point out that recognizing Japan's or China's claim over the islands could undermine Taipei's claim over its own sovereignty as an independent country, as well as deteriorate US' relations with one of the two other nations. Thus, the declaration of neutrality was calculated to prevent a potential conflict capable of harming US relations with any of the three East Asian nations. In sum, US policy was acceptable to the Japanese while providing enough ambiguity to avoid deterioration of relations with Taipei and Beijing. Since then, the islands have been disputed by China, Japan and the ROC, with escalation of tensions occurring in 1978, 1990, and 1996, as well as in 2004–2005, 2010, 2012, and onwards.

Obama's Pivot to Asia and Fading Neutrality

The ambiguous US policy of acknowledging, though not recognizing, the claims helped Washington achieve its foreign policy goals in East Asia during the Cold War. However, US neutrality and the attendant ambiguity thereof continued to impact the dispute into the 21st century. In fact, the adherence to neutrality has been fading over the past few years due to changes in the balance of power of East Asia, as well as changing perceptions by US leaders of China. When Barack Obama (2009–2017) assumed office, he discursively emphasized diplomacy, multilateralism, and respect for the international order as pillars of his foreign policy, aiming to distance himself from Bush's unilateralism (Brands 2017). Obama highlighted the need to promote greater restraint, cost cutting and precision in the use of US military power, to double diplomatic engagement with friends and rivals, and to rebalance American policy geographically, due to the emergence of the Asia-Pacific as the focal point of 21st century geopolitics and geoeconomics (Brands 2017).

Likewise, since the official implementation of the Pivot to Asia policy in 2012, there has been increased US involvement and interest in safeguarding its position of supremacy in East Asia. This promoted a greater US involvement in the region's territorial disputes, including the dispute over the Diaoyu Islands. During the escalation of the Sino-Japanese territorial dispute in both 2010 and 2012, the US government started to get more involved and discursively pointed out that the Diaoyu Islands were covered under the US-Japan Security Treaty. It is worth noting that the US policy of neutrality began to take clearer turn, with the US leaning towards favouring Japan.

On 23 September, for example, then-US Secretary of State Hilary Clinton made assurances that the Diaoyu Islands were under the protection of the Mutual Security Treaty between the US and Japan, and that any intervention or use of force was not welcome (Drifte 2013). Since 2010, it has been possible to observe an increase in the number of Chinese ships converging on the islands, precipitating an increase in US involvement in the region.

In another example of increased US involvement, after China demarcated an Air Defense Identification Zone (ADIZ) over the ECS in 2013, and amid the growing presence of Chinese naval assets in the surrounding waters of the Diaoyu Islands, Obama stated that the islands were under the umbrella of the US-Japan Security Treaty. Obama's statement is particularly significant because it was the first time that any sitting US president had overtly stated that the Diaoyu Islands fall within the US-Japan Security Treaty. Even though other high-level US officials had offered similar reassurances to Japan in the past, this had great symbolism. In response to the Chinese ADIZ, two American B-52 planes were dispatched on an overflight of the Diaoyu Islands (Drifte 2013; 2016).

In an April 2014 press conference, Obama reiterated the US commitment to fundamental principles such as freedom of navigation and respect for international law, stating that the 'treaty commitment to Japan's security is absolute, and Article 5 covers all territories under Japan's administration, including the Senkaku Islands' (Obama 2014). As pointed out by Grönning (2014), US diplomatic sources reveal that Japanese officials consistently encourage the United States to restate its commitment to defend the islands. His statement helped Obama gain leverage in bilateral issues involving Japan, and sent a signal to China that the United States would not tolerate any unilateral actions that the Chinese government might be tempted to pursue. The US government still holds that this position is not related to the sovereignty dispute between the two East Asian countries, and it continues to defend the US position of neutrality. However, this position of neutrality, in an era marked by increased Chinese belligerence, has served to strengthen US-Japan security relations[4].

By 2014–2015, Japan and China had signed a four-point consensus laying out their differences concerning the disputed islands. The bilateral discussions resumed in early 2015. In 2018, after nine rounds of high-level consultations, they launched a maritime and aerial communication mechanism (South China Morning Post 2018). However, even during the COVID-19 pandemic, tensions continue. For the last few years, Beijing's moves have put pressure on US officials to increase their commitment to Japan's security, and US authorities have publicly declared that unilateral actions by China would not affect the US acknowledgment that the islands are administered by Japan. The US Congress inserted in the FY2013 National Defense Authorization Act (H.R. 4310, P.L. 112–239) a resolution stating 'the unilateral action of a third party will not affect the United States'

---

[4]   In fact, as the threat posed by increased Chinese aggression has grown in the last few years, Japan's security policies and behaviour have shifted (Hughes 2017). Since the Abe administration, Tokyo decided to enhance Japan's deterrence capacity by improving Japan-US relations, as can be seen in the Japan's National Defense Program Guidelines published in the 21st century and the revision of the Guidelines for Japan-US Defense Cooperation.

acknowledgment of the administration of Japan over the Senkaku Islands.' Similar language appeared in a number of bills and resolutions concerning US interests in the ECS (Manyin 2021, 9).

Even if Obama's foreign policy was not consistent throughout the years, due to budget cuts, domestic political splits, and a lack of strategic cohesion on the concept of the pivot (later rebalancing) to Asia in government speeches and documents; the Pentagon managed to maintain its commitments in the Asia-Pacific, maintaining an active military presence in the region (Green 2017; Oliveira 2021). Washington's main goal can be seen as upholding and enhancing the US-led security architecture in the Western Pacific and maintaining a regional balance of power favourable to the US and its allies. When the Trump administration began, the US government adopted different policies that worsened US-China relations. The US foreign and security policy towards China evolved toward confrontation, based upon a perception of China as a revisionist power seeking regional hegemony (United States 2017). In the last few years, the United States has helped to strengthen the military capabilities of its allies in the region, particularly Japan, South Korea, the Philippines, and New Zealand (O'Rourke 2021).

On the issue of the disputed islands, the United States has constantly demonstrated its commitment through the statements made by its political leaders and military commanders. In 2020, for example, Lieutenant General Kevin Schneider, commander of US forces based in Japan, launched the joint US-Japanese exercise Keen Sword 21. Schneider said that 'our arrival today was simply to demonstrate the ability to move a few people, but the same capability could be used to deploy combat troops to defend the Senkaku [Diaoyu] Islands or respond to other crises and contingencies' (Zhou 2020). Backing up these words, the US Navy has shifted a greater part of its fleet to the Indo-Pacific region (O'Rourke 2021). The Department of Defense is assigning its most capable ships, aircraft, and personnel to the region and conducting increased operations and warfighting exercises, as well as developing new weapons and other technologies that could be crucial for the continued US presence in the East Asian region (O'Rourke 2021). Even now, Washington continues to emphasize its neutrality towards the islands. However, the American commitment to the defense of Japan and its growing presence in the region, demonstrate how US neutrality tends to serve US strategic interests in East Asia.

Conclusion

The US has consistently used its position of neutrality, and the ambiguity surrounding it, to prevent conflicts that could undermine its alliances in East Asia. The success of this strategy has been evident, especially during the political, ideological, and security tensions that arose in the 1970s. In the 21st century, this ambiguity has seen a renewed importance due to the US willingness to protect its East Asian allies like Japan, as well as a way of balancing revisionist threats, such as that posed by China.

Even after the Obama administration, the US presence in East Asia and its involvement in territorial disputes continue, whether through military cooperation or other commitments. In January 2021, White House press releases from the newly minted Biden administration sent a clear warning to Beijing against any expansionist intentions in Northeast and Southeast Asia. In multiple calls and statements, Biden and his top security officials have underscored 'US support for allies Japan, South Korea, Taiwan, and the Philippines, signalling Washington's rejection of China's disputed territorial claims in those areas' (Strait Times 2021). Other correspondence between high-level officials continued to reiterate the US commitment to defending the Diaoyu Islands, since they fall under Article 5 of the US-Japan Security Treaty (US Department of State 2021; Johnson 2021).

The US stance on the Diaoyu Islands dispute over the years shows how Washington's interests and statements on the issue have the power to shape the development of territorial disputes in East Asia. In the last few years, the US government has come to recognize in China a rival power with the potential to challenge US supremacy. Thus, it is not a surprise to see the US military presence in the Indo-Pacific grow and, as China's influence and military capabilities increase, the policy of neutrality is beginning to fade. Thus, in the years ahead, we may witness a more resolute US response in regards to the Diaoyu Islands dispute. Since the beginning, the United States has been one of the major players in the dispute, and even though Washington does not claim sovereignty over them, the islands are entangled in a discursive, military, and political power play closely related to US interests.

References

Brands, Hal. 2017. "Barack Obama and the Dilemmas of American Grand Strategy." *The Washington Quarterly* 39, no. 4: 101–125.

Drifte, Reinhard. 2013. "The Diaoyu Islands Territorial Dispute Between Japan and China: Between Materialization of the China Threat and Japan Reversing the Outcome of World War II?" *UNISCI Discussion Papers* 32, 9–62. Doi: 10.5209/rev_UNIS.2013.n32.44789.

Drifte, Reinhard. 2016. "Japan's Policy towards the South China Sea – Applying "Proactive Peace Diplomacy"?" *Peace Research Institute Frankfurt Report* 140.

Eldridge, Robert D. 2001. *The Origins of the Bilateral Okinawa Problem: Okinawa in Postwar US-Japan Relations, 1945–1952*. New York: Routledge.

_____. 2014. *The Origins of U.S. Policy in the East China Sea Islands Dispute: Okinawa's Reversion and the Senkaku Islands*. New York: Routledge.

Friedheim, Robert L. 2019. *Japan and the New Ocean Regime*. New York: Routledge.

Green, Michael. 2017. *By More than Providence: Grand Strategy and American Power in the Asia-Pacific Since 1783*. New York: Columbia University Press.

Gronning, Bjorn E. M. 2014. "Japan's Shifting Military Priorities: Counterbalancing China's Rise." *Asian Security* 10, no. 1: 1–21.

Hara, Kimie. 2007. *Cold War Frontiers in the Asia-Pacific. Divided Territories in the San Francisco Treaty*. Abingdon: Routledge.

_____. 2015. "Okinawa, Taiwan, and the Diaoyu Islands in the United States–Japan–China Relations." *The Asia-Pacific Journal. Japan Focus 13*, no. 28 (2).

Hughes, Christopher W. 2017. "Japan's Grand Strategic Shift. From the 'Yoshida Doctrine' to an 'Abe Doctrine'?" In *Strategic Asia 2017-18: Power, ideas, and military strategy in the Asia-Pacific*, edited Ashley J. Tellis, Alison Szalwinski, and Michael Wills, 73–105. Washington: The National Bureau of Asian Research.

Johnson, Jesse. 2021. "New U.S. Defense Chief Confirms Senkakus Fall Under Security Treaty." *Japan Times*, January 24, 2021. https://www.japantimes.co.jp/news/2021/01/24/national/politics-diplomacy/us-japan-defense-senkakus.

Komine, Yukinori. 2013. "Okinawa Confidential, 1969: Exploring the Linkage Between the Nuclear Issue and the Base Issue." *Diplomatic History* 37, no. 4: 807–840.

Manyin, Mark E. 2021. "The Senkakus (Diaoyu/Diaoyutai) Dispute: U.S. Treaty Obligations." Congressional Research Service, R42761. https://fas.org/sgp/crs/row/R42761.pdf

NSA [National Security Archive]. 1971. "Memorandum for Henry A. Kissinger, Day 1." https://nsarchive2.gwu.edu/NSAEBB/NSAEBB66/ch-34.pdf

NSC [National Security Council], 1949." Foreign Relations of the United States, 1949, The Far East and Australasia." Volume II, Part 2, NSC 13/3, Document 70. Report by the National Security Council on Recommendations With Respect to United States Policy Toward Japan. https://history.state.gov/historicaldocuments/frus1949v07p2/d70

NSC [National Security Council]. 1954. "Foreign Relations of the United States, 1952–1954, China and Japan." Volume XIV, Part 2, S/S–NSC files, lot 63 D 351, Document 820. https://history.state.gov/historicaldocuments/frus1952-54v14p2/d820.

Obama, Barack. 2014. "Joint Press Conference with President Obama and Prime Minister Abe of Japan." Accessed March 13, 2021. https://obamawhitehouse.archives.gov/the-press-office/2014/04/24/joint-press-conference-president-obama-and-prime-minister-abe-japan

Oliveira, Alana C. G. 2019. "Entre o Sol, a Águia e o Dragão: dinâmicas de poder e segurança entre Japão, EUA e China no Leste Asiático e o estudo de caso das ilhas Diaoyu no século XXI," PhD diss. Federal University of Rio de Janeiro.

_____. 2021. "From Panda to Dragon: An Analysis of China's Maritime Actions and Reactions in the East China Sea and Their Implications since 2012." *Contexto Internacional* 43, no. 1: 147–171.

O'Rourke, Ronald. 2021. "U.S.-China Strategic Competition in South and East China Seas: Background and Issues for Congress." Congressional Research Service, R42784. https://crsreports.congress.gov.

Park, Choon-Ho. 1973. "Oil Under Troubled Waters: The Northeast Asia Sea-Bed Controversy." *Harvard International Law Journal* 14, no. 2: 212–260.

Ryukyu Archives. 1965. "Sato-Johnson Communique, Washington, D.C." https://ryukyu-okinawa.net/pages/archive/sato65.html

_____. 1969. "Agreed Minute to Joint Communique of United States; President Nixon and Japanese Prime Minister Sato." https://ryukyuokinawa.net/pages/archive/wakai.html

Smith, Paul J. 2013. "The Senkaku/Diaoyu Island Controversy: A Crisis Postponed." *Naval War College Review* 66, no. 2: 27–44.

South China Morning Post. 2018. "China-Japan Hotline Launched to Avoid Sea, Air Clashes." June 8, 2018. https://www.scmp.com/news/china/diplomacy-defence/article/2149835/china-japan-hotline-launched-avoid-sea-air-clashes

Strait Times. 2021. "Biden Team Signals Rejection of China's Territorial Claims." January 29, 2021. https://www.straitstimes.com/asia/east-asia/biden-team-signals-rejection-of-chinas-territorial-claims

Suganuma, Unryu. 1996. "Historical Justification of Sovereign Rights Over Territorial Space of the Diaoyu/Senkaku Islands: Irredentism and Sino-Japanese Relations," PhD diss. Syracuse University.

US Congress. 1971. *Okinawa Reversion Treaty: Hearings Before the Committee on Foreign Relations, United States Senate, Ninety-second Congress, first session, on Ex. J. 92-1 the Agreement Between the United States of America and Japan Concerning the Ryukyu Islands and the Daito Islands*. Washington: U.S. Government Print Off.

US Department of State. 2021. "Secretary Blinken's Call with Japanese Foreign Minister Motegi." https://www.state.gov/secretary-blinkens-call-with-japanese-foreign-minister-motegi-2

United States. 2017. *The National Security Strategy of the United States of America*. Washington: President of the U.S.

USCAR [United States Civil Administration of the Ryukyu Islands]. 1952. "Provisions of the Government of Ryukyu Islands." https://www.spf.org/islandstudies/jp/wp/infolib/docs/01_history030_doc01.pdf

_____. 1953. "Civil Administration Proclamation No. 27. Geographical Boundaries of the Ryukyu Islands." http://ryukyu-okinawa.net/pages/archive/caproc27.html

Wakaizumi, Kei. 2002. *The Best Course Available; A Personal Account of the Secret U.S.-Japan Okinawa Reversion Negotiations*. Honolulu: University of Hawaii Press.

Worldjpn. 1967. "Joint Statement of Japanese Prime Minister Sato and U.S. President Johnson." https://worldjpn.grips.ac.jp/documents/texts/JPUS/19671115.D1E.html

Zhai, Xiang. 2015. "Rewriting the Legacy of Chiang Kai-shek on the Diaoyu Islands: Chiang's Ryukyu Policies From the 1930s to the 1970s." *Journal of Contemporary China* 25, no. 96: 1128–1146.

Zhou, Laura. 2020. "American Troops Could Be Sent to 'Defend the Senkaku Islands', US Commander Says." *South China Morning Post*, October 27, 2020. https://www.scmp.com/news/china/diplomacy/article/3107291/american-troops-could-be-sent-defend-senkaku-islands-us

8

Dashing Lines and Faking History: The Complicated History of Taipei's Maritime Claims

DEAN KARALEKAS

To understand Taiwan's claims in the South China Sea (SCS), one must first understand that Taiwan has no claims in the South China Sea. The student of history and geopolitics in the Indo-Pacific region is perhaps better advised to conceptualize the issue thusly: The Republic of China (ROC) has various claims in the South China Sea – as well as the East China Sea (ECS) – and the ROC also has claims over the island called Taiwan.

It is modern journalistic shorthand to conflate 'Taiwan' with 'the ROC' as the name of the nation, and this serves just fine in most usages. But it can lead to misperceptions when engaging in a deeper examination of issues, such as this one, in which a clear distinction must be made between the Republic of China – the government that came into being in 1912 after the overthrow of the Qing dynasty – and Taiwan, which was part of the Japanese Empire until 1945. Thus, for much of the formative part of its history, Taiwan was not even a part of the country for which it is today synonymous, and vice versa.[5]

Therefore, a usage note might be in order. In this chapter, the author will endeavour to be careful about referring to Taiwan and the Taiwanese as that island and peoples derived therefrom that are distinct to Formosa. Likewise, the term 'ROC' will be used in reference to the claims, laws, statutes, and

---

[5]   For an in-depth look at the history of Taiwan as a country, see Jonathan Manthorpe's (2016) Forbidden Nation.

other products of government that are properly the purview of the ROC administrative infrastructure now located on Taiwan, but which having been founded in China, are not necessarily Taiwanese. Of course, there is bound to be some overlap, but a distinction is essential to a proper understanding of the state of the ROC's maritime claims, their origins, and how they are seen today in Taiwan.

Identification as a Land Power

As a successor state to the Qing dynasty, the ROC departed little from its predecessor Chinese regime, at least in terms of culture and worldview. Part of the cultural identity of China has traditionally been that of a continental power, not a seafaring nation. Chinese emperors and bureaucrats have customarily exhibited a distrust of coastal inhabitants and seafaring peoples, and while there have been occasional dalliances with maritime expeditions during the long period of China's political history, such as the 15th century treasure ships of Admiral Zheng He, the pattern has been for the Chinese state to withdraw from these forays and resume an inward-focused, land-based orientation. This included the prevailing official opinion about Taiwan, with the Kangxi Emperor (reigned 1661–1722) famously opining that Taiwan was 'the size of a pellet; taking it is no gain; not taking it is no loss.' The island, considered 'a ball of mud beyond the sea, adding nothing to the breadth of China,' was not even depicted on imperial maps until parts of it were annexed by the Qing dynasty in 1683 (Nohara 2017; Calanca 1998; Teng 2004).

The designation of land power vs. sea power is not a trivial one. It has consequences not just for the cultural identity of the citizens, but for how that nation may be expected to behave in the international sphere. Military planners and security analysts must be especially attentive to such distinctions, as they are indicative of how the nation in question can be expected to react to crises. In the words of Napoleon Bonaparte, the policies of such states are inherent in their geography. Sea powers tend to have a culture of individualism, entrepreneurialism, and risk-taking. Venice and Rome were the sea powers of the ancient world, and later Portugal, the Netherlands, and England would rule the oceans. The United States inherited the Royal Navy's control of the world's waterways, and is the primary sea power of the modern day. In contrast, land powers tend to exhibit the qualities of community and security, and have a collective identity and strong central control. France under Napoleon, Germany under Bismarck, and Russia under the czars are examples of continental powers. The last great global land power was the Soviet Union. Notwithstanding Beijing's current efforts to transform the People's Republic of China (PRC) into a sea power, China has always been a land power, and can therefore be expected to exhibit the cultural tendencies that are associated with that history (Dasym 2016; Blagden et al. 2011; Berlin 2010).

China's land-based identity continued well into the modern era, with the Chinese Communist Party (CCP) – another successor regime of dynastic China – relying on a vast conventional land force versed in guerrilla warfare tactics, and largely content to leave control over river systems and littoral areas to its enemies. Mao Zedong exhibited a strong continental focus in his emphasis on the population as his source of strategic power, evincing little interest in maritime matters beyond mere coastal defense. Chairman Mao even went so far as to opine that Taiwan was entitled to its independence, conceding that this was derived from its right to self-determination. Later, on 21 October 1975, in conversation with then US Secretary of State and National Security Advisor Henry Kissinger, Mao said of Taiwan: 'if you were to send it back to me now, I would not want it.' This historical disinterest in maritime expansion is but one facet of how China exhibits the cultural qualities analysts ascribe to continental – as opposed to sea – powers (Simon 2017; Castro 2016; Nohara 2017; Foreign Relations of the United States 2010).

Dashed Lines and Dashed Hopes

Even a culture with a long-time tendency toward tellurocracy must concede to the realities of geopolitics, however, and the events in the Pacific Theater of the Second World War highlighted the importance of control over the South China Sea islands, even to ROC leaders. The navies of France and Japan had been competing throughout the 1930s over control of the region's archipelagos, with French forces claiming the Spratly Islands and occupying some of them in 1933, as well as occupying the Paracel Islands in 1938. In the run-up to the war, the Japanese Empire effected a military occupation of the Pratas, Paracel, and Spratly Islands, *inter alia*. Recognizing the importance of extending control over the SCS islands, immediately after the war ended, the ROC began pressing claims in an attempt to assert sovereignty over them, as evidenced by a trove of archival files that date to 1946, and which were declassified in 2009. The most recognizable of these claims is the map feature that has come to be known as the 'nine-dash line.' Also known as the 'U-shaped line' or the 'cow's tongue,' the cartographic delineation started life as the '11-dash line,' or 'Location Sketch Map of the South China Sea Islands,' which was sketched in rough form in 1946 and informed an official version promulgated the following year. Two years later, in 1949, the newly formed PRC adopted the same line, with a few changes, to define its own SCS claims. It is worth noting that previous versions of this line have been found that date back to the 1910s, but none was officially endorsed (Dzurek 1996; Chen 2017).

The results of extensive archival research conducted by Chris Chung (2016) on declassified official documents show that establishing sovereignty over these islands was high on the government's post-war priority list. The sketch map referenced above was mentioned in the minutes of a 1946 meeting of ROC leaders, who gathered to decide what territories and SCS islands they would press to receive from Japan. Chung interprets the phrasing of the report as being reflective of the prevailing mindset among participants in the meeting that the Paracel (Xisha), Pratas (Dongsha) and Spratly (Nansha) Islands, and Macclesfield Bank (Zhongsha) – and not to the waters surrounding them – were considered salient (Chung 2016).

In other words, the purpose of the U-shaped line was not to lay claim over exclusive navigation and other maritime rights over the waters delineated by the line, but strictly as an island attribution line. Following the promulgation of these measures, records of ROC protests against foreign incursions show that there was a focus only on infringements of island territory, with passage through the surrounding waters being tolerated. This is an important distinction: It can be argued that this interpretation of what is claimed within the U-shaped line (to wit: only the land formations) would not be inconsistent with the current state of maritime rights according to the United Nations Convention on the Law of the Sea (UNCLOS) (Chen 2018a; Chung 2016).

The actions taken to assert ROC sovereignty over the SCS islands in the months that followed Japan's defeat included building weather stations, conducting surveys, and deploying soldiers to Pratas (Dongsha) Island, Woody (Yongxing) Island, and Itu Aba (Taiping Island). In late 1946, a naval expedition led by Rear Admiral Lin Zun and Captain Yao Ruyu sailed to the islands in question to formally reclaim them from Japan in the name of the ROC. These steps were taken despite the pressures of the seemingly endless Chinese Civil War that had been raging since 1927, as well as of obstructionist efforts by the French colonial government in Vietnam, to say nothing of the northeast monsoon rains and rough seas that harried the men undertaking this storied mission (Chen 2017; Granados 2006; Chung 2016).

Historical Claims and Shady Evidence

As described above, the ROC government was desperate to establish a strong case for ownership over the islands of the SCS, both in the run-up to and in the immediate aftermath of the Second Sino-Japanese War, known in China as the War of Resistance against Japanese Aggression. This desperation led to actions and intentional misrepresentations that are still being unravelled today, and which illustrate one of the dangers of putting too much stock in territorial claims based solely on history.

Two historical incidents that illustrate this danger have been described by French geographer François-Xavier Bonnet, who conducted extensive archival research on this issue and who outlined his findings in a provocative conference presentation in 2015. The first such incident involved a secret mission to the Paracel Islands in June of 1937 undertaken by Huang Qiang, an ROC regional military commander. There had been intel that Japanese forces had been harrying the Paracel Islands, and Huang was dispatched to investigate the veracity of these reports. His other assignment was to secure ROC sovereignty over the territory, visiting several islands in the Amphitrite Group including the largest of the Paracels, Woody Island. In his *Confidential Report of 31 July 1937*, Huang describes loading 30 sovereignty markers aboard his ship in preparation for the voyage. Of these stone tablets, none was dated 1937: rather, most of the markers were dated either 1921 or 1912, as well as four that went back to the Qing dynasty. These latter were removed from the city of Guangdong by Huang's team and were dated 1902 (Bonnet 2015; Nery 2015).

Like salting a gold mine, Huang and his crew planted the antedated stone markers on various islands in the Paracels in order to bolster the ROC's claim, on historical grounds, to sovereignty over these features. The annex of his report, reprinted by the Committee of Place Names of the Guangdong Province (1987) contains Huang's detailed record of which markers were buried where. The following are excerpts from this record:

> (1) One stone tablet can be found beside the old tree on the southern side of Shi Dao (Rocky Island) facing Lin Dao (Woody Island), which is 50 feet from shore. The tablet's base was buried at a depth of 1 foot. 'Commemorating the Inspection of 1911,' was carved on the tablet;…

> (6) At the center of northern Lingzhou Dao (Lingzhou Island), a stone tablet can be found under the tree with the inscription 'Commemorating the Inspection of 1911' with its base buried 8 feet into the ground;…

> (13) At the northern shore of Bei Dao (North Island), a tablet can be found with the inscription 'Commemorating the Inspection of 1902.' (Committee of Place 1987; Carpio 2016).

At least a dozen stone tablets were planted on the Paracel Islands during that 1937 voyage, all dated between 1902 and 1921. Owing to the clandestine nature of this mission, these markers were lost to time until being rediscovered by Chinese archaeologists and soldiers of the People's

Liberation Army (PLA) in the mid to late 1970s, at which time they were leveraged to bolster the PRC's history-based claim over the archipelago (Bonnet 2015).

The second historical incident is similar to the first, though this tale begins in 1956, and ends 10 years earlier, in 1946. The story begins with Tomas Cloma, a Philippine national who made a personal claim to sovereignty over the Spratly Islands based on an interpretation of the law governing *terra nullius* (no-man's land). On 15 May 1956, Cloma issued a 'Notice to the Whole World' that his brother, Filemon Cloma, and a crew of 40 men had taken physical possession of each of the islands in the Spratly archipelago, as was their right after Japan gave up ownership over the islands in the 1951 San Francisco Peace Conference. Cloma named his new micronation the 'Free Territory of Freedomland' (Raine and Le Mière 2013).

Records show that the ROC dispatched several patrols to these islands later that year in response to the Cloma claim. In addition to detaining Filemon and confiscating his weapons and navigational charts, the Chinese nationalist agents tried to force the captain and his officers to sign a statement recognizing Freedomland as ROC territory. It was during three voyages in late 1956 that ROC sailors landed on various islands in the Spratly group to conduct flag ceremonies, remove or destroy structures built by competing claimants, and erect antedated markers. Specifically, two markers (both dated December 1946) were planted: one on Nam Wei Dao (Spratly Island), and one on Xi Yue Dao (West York Island). For decades afterwards, the history books attributed the presence of these markers to a 1946 voyage led by Commander Mai Yun Yu, who in the mid-1970s would publicly admit that, while his expedition did indeed visit Taiping Dao (Itu Aba Island) in December 1946 on a mission to destroy the Japanese tablets there and plant two ROC sovereignty markers (in the north and south of the island), his team never set foot on Spratly island or West York island (Samuels 2013; Bonnet 2015; Carpio 2016).

While the ROC officially claims the islands encompassed by the aforementioned U-Shaped Line, it is in direct control of a total of 166 islands, though the vast majority of these are the islands surrounding Taiwan proper (Formosa Island; consisting of 22 islands) and Penghu (the Pescadores; 90 islands). The remainder form part of the geographical units referred to as the outlying islands of Kinmen (Quemoy; 14 islands, including Wūqiū) and Matsu (Mǎzǔ; 36 islands), as well as Nansha (consisting of Itu Aba [Taiping Island] and the adjacent Zhongzhou Reef) and Dongsha. And then there's the Senkakus.

East China Sea Claims

The Senkakus are a group of five uninhabited islands and three rocks located north of the south-western end of the Ryukyu Islands in the East China Sea. In Taiwan, they are known as the Tiaoyutai Islands; in China, as the Diaoyu Islands. They are claimed by the ROC, the PRC, and Japan, the latter of which is in effective control of the archipelago and therefore has the strongest claim. If nothing else, possession is still nine-tenths of the law – even international law.

The ROC's ECS claims are almost the inverse of its SCS claims, at least in terms of proximity and level of control exerted: Taiping Dao lies 1,600 km from Kaohsiung, and 1,150 km from ROC-controlled Pratas Island. In the event of an armed conflict, such great distances would make it difficult for Taipei to deploy military assets quickly enough to protect its claim, and hence the facilities and uniformed personnel stationed there. The Senkakus, on the other hand, remain uninhabited and undeveloped, yet lie just 102 nautical miles northeast of Keelung, in Taiwan's north (Chen 2011).

The root cause of the Senkakus dispute stems from two very different conceptions of what constitutes a valid sovereignty claim. On one side, the global order is informed by Western norms of sovereignty and international law in such matters, particularly UNCLOS. China, on the other, eschews this view and instead presses primarily for the use of historical arguments to determine sovereignty. The Chinese reasoning is salient here, as it rests, ironically enough, upon recognition of the Senkaku Islands as being under Taiwan administration: Despite the clear enmity between the PRC and the ROC, the two governments do agree on the view that the Senkakus are part of Toucheng Township, in Taiwan's Yilan County. With the Senkakus clearly belonging to Taiwan, the only real difference of opinion is on the question of to whom Taiwan belongs (Valencia 2014).

Historically, neither the Republic of China nor the People's Republic thereof had evinced any interest in claiming the Senkaku Islands, at least not until the late 1960s. In 1968, a geological survey revealed that there might be rich deposits of petroleum resources under the seabed there, and after the results of this survey were published, the ROC initiated its first territorial claim to the islands, with the PRC following suit soon thereafter. Both employed a historical-based argument, which posits that the first, albeit vague, mention of the Diaoyu Islands can be found in an ancient Chinese document dating back to the 15th century. By the 17th century, the boundary between the Diaoyu Islands and the Ryukyus was being referred to in Chinese texts as the Black Water Trench, or *Heishuigou*. The islands are mentioned again by Xu Baoguang, a Chinese official who was dispatched in 1720 to confer robes of office upon the king of Ryukyu, which at the time was a vassal state of the Qing dynasty. Xu identified the western demarcation line of the Ryukyuan kingdom as being at Kume-jima, just south of the Black Water Trench, suggesting that the Senkaku Islands – and anything else situated to the west of Kume-jima – must belong to China. Tokyo was loath to put any credence in this historical claim to Chinese ownership – one predicated on the former Ryukyuan Kingdom having been a tributary state of Imperial China. Japanese leaders feared it was a slippery slope and could eventually lead to China claiming Okinawa – a step that hawkish Chinese academics and media commentators have been urging Beijing to take since 2013 (Smith 2013; Nakayama 2015; Perlez 2013).

From the Japanese perspective, the Ryukyus' tributary relationship to the Qing had been officially tolerated since 1655, because the Ryukyuan kings – unbeknownst to the Qing Emperor – had been simultaneously paying tribute to the Japanese Shōgun. Indeed, these kings were chosen in Japan, though the Qing still believed them to be loyal subjects. This tributary relationship came to an end in the mid-1870s, when the Japanese Home Ministry assumed full jurisdiction. In 1895, after the Chinese defeat in the First Sino-Japanese War, the Qing court dropped any remaining claims over the Ryukyus via the Treaty of Shimonoseki. This is the justification for their inclusion in Japan's territories as laid out in the 1952 San Francisco Peace Treaty (Economy 2017; Zhang and Li 2017).

At the end of the 19th century, agents of the Japanese government erected sovereignty markers on the Senkaku Islands, officially incorporating them as national territory via the laws governing *terra nullius* and the right to acquisition through occupation. In 1895, a Japanese businessman named Koga Tatsushirō built a settlement on the island, where about 200 residents operated a bonito processing facility. The enterprise was ultimately unsuccessful, however, and the islands have been uninhabited since the plant closed in 1940. The islands were administered by the US occupying forces from the end of the war until 1972, although the Americans did not equate this administration with actual US sovereignty. In light of this ambiguity, a resolution was passed by the Okinawa Legislative Assembly in 1970 declaring the Senkaku Islands to be Japanese territory. The Japanese, whose own claim is more consistent with the norms of international law, generally view the ROC and PRC historical-based counterclaims as being driven by a thirst for the oil in the seabed below (Pan 2007; Moteki 2010).

Officially, Taipei has been largely silent on the issue, and even the hard-line factions that demand a tough stance are marginal forces that are largely ineffectual. For example, in 2012, an activist from Taiwan, Huang Xilin, travelled to the Senkakus to raise the flag and demonstrate ROC sovereignty over the archipelago. Through a failure to pack properly for the voyage, Huang – who at the time was serving as president of a group calling itself the World Chinese Alliance in Defense of the Diaoyu Islands – arrived at the designated island and, rather than planting an ROC flag, unfurled the five-star red flag of the PRC. When interviewed later by Taiwan media, Huang claimed to have forgotten his ROC flag at home. Huang's misadventure may be comical, but it is indicative of a larger trend in Taiwan, wherein that part of the population most passionate about aggressively pressing the ROC's ECS claims tend also to be pro-China in their orientation (or, at the very least, tend to be supportive of some form of 'greater China' conceptualization, of which they see Taiwan a part). This hard-line stance over the islands is not reflected in Taipei's official policy. For one thing, there is no widespread support in Taiwan for launching a military effort to occupy the islands and taking them by force from Japan, a fellow democracy (Zhang 2015; Wang 2014).

Personal Connections and Policy

The manner in which the ROC government prosecutes its claims over the Senkaku Islands – as well as how it behaves in the South China Sea maritime territorial disputes – is greatly dependent upon which of Taiwan's two main political parties, the Kuomintang (KMT) and the Democratic Progressive Party (DPP), is in power. Broadly speaking, due to what amounts to personal convictions on the part of certain party leaders, the DPP has a track record of showing greater concern with the South China Sea, while the KMT has focused more on the Senkaku Islands in the East China Sea.

Chen Shui-bian

The DPP administration of President Chen Shui-bian, which ran from year 2000 to 2008, was marked by a focus on the South China Sea, and particularly Taiping Island. Chen – a maritime lawyer by trade – was elected amid a wave of pro-Taiwanese sentiment. He had been thrust into the public arena after representing anti-KMT dissidents in court in the days when Taiwan was still the KMT's one-party state. He became a political player after several attempts on his life, as well as the crippling of his wife (she was hit by a truck, which then backed up and ran over her two more times in what was officially deemed an accident and in no way politically motivated). These tragedies, and Chen's role in the struggle against authoritarianism, played no small part in the development of his worldview and hence the direction taken by his policies (Lynch 2006; Robinson 2000; Danielsen 2012).

The grand narrative of Chen's presidency was the 'Localization' (read: de-Sinization) of Taiwan through a series of policies designed to erase the sense of 'shared Chineseness' that had been developing between the ROC and the PRC. Nowhere was this more important than in the handling of the respective governments' island claims. There had been a dalliance by the previous KMT administration with supporting PRC activities in the South China Sea, such as allowing PLA warships to resupply at Taiping Dao during China's 1988 skirmish with Vietnam over the Spratly Islands. Chen sought not just to end this cooperation on island claims, but to distinguish the claims of the ROC from those of China despite their several commonalities. Indeed, he paid the matter inordinate attention, even becoming the first ROC president ever to personally set foot on Taiping Dao (Danielsen 2012; Elleman 2013; Hsue 2007).

Chen engaged in a two-pronged approach to handling the island disputes. The first was to solidify the ROC sovereignty claims to the islands that it did control. He did this by initiating construction of a 1,150-meter-long runway on Itu Aba, for example, designed to increase the operational capabilities of the island as a potential forward-operating base. In an effort to placate Beijing as well as to demilitarize the situation to an extent, he also replaced the detachment of ROC Marines stationed on the island with members of the Coast Guard, a less threatening branch of the service. The second prong was a reconceptualization of the multiple and overlapping SCS claims (various ROC claims and those of the PRC are contested by Brunei, Malaysia, the Philippines, and Vietnam) from an exercise in competition to one of cooperation. In early 2008, the Chen administration launched its Spratly Initiative, in which it reached out to other SCS claimants and entreated them to 'shelve sovereignty disputes and jointly explore resources based on the principle and spirit of the UN Charter, [UNCLOS] and the Declaration on the Conduct of Parties in the South China Sea' (MOFA 2008; Lin 2016).

Global warming and rising sea levels had become high-visibility issues, so the Chen administration began calling for cooperation on environmental protection, ecological preservation, and – most importantly – joint resource exploitation. The entire South China Sea should be designated a marine ecological sanctuary, where environmental scientists and protection groups from all claimant nations could cooperate on field research, according to the proposals. This multilateral approach was designed to create a 'united front' of sorts to counter China's unilateral actions in the SCS and frustrate Beijing's preferred method of using bilateral negotiations as a divide-and-conquer approach. Moreover, the purpose of this paradigm shift was not just to calm regional tensions: it was also to aid in the fight against China's diplomatic blockade and to raise Taiwan's profile in the regional and international fora that would be erected to discuss the SCS issue: Whether or not the ROC was a valid country, it was undeniably a valid claimant, and therefore any forum that excluded Taipei would lose all legitimacy. It was an elegant way to reframe the island disputes to Taipei's advantage and proved so popular that even the subsequent KMT administration would borrow from it (McManus et al. 2010; Song 2010).

Ma Ying-jeou

Upon assuming the ROC presidency in 2008, Ma Ying-jeou and his new KMT administration immediately set about repairing the relationship with China, primarily as a means of boosting the economy by hitching it to China's meteoric economic rise, but also in the hopes that the Beijing authorities would grant Taipei more international diplomatic space. He also managed to secure an implicit 'diplomatic truce' with the PRC, in which each side would stop trying to poach the other's diplomatic allies. Given this positioning, it was natural that the Ma administration went out of its way to avoid butting heads with Beijing over the SCS claims. Instead, it focused more on the East China Sea disputes with Japan. Ma himself had a strong personal connection to the Senkaku Islands issue, going back to his days as a student activist during the 1970s (Atkinson 2010).

On 17 June 1971, for example, Ma led students from National Taiwan University in a march on the US and Japanese embassies to deliver a list of demands concerning the Islands. He became affiliated with a protest movement called *Baodiao*, which is a portmanteau of *Baowei Diaoyutai*, meaning 'defend the Diaoyu Islands.' Ma's interest in the Senkaku issue extended to his academic work as well, it being the focus of his Doctor of Juridical Science dissertation at Harvard University. Titled 'Trouble Over Oily Waters: Legal Problems of Seabed Boundaries and Foreign Investments in the East China Sea,' the thesis identifies the key sovereignty issue as the dispute between China and Japan over the seabed boundary delimitation in the East China Sea. Examining this from an international law perspective, Ma argues in favour of treating the seabed issue as separate from the territorial dispute over the islands. Both the activism and the dissertation shed light on Ma's position vis-à-vis the Senkaku Islands, and undoubtedly influenced the direction his policy would take while serving as ROC president (Chen 2018b; Ogasawara 2015).

It would not take long for the Senkaku issue to dominate the agenda of the newly minted Ma administration. In June 2008, a private Taiwanese vessel called the *Lianhe Hao* sank after colliding with a Japanese Coast Guard patrol ship. Her three crewmembers and 13 passengers were rescued by Japanese Coast Guard, and subsequently held for territorial violations. In a rare display of Taiwanese belligerence, Ma demanded that Tokyo pay compensation for the sinking – an outcome that would be seen by some in

Taiwan as a Japanese concession of ROC rights over the Senkakus (Wang 2010).

Despite the KMT administration's wider foreign policy goal of engineering a rapprochement with Beijing, and the concomitant distancing with other powers in the region, Ma showed considerable restraint in refusing Beijing's pressure to harmonize the ROC maritime claims with the PRC's, or indeed to engage in any sort of cooperation on the issue. Moreover, his administration completed a number of endeavours related to the SCS islands begun by his predecessor, including promoting the Pratas Islands as a center of maritime research, completion of a geological exploration and marine survey in the Pratas and Spratly Islands, and construction of a photovoltaic system in order to reduce carbon emissions in the Spratly Islands. Two of Ma's most remarkable triumphs on the maritime portfolio were unrelated to the Chinese claims. His high-profile proposal in 2012 of an East-China Sea Peace Initiative, for example, was received enthusiastically (by the global media, if not the policymakers of the region) for its promotion of such cooperative mechanisms as multilateral cooperation, preventive diplomacy, and the peaceful settlement of disputes. Though Beijing ultimately put the kibosh on the effort, it painted Ma as a peacemaker and capable regional leader. Moreover, it raised Taiwan's international profile and showed that Taipei's interests in the region were, at least rhetorically, aligned with Washington's own (MOFA 2012; Souza and Karalekas 2015; Valencia 2014).

Ma scored another high-profile success with the April 2013 inking of a fisheries agreement with Japan. Negotiations over this agreement had been on-again, off-again for 17 long years, and it was only due to the increased tensions in the region that Washington put pressure on Taipei and Tokyo to finally close the deal. Following the spirit of the American political proverb that 'only Nixon could go to China,' it would seem that only Ma Ying-jeou, with his history of nationalistic activism and hardline stance on the Senkakus, could make peace with the Japanese over shared resources in the waters surrounding the contentious islands (MOFA 2013; Leng and Chang Liao 2016).

Tsai Ing-wen

In 2016, the DPP once again won at the ballot box, and President Tsai Ing-wen was inaugurated. Unlike Chen and Ma, Tsai had had no previous personal connections to maritime claims and counterclaims, and was not expected to devote much political capital to the issue given the party's Taiwan-centered orientation, as well as the perception that the new administration would be amenable to developing deeper Taiwan-Japan ties. It therefore came as somewhat of a surprise when Tsai responded with a tough stance against Tokyo over the Senkaku claims, after the city council of Okinawa's Ishigaki-shi approved legislation in 2020 to change the district name of the Senkaku Islands from *Tonoshiro* to *Tonoshiro Senkaku*. Tsai swiftly denounced the move and pledged to protect ROC sovereignty and fishing rights over the territory. In fact, the strong response speaks less to the importance of the Senkaku claims among the Taiwanese electorate and more to the horse-trading that characterizes domestic politics in Taiwan (South China Morning Post 2020).

Just weeks prior to the incident, on 4 June 2020, the Executive Yuan – the executive branch of the ROC government – released the country's first-ever Marine Policy White Paper. At the time, China had been aggressively militarizing the SCS islands over which it had wrested *de facto* control over the previous decade, and the maritime security environment in both the East and South China seas had become volatile (Taiwan News 2020).

The white paper was the next step in implementing a framework designed to streamline the country's ocean management, approved by the Legislative Yuan in November 2019. Known as the Basic Act For Ocean Affairs, the legislation was aimed at integrating the multitude of government agencies that shared purview over marine and maritime issues. Until this initiative, ocean-related matters in the ROC involved more than 15 different agencies with sometimes overlapping jurisdictions, ranging from ministry-level bodies to technical departments. As a result of these intersecting responsibilities, scopes, and structures, inter-agency rivalries developed, making coordination of the administration of maritime affairs a bureaucratic challenge. Compounding this Byzantine nightmare was domestic inertia and party rivalry, marked by inter-party conflicts over maritime ideology. Thus, for years Taipei had been hamstrung in efforts to respond swiftly and efficiently to its urgent marine and maritime challenges (Souza and Karalekas 2020; Shih 2020).

The Tsai administration therefore worked hard to implement more coherent and coordinated ocean policies through the white paper, and for this to succeed, it needed cooperation from the many government agencies that would be affected, as well as by both ends of Taiwan's unique political spectrum. Thus, a *modus vivendi* had to be found between the Blues and the Greens (Kuomintang and DPP) if the initiative was to move forward. With this in mind, Tsai's tough talk in response to Japan's redesignation of the Senkaku Islands makes more sense: it was likely conceived as an olive branch offered to the Pan-Blue coalition – not just the professional politicians, but the many career civil servants employed in the relevant ministries and departments known to have blue-leaning sympathies. This is a Herculean task. Not only is it necessary to unite political factions for the good of the nation's maritime endeavours, but the Tsai administration must, in a sense, unite disparate paradigms: the Pan-Green Camp's localized perspective, with its focus on an environmental-protection discourse viewing Taiwan as an island culture; and the Pan-Blue camp's terrestrial or land-oriented worldview, inherited from the Chinese tradition from which this party evolved. Tsai's willingness to take the concerns of this tellurocratic mentality into account in devising her response to the Japanese – despite that response being perhaps more assertive than it needed to be – is therefore heartening.

Conclusion

No matter which political party happens to be in power in Taipei, voters in Taiwan expect their leaders to safeguard their interests, especially when it comes to the country's maritime issues. Unfortunately, Taipei's arguments to support its claims of sovereignty suffer from the same deficiencies as those of China: to wit, they are predicated on historical sources, and shaky ones at that. As this chapter discusses, there are great many problems inherent in using a historical argument as the basis for claims over territorial sovereignty, not the least of which is the questionable reliability of so-called historical and archaeological evidence.

Like the PRC, the ROC inherited a cultural identity and worldview of a continental power, not a seafaring nation. Over the years of its exile on Taiwan, however, it has begun to incorporate aspects of the maritime identity of the islanders living there when the ROC arrived in 1949. It therefore behooves military and IR analysts to include a culturalist perspective when dealing with the complicated and overlapping island claims in the East and South China Seas, especially as these have become potential flashpoints that threaten regional peace and stability.

Figure 8.1. Nine-Dash Map/U-Shaped Map. Source: Secretariat of Government of Guangdong Province, Republic of China - Made by Territory Department of Ministry of the Interior, printed by Bureau of Surveying of Ministry of Defence. Now in Sun Yat-sen Library of Guangdong Province, China. https://commons.wikimedia.org/w/index.php?curid=4002269

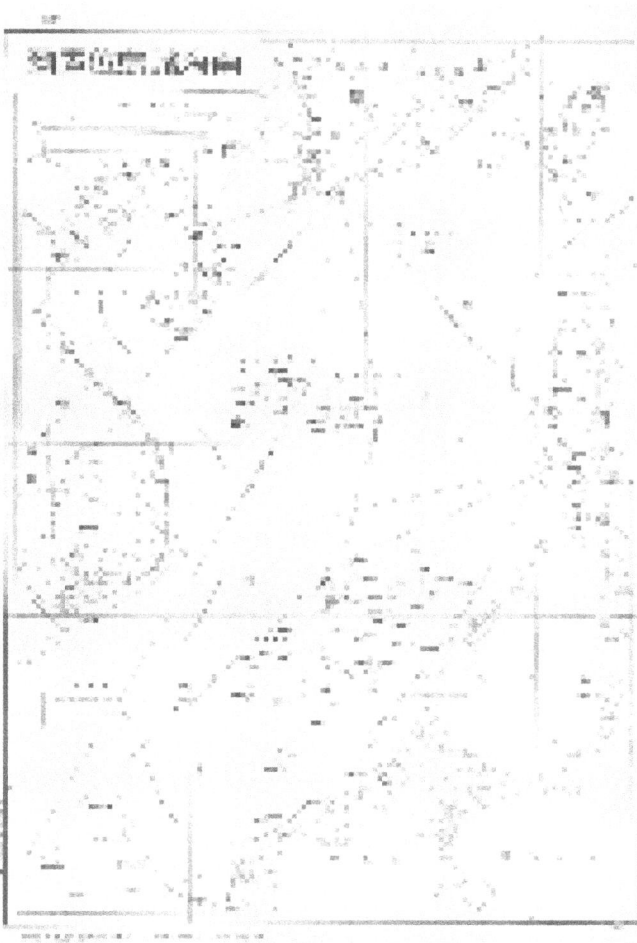

References

Atkinson, Joel. 2010. "China-Taiwan Diplomatic Competition and the Pacific Islands." *The Pacific Review* 23, no. 4: 407–427.

Berlin, Don. 2010. "Sea Power, Land Power and the Indian Ocean." *Journal of the Indian Ocean Region* 6, no. 1: 52–66.

Blagden, David W., Jack S. Levy, and William R. Thompson. 2011. "Sea Powers, Continental Powers, and Balancing Theory." *International Security* 36, no. 2: 190–202.

Bonnet, Francois-Xavier. 2015. "Archaeology and Patriotism: Long Term Chinese Strategies in the South China Sea." In *Southeast Asia Sea conference*, Ateneo Law Center, Makati, Manila, 27 March, 2015.

Calanca, Paola. 1998. "From a Forbidden Ocean to an Ocean Under Close Watch: The Ming and Early Qing Governments and the Maritime Problem." *Ming Qing Yanjiu* 7, no. 1: 13–47. https://doi.org/10.1163/24684791-90000372.

Carpio, Antonio T. 2016. "The South China Sea Dispute: Philippine Sovereign Rights and Jurisdiction in the West Philippine Sea." Phil. LJ 90: 459.

Castro, Sara. 2016. *Improvising Tradecraft: The Evolving U.S. Intelligence Regime and the Chinese Communist Party In the 1940s.* https://doi.org/10.17615/1g6m-kv39.

Chen, Hurng-Yu. 2018a. "The Phantom of the U-shaped Line: A Challenge for Southeast Asia's Security." *AMTI Brief, CSIS,* May 9, 2018. https://amti.csis.org/phantom-u-shaped-line.

Chen, Mumin. 2018b. "Managing Territorial Nationalism in the East and South China Seas." In *Assessing the Presidency of Ma Ying-jiu in Taiwan: Hopeful Beginning, Hopeless End?,* edited by André Beckershoff and Gunter Schubert, 317–333. New York: Routledge.

Chen, Qianping. 2017. "The Nationalist Government's Efforts to Recover Chinese Sovereignty Over the Islands in the South China Sea After the End of World War Two." *Journal of Modern Chinese History* 11, no. 1: 72–96. DOI: 10.1080/17535654.2017.1313527.

Chung, Chris P. C. 2016. "Drawing the U-Shaped Line: China's Claim in the South China Sea, 1946–1974." *Modern China* 42, no. 1: 38–72. https://doi.org/10.1177/0097700415598538.

Committee of Place Names of the Guangdong Province [Guangdong sheng di ming wei yuan hui]. 1987. Compilation of References of the Names of all the South Sea Islands [Nan Hai zhu dao di ming zi liao hui bian], *Guangdong Map Publishing Company [Guangdong sheng di tu chu ban she]*.

Danielsen, Michael. 2012. "On the Road to a Common Taiwan Identity." In *National Identity and Economic Interest*, edited by Peter C. Y. Chow, 135–151. New York: Palgrave Macmillan.

Dasym. 2016. *Sea Versus Land Powers*. December 23, 2016. https://www.dasym.com/sea-versus-land-powers

Dzurek, Daniel J. 1996. "The Spratly Islands Dispute: Who's on First?" *Maritime Briefing* 2, no. 1.

Economy, Elizabeth C. 2017. "History with Chinese Characteristics: How China's Imagined Past Shapes Its Present." *Foreign Affairs* 96, no. 4: 141–148. Accessed March 24, 2021. http://www.jstor.org/stable/44823900

Elleman, Bruce. 2013. "PRC Disputes with the ROC on Taiwan." In *Beijing's Power and China's Borders: Twenty Neighbors in Asia*, edited by Bruce Elleman, Stephen Kotkin, and Clive Schofield, 267–282. England: M.E. Sharpe.

Foreign Relations of the United States. 2010. *Foreign Relations of the United States 1969–1976, Volume XVIII, China, 1973–1976. The Summit in Beijing, August–December 1975*. Washington: Government Printing Office.

Granados, Ulises. 2006. "Chinese Ocean Policies Towards the South China Sea in a Transitional Period, 1946 – 1952." *China Review* 6, no. 1: 153–81. Accessed March 24, 2021. http://www.jstor.org/stable/23462012

Leng, Tse-Kang, and Nien-chung Chang Liao. 2016. "Hedging, Strategic Partnership, and Taiwan's Relations with Japan Under the Ma Ying-jeou Administration." *Pacific Focus* 31, no. 3: 357–382.

Lin, Ting-Hui. 2016. "South China Sea Disputes: Taiwan's Opportunities and Challenges." In *Asia Pacific Countries and the US Rebalancing Strategy*, edited by David W.F. Huang, 241–257. New York: Palgrave Macmillan.

Lynch, Daniel. 2006. "Taiwan Adapts to the Network Society." In *China's Rise, Taiwan's Dilemmas and International Peace*, edited by Edward Friedman, 158–174. New York: Routledge.

Manthorpe, Jonathan. 2016. *Forbidden Nation: A History of Taiwan*. New York: St. Martin's Griffin.

McManus, John W., Kwang-Tsao Shao, and Szu-Yin Lin. 2010. "Toward Establishing a Spratly Islands International Marine Peace Park: Ecological Importance and Supportive Collaborative Activities with an Emphasis on the Role of Taiwan." *Ocean Development & International Law* 41, no. 3: 270–280.

MOFA [Ministry of Foreign Affairs] of ROC [Republic of China]. 2008. *The Government of the Republic of China (Taiwan) Reiterates its Sovereignty over the Spratly Islands and Has Proposed a Spratly Initiative that Focuses on Environmental Protection Instead of Sovereignty Disputes*. Taipei: Press Release.

_____. 2012. *The Republic of China's Sovereignty Claims over the Diaoyutai Islands and the East China Sea Peace Initiative*. Catalog Card No.: MOFA-EN-FO-102-016-I-1. Ac.

_____. 2013. *Republic of China (Taiwan) Signs Fisheries Agreement with Japan*. Taipei: Press Release.

Moteki, Hiromichi. 2012. "The Senkaku Islands Constitute an Intrinsic Part of Japan." Society for Dissemination of Historical Fact. – Режим доступа: www. sdhьfact. com. – Дата доступа 1, 12.

Nakayama, Toi. 2015. "An English Translation of Xu Baoguang's Poems on the Eight Views of the Ryukyu Kingdom." *The Meio University Bulletin* 20, 135–139.

Nery, John, 2015. "A Chinese Strategy: Manipulating the Record." *Philippine Daily Inquirer*, 21 April, 2015.
https://opinion.inquirer.net/84307/a-chinese-strategy-manipulating-the-record

Nohara, Jun J. 2017. "Sea Power as a Dominant Paradigm: the Rise of China's New Strategic Identity." *Journal of Contemporary East Asia Studies* 6, no. 2: 210–232.

Ogasawara, Yoshiyuki. 2015. "Ma Ying-Jeou's Doctoral Thesis and Its Impact on the Japan–Taiwan Fisheries Negotiations." *Journal of Contemporary East Asia Studies* 4, no. 2: 67–92.

Pan, Zhongqi. 2007. "Sino-Japanese Dispute over the Diaoyu/Senkaku Islands: The Pending Controversy from the Chinese Perspective." *Journal of Chinese Political Science* 12, no. 1: 71–92.

Perlez, Jane. 2013. "Calls Grow in China to Press Claim for Okinawa." *New York Times*, June 13, 2013.

Raine, Sarah, and Christian Le Mière. 2013. "Chapter One: Mapping the History." *Adelphi Series 53, no. 436–437: Regional Disorder: The South China Sea Dispute*, 29–54. DOI: 10.1080/19445571.2013.779488.

Robinson, James A., and Deborah A. Brown. 2007. "Chen Shui-Bian and Taiwan's Political Development." *American Asian Review* 18, no. 4: 207.

Samuels, Marwyn. 2013. *Contest for the South China Sea*. New York: Routledge.

Shih, Yi-Che. 2020. "Taiwan's Progress Towards Becoming an Ocean Country." *Marine Policy* 111, 103725.

Simon, Scott. 2017. "Why Taiwan is an International Issue." *Centre for International Policy Studies*, September 20, 2017.

Smith, Paul J. 2013. "The Senkaku/Diaoyu Island Controversy: A Crisis Postponed." *Naval War College Review* 66, no. 2: 27–44.

Song, Yann-Huei. 2010. "The South China Sea Workshop Process and Taiwan's Participation." *Ocean Development & International Law* 41, no. 3: 253–269.

South China Morning Post. 2020. "Japan City Renames Area Covering Senkaku Islands, Triggering China to Warn of Reprisal." June 22, 2020. http://archive.today/2021.03.22-222947/https://www.scmp.com/news/asia/east-asia/article/3090077/japan-city-renames-area-covering-senkaku-islands-triggering

Souza, Moises de, and Dean Karalekas. 2015. "Domestic Politics and Personal Beliefs in Taiwan's Territorial Claims." *Panorama of Global Security Environment 2015–2016*, 409–420.

_____. 2020. "Confronting Japan to Defend Against China: Senkaku as a Case Study in Taiwan's Politics." *Global Security Review*, July 20, 2020.

Taiwan News. 2020. "Cabinet Passes Taiwan's First Marine Policy White Paper." June 4, 2020. https://www.taiwannews.com.tw/en/news/3944805

Teng, Emma. 2004. *Taiwan's Imagined Geography: Chinese Colonial Travel Writing and Pictures, 1683–1895*. Cambridge: Harvard University Asia Center.

Valencia, Mark J. 2014. "The East China Sea Disputes: History, Status, and Ways Forward." *Asian Perspective* 38, no. 2: 183–218.

Wang, Kuan-Hsiung. 2010. "The ROC's Maritime Claims and Practices with Special Reference to the South China Sea." *Ocean Development & International Law* 41, no. 3: 237–252.

Wang, Vincent Wei-Cheng, and Gwendolyn Stamper. 2014. "Taiwan's Policy Toward the Diaoyu/Senkaku Islands Dispute and the Implications for the US." *Education About Asia* 19, no. 2: 45.

Zhang, Haipeng, and Guoqiang Li. 2017. "The Treaty of Shimonoseki, the Diaoyu Islands and the Ryukyu Issue." *International Critical Thought* 7, no. 1: 93–108.

Zhang, Ketian. 2015. "Patriots' with Different Characteristics: Deconstructing the Chinese Anti-Japan Protests in 2012." *MIT Political Science Department Research Paper No. 2015–18.*

9

Sino-Indian Border Dispute: A Brief Introduction

MAYURI BANERJEE

The year 2020 marked the 70th anniversary of Sino-Indian relations and also became one of the watershed years in the history of bilateral ties between India and the People's Republic of China (PRC). Following disagreements between the two countries over territorial delineation and their armies setting up military posts in or near disputed areas, Chinese and Indian troops clashed fiercely at Galwan Valley near Ladakh on 15 June 2020, leading to the death of 20 Indian soldiers and an unidentified number of Chinese troops (BBC 2020).

The localized conflict escalated rapidly into a full-blown crisis, with both sides deploying additional troops, missile launchers, and armed helicopters. By all appearances, China and India were on the brink of another war. Further escalation was prevented by a timely intervention by political and military officials, however, the brutality and magnitude of the violence witnessed during the few days that the crisis lasted has complicated the disengagement process, since neither country wanted to be seen as compromising on its national interests (Peri 2021). The Galwan Valley clash was significant for two reasons; first because it shattered the 1988 consensus of keeping the border dispute divorced from the broader relationship and repositioned the border dispute at the centre of bilateral ties, making diplomatic and economic relations contingent upon developments on the border (Vasudeva 2020). Second, the animosity exhibited by the two sides reversed years of hard-won diplomatic and political improvements that had strengthened cooperative structures, setting bilateral ties back years and placing the Sino-India relationship at crossroads where prospects for a major reset appear bleak. The first attribute is perhaps more damaging because the border dispute was already a major driving factor in Sino-Indian rivalry, and its increased prominence is likely to intensify feelings of hostility in New Delhi and Beijing. Moreover, as the existing bilateral border management framework appears to be severely compromised, the rise of border tensions portend a new era of uncertainty where bilateral interaction will be more adversarial, conflict-prone, and volatile.

This chapter examines the origin of the border dispute, its colonial legacy, and the factors that have contributed to its recent entrenchment. It will then discuss the divergent positions held by the two countries on the border issue, and the various bilateral dialogues and confidence-building measures adopted by the two countries. It concludes with an assessment of the effectiveness of these bilateral endeavours toward effective border management, addressing the trust deficit, and finding a final resolution of the border dispute, followed by policy recommendations the two countries can contemplate.

Genesis of Sino-Indian Border Dispute

Over its seven decades, the Sino-Indian border dispute has become an intractable disagreement, with no resolution in sight. The question of a disputed border emerged in the early 1950s when the PRC effected its occupation of Tibet, a move which created for China and India one of the longest undemarcated borders of the world. The proximity of the Chinese military presence so close to the undemarcated frontier created considerable consternation in New Delhi. Factions of Indian policy elites led by India's first home minister and also its first deputy prime minister, Sardar Vallabhbhai Patel, and then-Bombay Governor Girija Shankar Bajpai urged the government of then-Prime Minister Jawaharlal Nehru to enhance the military and administrative presence along India's north-east region (Raghavan 2012, 80). However, both Nehru and India's ambassador to China, K.M. Pannikar, were reluctant to annoy their powerful northern neighbour and decided that India would not actively pursue the border question with Beijing, but would explicitly announce their endorsement of the McMahon Line as India's border (Luthi and Das Gupta 2017, 8–10). Beijing, on the other hand, was less perturbed by the status of the common border as the new communist regime was more engaged in consolidating its authority at home, supressing rebellions, dealing with poverty, agrarian crises, and fears of invasion by the United States and the exiled nationalist government of the Republic of China, then in exile in Taiwan. Accordingly, the leadership of the Chinese Communist Party (CCP) saw fit to put the boundary issue on the backburner until they were well-prepared to address it (Chaowu 2017, 70).

The border dispute came to the fore in 1958, when Chinese Premier Zhou Enlai, responding to Nehru's protests against the Aksai Chin Road – 179 kilometres of which ran through the Aksai Chin region claimed by India – as well as acquisitive Chinese maps, denied for the first time the presence of any formalised border between China and India. Central to the border dispute was two flanks of territories lying at the two extremities of the vast border; the Aksai Chin region in the western sector, and the India-controlled and administered North Eastern Frontier Agency (NEFA), now Arunachal Pradesh, in the eastern sector. While New Delhi extended its claims on the basis of maps inherited from the British, Beijing claimed that these territories were historically part of Tibet. Over the next few years, the territorial disagreements between the two countries only deepened as the Tibet crisis, Dalai Lama's refuge in India, and New Delhi's Forward Policy only intensified the mutual distrust and led to the 1962 war (Shankar 2018, 29–34).

The Border Dispute: A Colonial Legacy

Ambiguity about the Indian frontier with China dates back to the colonial era, and can be attributed as one of the foremost causes of the territorial conundrum facing the two countries (Sidhu and Yuan 2001, 11). The British initiatives to demarcate the Himalayan frontiers were guided primarily by its strategic competition with Russia. Accordingly, the urgency to delineate the boundaries of the British Empire arose only when the Great Game intensified between the two superpowers. British administrators up until then held no clear view of India's territorial limits along the massive Indo-Tibetan boundary. In the western sector, the first attempt to fix a boundary line was taken in 1865. Then-Surveyor General of India Sir W. H. Johnson, in a bid to impress the Dogra ruler, produced expansive boundary claims stretching the Dogra state border to the Kunlun Mountains and including all of Aksai Chin (Chakravarty 2020). Since other British officials were sceptical about Johnson's claims, the boundary proposition died a natural death, until it was revived in 1897 by the director of the British military intelligence Sir John Ardagh, who believed that implementation of the forward positions in Johnson's line would secure strategic leverage against Russia in the event of an Anglo-Russian confrontation. This boundary came to be known as the Ardagh-Johnson line, and later formed the basis of India's claims to Aksai Chin.

It is noteworthy that between 1865 and 1897, colonial administrators depicted different versions of the northern and north-eastern boundary of Kashmir, the line fluctuating according to the degree of perceived threat from Russia (Palit 1991, 32). Also, China never acquiesced to any of the boundary propositions made during this period. The 1899 Macartney–MacDonald Line, which was the only formal boundary proposition ever presented to Beijing, was never officially acknowledged by the Manchu dynasty then ruling China (Palit 1991, 32).

The urgency to secure British India's northern boundaries was lost with the removal of threat of invasion due to fall of Tsarist Russia in 1917. Post-1945, a map published by Survey of India did imply claims to the Aksai Chin region, but the British military remained non-committal on that boundary (Chakravarty 2020). In effect, the British administration exercised such benign neglect that sometimes the Macartney-MacDonald or the Ardagh-Johnson Line were treated as informal boundaries, depending on the administration's inclination. Therefore, when the British left in 1947, there was no clear indication of exactly where the northern boundaries were. Major General D.K. Palit, who was a brigade commander during the 1962 war with China, opined that, had the British suggested that the newly formed Indian government follow the 1899 boundary proposition that left out the north-eastern Aksai Chin (through which the strategic Chinese road runs), the Nehru government would have certainly accepted the suggestion, and consequently the whole confrontation could have been avoided (Palit 1991, 34–36).

A similar reticence was displayed by colonial administrators in the eastern sector as well. The British had long been content to occupy the Brahmaputra plains, and did not extend their jurisdiction to the mountains, for these mountains were neither of commercial nor strategic value. However, in order to delineate the limit of British responsibility, the foothills were divided by an Outer Line representing the external territorial frontier of the British Empire, and an Inner line which was forbidden to cross without a permit. In the absence of any perceived threat from Russia or China, the vague demarcation continued.

The British began consolidating India's eastern boundaries with Tibet in the early 1900s, as the administration became paranoid about Russia's increasing influence in that country. A military expedition under Francis Younghusband was sent to Lhasa in 1903 to secure British India's diplomatic and economic rights, which in turn triggered the perception of a threat by China, which responded with an expedition of its own to assert control over Lhasa. The operation's leader Zhao Erfeng, who had earned the nickname 'the Butcher of Kham' for his actions extending Chinese rule into that Tibetan province, reached Lhasa in 1910 with 2,000 troops, securing the city and spurring the 13th Dalai Lama to flee toward India.

Britain, sensing the potential of a threat from China's counter-moves, for the first time ordered a series of surveys to determine the extent of the tribal areas and to bring the area of Assam Himalaya (later NEFA) under British jurisdiction. Although, the sudden collapse of the Manchu dynasty in 1911 eased some of the pressure, the new republican government appeared equally assertive toward Tibet. At this point, the British government began to contemplate a tripartite conference to settle such issues as the eastern borders of Inner and Outer Tibet, China's degree of control in Inner Tibet, and alignment of the Indo-Tibetan border.

A tripartite conference which ultimately convened at Simla in October 1913 was fraught with controversy from the very beginning. For instance, the Chinese objected to Tibet's equal representation, and were adamant about pushing Tibet's Inner Line as the Outer Boundary. After negotiations dragged on, eventually in March 1914 the Chinese representative reluctantly agreed to a line drawn by McMahon on the map that ran along the highest crest of the Assam Himalayas and included Tawang within British Indian territory.

The Simla Conference ultimately failed to align the Indo-Tibetan border: the Chinese government never ratified the McMahon line, and since the Assam government was never informed about the Simla Conference proceedings, areas of Dirang and Tawang claimed by the McMahon Line remained under Tibetan control. In 1938, the Assam government attempted to occupy Tawang, but it back-pedalled after vehement protests from Lhasa, as well as when the British government during World War II excluded Tawang from its defensive efforts against a Japanese invasion, despite fortifying nearby Walong and Dirang. China too, its hands full fighting both the Second Sino-Japanese War (the Chinese theatre of World War II) as well as the Chinese Civil War against communist revolutionaries, paid scant attention to the Indo-Tibetan border issue. Therefore, the British left the Indian subcontinent without making any definite provisions for either NEFA or Tawang (Palit 1991, 38–44).

The Entrenchment of the Border Dispute

After India's independence, three major factors contributed to the entrenchment of the border dispute. First was the reluctance of both India and China to broach the subject in the initial phase from 1950 to 1957, when Sino-Indian ties were peaceful and amicable and the two countries had many high-level diplomatic exchanges, which provided the leaders with ample opportunities to settle the ambiguities left over from the colonial period. However, the two countries not only circumvented the boundary issue but also followed unilateral policies. The Indian government failed to consult China before declaring the forward-most posts in the eastern and western sectors (EPW 2020); it annexed Tawang in 1951; and it published new maps reflecting India's unilateral demarcation, interpreted China's silence as tacit consent. Nehru himself admitted in 1953 that even while India inherited the McMahon Line from the British, he was not willing to raise the subject lest it awaken sleeping dogs (Luthi 2017, 32). Similarly, Mao Zedong's instructions, the PRC followed a delaying strategy, with China deciding to refrain from formally protesting against New Delhi's unilateral moves until they had consolidated their administrative and military position in Tibet, as China had begun building the Xinjiang National Highway in 1951 – a road that would not be completed until 1957 (Chaowu 2017, 69–71). Moreover, during 1954 negotiations on Tibet, China chose not to raise the issue of border alignment despite having the opportunity, and in 1956, when Nehru for the first time referred to the boundary issue, Zhou Enlai suggested that the Chinese government would be willing to recognize the McMahon Line (Das Gupta 2017, 53).

Later scholarly works reveal that a combination of domestic and international factors influenced the policy choices of both countries. For instance, New Delhi's trauma from previous territorial losses due to Partition and also Nehru's desire to maintain friendly relations with China weighed heavily on Indian decision-makers. Simultaneously, Beijing, too embroiled in China's internal struggles and facing international diplomatic isolation, was reluctant to immediately open another confrontational front with India. In retrospect, however, the deferral policy followed by both countries proved to be disastrous, because as suspicion and misperceptions mounted on both sides, the window of opportunity to settle the border dispute only became narrower.

Tibet is the second factor which contributed to the entrenchment of the border dispute. From the very beginning, Tibet had become a point of contention between India and China. China's military occupation of Tibet in 1950 was seen as a security threat in New Delhi and led to massive public outcry against China. Similarly, India's close ties with the Dalai Lama and Nehru's attempts to mediate between Lhasa and Beijing was perceived by the Communist regime as interference in China's internal matters. The 1954 Panchsheel Agreement provided only partial relaxation of tensions as China's coercive practices to Sinicize Tibet, and India's clandestine aid to the unarmed Tibetan resistance, kept suspicions lingering on both sides. In this context, the spontaneous 1959 Lhasa uprising further aggravated mutual misgivings, which in turn hardened their positions on the border dispute (Sikri 2011).

At the outbreak of the insurgency, Beijing immediately held India responsible for inciting the violence. Although the People's Liberation Army (PLA) quickly crushed the rebellion, the 14th Dalai Lama's flight to India and his subsequent granting of political asylum by New Delhi infuriated the CCP and strengthened its conviction about Indian malfeasance. An internal intelligence report even suggested that India had been complicit in fomenting rebellion in Tibet to compel China into accepting India's territorial claims. Accordingly, Beijing directed intense criticism against Nehru, accusing him of continuing imperial policies in Tibet. The polemical attack not only shocked Nehru but also created trepidation in New Delhi that China might now try to push through the disputed areas (Westcott 2017). Evidently, an atmosphere of distrust and suspicion surrounding events in Tibet strained bilateral political and military ties. At the operational level, the PLA and the Indian army began to clash quickly since both militaries had begun conducting forward patrols, primarily in the eastern sector, and in August 1959, the first exchange of fire took place at Longju, NEFA, which significantly impacted relations (Raghavan 2012, 126). Concurrently, an exchange of letters between Zhou Enlai and Jawaharlal Nehru in September demonstrated significant hostility between the two leaders over the border dispute: China retracted its earlier willingness to accept the McMahon Line and accused the government of India of pressuring China, and Nehru replied by demanding the withdrawal of Chinese forces from posts on the Indian side as a precondition to border talks. Over the next few months, as bilateral ties continued to deteriorate following more clashes, deaths of Indian soldiers, rhetorical statements, and unfriendly correspondence, both China and India increasingly developed unyielding and aggressive attitudes toward the border question (Raghavan 2012, 132–149). Therefore, even though the original incident sparking the Tibet uprising had subsided, the resultant bitterness persisted to such an extent that in 1960, when representatives from the two countries met for final talks before the fateful war, there was little room left to manoeuvre.

Compounding the impact of the first two factors discussed above, the post-imperial ideology harboured by the two countries contributed to the entrenchment of the border dispute. While the deferral policy and the Tibet crisis both underscore how the border dispute had attained such complexity by 1960, the post-imperial ideology helps understand why the 1960 negotiations failed, ultimately leading to a deadlock.

Due to the intense trauma and violence suffered during colonization, China and India operated under a post-imperial ideology after their independence, which was aimed at gaining recognition of their victimhood and maximizing their prestige due to the humiliations suffered in the past (Chatterjee 2013, 253–260). This tendency was observed at the 1955 Bandung conference, at which the leadership of both newly decolonized countries highlighted their intense suffering and anti-colonial struggle. However, it also resulted in a simmering competition between India and China that intensified in the months following the Tibetan crisis, due to China's negative publicity and India's loss of territory and military casualties (Chatterjee 2013, 261). Accordingly, establishing their claims of victimhood over the other and resistance to further humiliation in the form of territorial loss heavily informed China and India's attitude when their delegates met again in 1960 to try to resolve the boundary question.

Both Zhou Enlai and the Indian leaders were insistent on securing acknowledgement of their victimhood and acceptance of the disputed territories as historically significant and integral to their respective countries. For instance, the Chinese premier emphasised in the aforementioned meetings that Tibet – which he averred had been part of China since the Manchu dynasty – was made a protectorate by the British government of India through the signing of the Anglo-Tibetan Treaty in 1904 and the Simla Convention, where the McMahon Line was determined. This, Zhou maintained, was essentially a humiliation imposed on China. With regard to Aksai Chin, Zhou asserted that the region was under the jurisdiction of Xinjiang province, and therefore indisputably part of China. It is noteworthy here that one of the major national goals of the CCP was to restore China's former glory, and therefore regaining control of Xinjiang and Tibet was seen as essential to this restoration (Chatterjee 2013, 266–267). On the Indian side, Nehru and other Indian leaders argued along similar lines, stating that the British Raj merely formalised boundaries that had been in place for centuries. In the case of Ladakh-Tibet, the boundary was historically accepted and recognised, and did not require any formal delimitation, and for the western sector the McMahon Line established a boundary that had been administered by Indian rulers since even before the Christian era. In other words, the government of India proclaimed a civilizational glory on the basis of timeless borders which were only concretised during colonial rule (Chatterjee 2013, 268–269). Following the logic of post-imperial ideology, the 1960 border talks failed on two accounts; first, neither party made any new territorial claims but simply reiterated what was rightfully theirs; and second, both were eager to establish that they had been victimised in the past and were being victimised again (Chatterjee 2013, 270).

Divergent Positions on the Border Dispute

The negotiations between Zhou and Nehru continued for five days and ended in complete failure. Nehru rejected the Chinese premier's package deal that offered Beijing's acceptance of the Indian position in the eastern sector in return for New Delhi's acceptance of the Chinese position in the western sector. The Chinese delegation returned to Beijing with the conviction that the Indians were not interested in negotiating. Tensions escalated over the next two years, with the Indian army pushing northward via the controversial Forward Policy, and PLA units responding tit-for-tat, resulting in small skirmishes. War erupted on October 20, 1962, when the PLA launched a massive offensive across the entire disputed border. It was a short and swift campaign that lasted a month and resulted in the complete defeat of the Indian army (Sidhu and Yuan 2003, 15). However, the war failed to ensure a permanent solution to the border dispute. Instead, the political rift that was created continues to dampen bilateral ties, especially as regards border negotiations. Indeed, the divergent positions adopted by India and China on the border dispute have seen their differences evolve and widen in the post-war years.

India argues that the western sector was demarcated by the 1842 agreement between Tibet and Kashmir and that the eastern sector was finalised by the Simla Agreement in 1913–1914. Therefore, no further demarcation is required. China in turn states that no formal treaty or agreement has ever been signed between the Indian and Chinese governments, for China neither sent any representative to the India-Tibet negotiations nor ratified the McMahon Line. In this context, China views the establishment of the state of Arunachal Pradesh as a unilateral step by India, and that this amounts to an illegal occupation of China's Tibet (Fang 2014, 88; Panda 2017, 35).

From a broader perspective, the two countries disagree first on the size of the border and the locations which are disputed. The Indian position is that the Sino-Indian boundary is a total of 3,488 kilometres in length (including 523 km of what India calls the Pakistan Occupied Kashmir-China section), with the western sector being 1,597 kilometres, the middle sector 545 kilometres, and the eastern sector 1,346 kilometres in length (Kumar 2020). Here, India accuses China of occupying 38,000 square kilometres of land in the Kashmir region, along with 5,180 square kilometres of land in the Kashmir region which was ceded to it by Pakistan. Also, India claims Aksai Chin to be part of India's Ladakh region, and India has no dispute as far as the eastern sector is concerned (Panda 2017, 35).

The Chinese position is that the Sino-Indian border is not more than 2,000 kilometres, the western sector roughly covers Karakoram Mountain and is about 600 kilometres long, the disputed area in this sector is 33,000 square kilometres and currently lies under Chinese control. The middle sector is roughly 450 kilometres long and has a disputed area of 2,000 square kilometres, and the eastern sector is 650 kilometres and has a disputed area of 90,000 square kilometres occupied by India (Lin 2020). Contrary to India's position, China asserts that the eastern sector of the border is the most contentious part as the McMahon line is illegitimate and China therefore claims the Indian state of Arunachal Pradesh. In the western sector, China contends that Ladakh is a disputed region (Panda 2017, 35).

Another major area of contention between the two countries is the determination of the Line of Actual Control (LAC). India rejects the Chinese version of the LAC, describing it as a series of disconnected points on the map. New Delhi also claims that the LAC should be based on military positions before China's 1962 attack, discounting any gains made during that war (Menon 2016, 14). China on the other hand insists that the LAC should be the *status quo* attained after the 1962 war; which is incidentally the territorial arrangement suggested by Zhou Enlai during the 1960 negotiations. On the eastern side, it coincides mostly with the McMahon Line, while in the western and middle sectors, the LAC follows the traditional customary line pointed out by China. However, China only describes it in general terms without precise scales on the map (Menon 2016, 15–16). Owing to such disagreements between the two countries, the LAC, even after fifty years of conflict, remains undemarcated.

The demarcation and implementation of the LAC is intrinsically associated with the larger process of negotiations on border alignment. The Chinese leadership and officials hold the determination of the LAC to be a critical matter, and have usually followed an extremely reserved approach. In 1999, the issue of demarcation of the LAC gained momentum, during the visit of India's then-External Affairs Minister Jaswant Singh. The two sides also formally exchanged their respective maps of the middle sector in 2001, however one-year later, an Indian proposal to set a time frame for exchanging maps and addressing the clarification of the western and eastern sectors failed to elicit a cogent response from China, and the matter stagnated (Yuan 2007, 133).

Indian experts observe that the Chinese lack of interest in providing clarification on the LAC is related to Beijing's shift in policy on the border dispute. In the post-war period, China has withdrawn the package deal originally proposed by Zhou Enlai and now claims the entire state of Arunachal Pradesh. Although initially, Chinese interests in Arunachal Pradesh were limited only to Tawang, in recent years their claims have expanded to include the entire state. For instance, in 2006, before the visit to India by China's then-President Hu Jintao, the PRC ambassador to India Sun Yuxi declared all of Arunachal Pradesh to be Chinese territory, and that Tawang was merely a small portion of it. Chinese commentators lament that it was a great political mistake on China's part to give up NEFA or modern day Arunachal Pradesh (Chaudhury 2006; Panda 2017, 39). In 2007, Chinese Foreign Minister Yang Jiechi stated that mere presence in populated areas would not affect China's claims: a stance that is problematic because it is a clear reversal of Beijing's earlier agreement to abide by the principle to safeguard the interests of the settled populations in the border areas. It also suggests that, in the future, China might unilaterally reject any principle that is inconvenient to its national interests (Panda 2017, 40). In response to Indian allegations, China argues that there are two reasons why China is reluctant to demarcate the LAC; first because such a process will take both countries back to the historical disputes and once again entrap bilateral ties within the historical and legal approach, which in turn will inhibit the overall development of Sino-Indian relations. Second, China is charging New Delhi with taking advantage of the clarification process to increase the disputed area into places where no dispute existed before, although Beijing is unable to provide any concrete evidence to support this claim (Lin 2020, 83).

Managing the Border Dispute

After 1962 war it took India and China ten years to restore diplomatic ties, and post-normalisation, the two countries were faced with the dual challenge of resolving the border dispute while simultaneously maintaining peace along the undemarcated border. The Indian foreign minister, Atal Bihari Vajpayee, visited China in 1979, helping to ease tensions in bilateral ties, and Sino-Indian talks on the border dispute started in the 1980s. However, confidence-building measures were initiated only in the 1990s when border patrols of the two countries had begun to clash again (Hussain 2019, 262).

In 1981, border talks commenced at the vice-ministerial level, and were followed by seven more separate rounds of meetings. Although bilateral ties deteriorated due to the military standoff during the Sumdorong Chu crisis, however, Indian Prime Minister Rajiv Gandhi's visit turned out to be a definitive moment. The two countries agreed to set up the Joint Working Group for settlement of the boundary question with a twin mandate of ensuring peace and tranquillity along the LAC and working toward a fair, reasonable and mutually acceptable settlement of the boundary question (Scott 2012, 204; Sidhu and Yuan 2003, 23–24).[1] A major breakthrough was achieved in 1993, during P.V. Narasimha Rao's visit to Beijing. The two leaders penned the *Agreement on the Maintenance of Peace and Tranquillity*, which called for a renunciation of the use of force, recognition of and respect for the LAC, and the resolution of the border issue through negotiations (Stimson Centre 1993). Another high point of border dispute management was reached with 1996 signing of the *Agreement on Confidence Building Measures in the Military Field along the LAC in the India-China Border Areas* (United Nations 1996). The agreement laid down pledges on non-aggression, prior notification of large troop movements, and exchange of maps to resolve disagreements over the LAC. The two documents remain significant in the context of Sino-Indian border negotiations, because both countries finally acknowledged that certain problems exist in their border regions and that there is need for institutional mechanisms to manage these problems.

Following the successful conclusion of these two agreements, China and India in June 2003 adopted the *Declaration on Principles for Relations and*

---

[1]   From 1989–2005, India and China have held 15 Joint Working Group Meetings, addressing issues relating to maintenance of peace and tranquillity along the border, review of confidence-building measures, and exchange of maps.

Comprehensive Co-operation between India and China, whereby each side agreed to appoint special representatives to explore ways for settlement of the boundary dispute keeping in view the political perspectives of both countries (Sidhu and Yuan 2001). It should be noted that the Special Representative Dialogue[2] mechanism has become one of the crucial negotiation strategies in recent years, and through the Special Representative talks the two countries have reached a broad consensus on outlining guidelines for the settling of the boundary dispute. A supporting mechanism for the Special Representative Talks was established in 2012 in the form of the Working Mechanism for Consultation and Co-ordination on India-China Border Affairs. This apparatus was specially tasked to address and manage issues arising out of tensions in the border regions (Panda 2017, 43–45).

A more concrete framework for settlement of the territorial dispute was instituted in 2005 with the signing of *The Political Parameters and Guiding Principles for the Settlement of India-China Boundary Questions.* According to this protocol, the two countries recognised the need to initiate the process of early clarification and confirmation of the alignment of the LAC along with undertaking meaningful and mutually acceptable adjustments to their respective positions on the boundary question. The most recent document inked between the two countries, the Border Defence Co-operation Agreement (2013), was signed following the Depsang Valley incident (Panda 2017, 43–45).

Assessing the success of Border Dispute Management Talks and Confidence-Building Measures

The success of the bilateral dialogue mechanisms and confidence-building measures described above needs to be assessed according to three aspects; management of border conflict, addressing the bilateral trust deficit, and resolution of the border dispute.

A cursory review of the state of affairs indicates that, in all three aspects, both countries have achieved minimal success. For instance, in the matter of border conflict management, the maintenance of peace and tranquillity along the LAC has been one of the most important stated objectives. Although China and India have been able to avert a major 1962-style confrontation, the number of military incursions by China has risen sharply, from 334 in 2014 to 606 in 2019 (Bhonsale 2018). Also, military standoffs between the two countries have grown longer and more difficult to resolve; the 1987

---

[2]   From 2003–2015, there have been eighteen rounds of Special Representative meetings, addressing formulation of guidelines and a framework to resolve the border dispute.

Sumdorong Chu standoff continued for eight months, the 2013 Daulat Beg Oldi incident continued for a full month, the Doklam crisis in 2017 lasted for 70 days, and the Galwan Valley military standoff led to severe military clashes; and the stalemate continues. Simultaneously, local feuds between the armies have inclined toward more violence, that is from fist fights and throwing stones, the armies of the two sides have resorted to more violent measures including the use of clubs studded with nails or wrapped with metal barbed wire (Gettleman, Kumar, and Yasir 2020). These instances point toward a lack of local-level communication and understanding, which persists amid the backdrop of diplomatic proclamations of friendship and cooperation.

Likewise, despite high level political and diplomatic exchanges and frequent meetings of the top leadership, the trust deficit between the two countries has only widened. There exists the perception of a considerable security threat on both sides as India and China have moved rapidly to upgrade their border infrastructure and military capabilities along the disputed border on the sidelines of the Special Representative Talks and Joint Working Group meetings. In recent years, a vigorous border infrastructure race has developed between the two countries, wherein both sides have engaged in building extensive road and railway connections on their respective sides of the border, upgrading military facilities, and increasing overall troop deployments for quick mobilisation. This in turn has aggravated insecurities in both countries and is considered one of the primary reasons for the frequent border skirmishes along the LAC. In particular, the Doklam (2017) and Galwan Valley (2020) clashes were triggered by road-building activities undertaken by China and India, respectively (Jakhar 2020). Apart from upgrading military infrastructure along the border, both sides have also invested heavily in modernising their conventional and non-conventional combat forces as an indication of battle preparedness to the other (Ramachandran 2016). In view of increasing military capabilities, assertive behaviour and intense distrust, the notion of peace along the LAC seems dependent on the political wisdom of their respective governments.

Even after fifteen rounds of Joint Working Group meetings and eighteen rounds of Special Representative Dialogues, the border dispute is far from being resolved. Even though the negotiation process follows a generous principle of package settlement through a sectoral approach, the two countries have failed to go beyond routine delegation meetings and joint declarations. The ascent to power of Xi Jinping in China and Narendra Modi in India, known for their strong leadership and corporate style of politics, had raised hopes for a final settlement of the border dispute, but domestic political considerations and strategic threat perceptions continue to severely constrain the ability of these political leaders to undertake sweeping decisions to resolve the dispute.

Conclusion: The Road Ahead

The border dispute undeniably remains one of the major issues impinging on Sino-Indian bilateral ties. Experts contend that there are multiple factors today which sustain the border dispute. The first is the geographical constitution of the disputed areas: The rugged, featureless terrain and extreme weather conditions make determination of the precise alignment challenging. Subsequently, implementation of border agreements on the ground also remains elusive. Second, there is asymmetry in the level of urgency for the settlement of the border dispute. In contrast to New Delhi's endeavours seeking a quick settlement, Beijing has staunchly resisted any fast-tracking of the resolution process, arguing that the border dispute is a complicated question and should be negotiated only when conditions are favourable. The primary reason for this difference in approaches is that the disputed border does not pose a security threat to China, and therefore Beijing is willing to wait for a more beneficial resolution. In contrast, New Delhi sees the border dispute as source of instability and worries and that China would use the unresolved border to bully India. The third factor inhibiting the resolution of the border dispute is intense nationalism in both countries. For China, the border dispute is intrinsically linked to Tibet and the Dalai Lama, and since the CCP has always projected the Tibetan government-in-exile in a negative light, territorial concessions involving Tawang will not only endanger China's own rule in Tibet but will also be seen domestically as sign of weakness; a terrifying prospect for the Chinese leadership. As for India, no political party would be able to propose a territorial exchange with China without seriously jeopardising its electoral prospects, as the memories of 1962 war continue to haunt the Indian national psyche. Lastly, along with the boundary dispute, new issues have begun to stir trouble in Sino-Indian bilateral ties. India's concerns regarding China's diversion of the Yarlung-Tsangpo/Brahmaputra river water, the China-Pakistan Economic Corridor, and China's growing influence in South Asia have emerged as new irritants for Indian policy makers. Similarly, Beijing too is annoyed by India's increasing proximity with Southeast Asian countries and its diplomatic-military exchanges with the United States, Japan, and Australia. These issues further erode political will in both countries and in this context territorial exchange by swap or political settlement appears a daunting task.

As evinced by the recent Galwan Valley clashes, managing the border dispute is both a political and an economic exigency for India and China because any major confrontation between the two countries will not only hurt the long-term prospects for development of both, but will also have significant repercussions on Asian stability and prosperity. Therefore, the policy-making elites of both countries need to frame innovative solutions like creating soft borders through civilian, cultural, and economic exchanges, and involving local communities in managing the border (Ranjan 2021). Such an approach can help reduce the number of military encounters between the two countries and create an enduring peace in the border region. The two countries should also aim toward building strategic trust through open dialogue, exchange of information, and verification mechanisms along the disputed border. Enhancing military-to-military communication, technological collaboration and engagement on multilateral platforms remain indispensible toward building trust. Public perception is another key area that needs to be urgently addressed through civilian exchanges. This would go a long way toward dispelling stereotypes and negative perceptions. Track-II dialogue involving strategic-affairs experts and academics from the two countries could also be organized to identify new areas for cooperation. For the foreseeable future, the border dispute will remain a pressing challenge in Sino-Indian ties, however, it is in the national interest of both countries to prioritise their larger bilateral relationship, while at the same time erecting confidence-building measures and dialogue mechanisms to better preserve the benefits accruing from the relationship.

Figure 9.1. Aksai Chin Sino-Indian border Map. Source: The Discoverer/ Wikimedia commons.
https://commons.wikimedia.org/w/index.php?curid=27897154

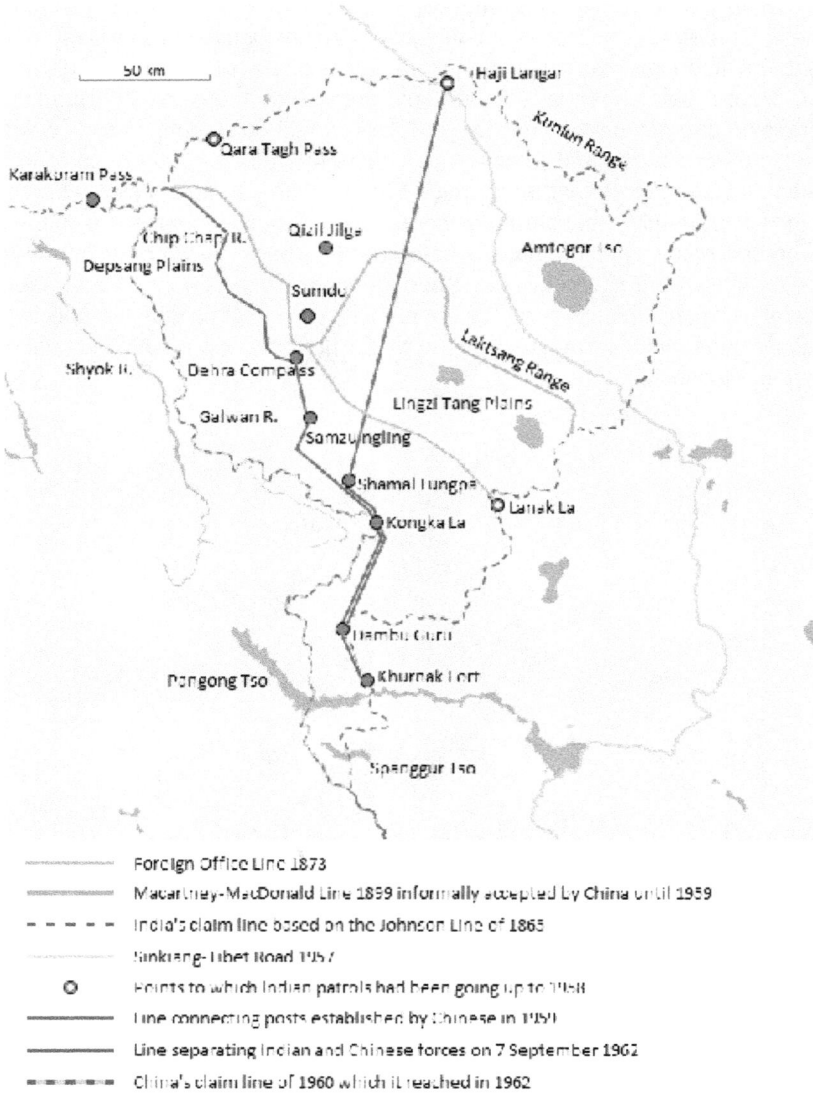

Legend:

- Foreign Office Line 1873
- Macartney-MacDonald Line 1899 informally accepted by China until 1959
- India's claim line based on the Johnson Line of 1865
- Sinkiang-Tibet Road 1957
- ○ Points to which Indian patrols had been going up to 1958
- Line connecting posts established by Chinese in 1959
- Line separating Indian and Chinese forces on 7 September 1962
- China's claim line of 1960 which it reached in 1962

References

BBC. 2020. "India-China Clash: 20 Indian Troops Killed in Ladakh Fighting." Accessed April 15, 2021. https://www.bbc.com/news/world-asia-53061476

Bhonsale, Mihir. 2018. "Understanding Sino-Indian Border Issues: An Analysis of Incidents Reported in the Indian Media." *ORF Occasional Paper* 143. https://www.orfonline.org/research/understanding-sino-indian-border-issues-an-analysis-of-incidents-reported-in-the-indian-media

Chakravarty, Ipsita. 2020. "How British Ambiguity About Frontier Between India and China Paved Way for a Post-Colonial Conflict." Scroll.in. Accessed May 30, 2021, https://scroll.in/article/965502/how-british-ambiguity-about-frontier-between-india-and-china-paved-way-for-a-post-colonial-conflict

Chaowu, Dai. 2017. "From 'Hindi-Chini Bhai Bhai' to 'International Class Struggle' Against Nehru: China's India Policy and the Frontier Dispute 1950-1962." In *The Sino-Indian War of 1962: New Perspectives*, edited by Amit Das Gupta and Lorenz M. Luthi, 68–84. Abingdon: Routledge.

Chatterjee, Manjari. 2013. "Recollecting Empire: Victimhood and the 1962 Sino-India War." In *India's Foreign Policy: A Reader*, edited by Kanti P. Bajpai and Harsh V. Pant, 248–280. Delhi: Oxford University Press.

Chaudhury, Nilova R. 2006. "China Lays Claim to Arunachal." *Hindustan Times*, November 19, 2006. https://www.hindustantimes.com/india/china-lays-claim-to-arunachal/story-QDVTkQ1kDNBBf9QMvsDdBM.html

Das Gupta, Amit. 2017. "Foreign Secretary Subimal Dutt and the Prehistory of the Sino-Indian Border War." In *The Sino-India War of 1962: New Perspectives,* edited by Amit Das Gupta and Lorenz M. Luthi, 48–67. Abingdon: Routledge.

EPW [Economic and Political Weekly]. 2020. "Why Nationalism Alone Cannot Solve the Sino-Indian Border Dispute." Accessed March 19, 2021. https://www.epw.in/engage/article/why-nationalism-alone-cannot-solve-sino-indian

Fang, Tien-Sze, ed. 2014. *Asymmetrical Threat Perceptions in India-China Relations.* India: Oxford University Press.

Gettleman, Jeffrey, Hari Kumar, and Sameer Yasir. 2020. "Worst Clash in Decades on Disputed India-China Border Kills 20 Indian Troops." *New York Times*, June 16, 2020. https://www.nytimes.com/2020/06/16/world/asia/indian-china-border-clash.html

Hussain, Nazia. 2019. "The Border Dispute in Sino-Indian Relations." In *China's Omnidirectional Peripheral Diplomacy*, edited by Jianwei Wang and Tiang Boon Hoo, 257–280. World Scientific Publishing Company.

Jakhar, Pratik. 2020. "India and China Race to Build Along a Disputed Frontier." BBC. Accessed August 15, 2020. https://www.bbc.com/news/world-asia-53171124

Kumar, P. R. 2020. "India's Perception of the India-China Border Issue and the Way Forward." In *India and China Building Strategic Trust*, edited by Rajiv Narayanan and Yonghui Qiu, 59–74. New Delhi: Vij Books Pvt Ltd.

Lin, Minwang. 2020. "China's Stance on the Sino-Indian Border Issue and Roadmap for a Resolution." In *India and China Building Strategic Trust*, edited by Rajiv Narayanan and Yonghui Qiu, 75–85. New Delhi: Vij Books Pvt Ltd.

Luthi, Lorenz M. 2017. "India's Relations with China 1945-74." In *The Sino-India War of 1962: New Perspectives,* edited by Amit Das Gupta and Lorenz M. Luthi, 29–41. Abingdon: Routledge.

Luthi, Lorenz M., and Amit Das Gupta. 2017. "Introduction." In *The Sino-India War of 1962: New Perspectives,* edited by Amit Das Gupta and Lorenz M. Luthi, 8–10. Abingdon: Routledge.

Menon, Shivshankar. 2016. "Pacifying the Border." In *Choices: Inside the Making of Indian Foreign Policy*, edited by Shivshankar Menon, 7–32. Washington: Brookings Institution Press.

Palit, George D. K. 1991. *War in High Himalaya: The Indian Army in Crisis, 1962*. India: Lancer International.

Panda, Jagannath P. 2017. "From Boundary to Bordering Territory: The Enduring Dispute." In *India-China Relations: Politics of Resources, Identity and Authority in a Multipolar World Order*, edited by Jagannath P. Panda, 34–52. Abingdon: Routledge.

Peri, Dinakar. 2021. "The Disengagement Plan Between India and China Along the LAC." *The Hindu*, February 15, 2021. https://www.thehindu.com/news/national/explained-the-disengagement-plan-between-india-and-china-along-the-lac/article33841285.ece

Raghavan, K. N. 2012. *Dividing Lines: Contours of India-China Conflict.* Mumbai: Leadstart Publishing Pvt. Ltd.

Ramachandran, Sudha. 2016. "China and India's Border Infrastructure Race." Jamestown Foundation. Accessed May 16, 2021. https://jamestown.org/program/china-and-indias-border-infrastructure-race

Ranjan, Rajiv. 2021. "The Local Solution." *India Express*, February 19, 2021. https://indianexpress.com/article/opinion/india-china-border-standoff-ladakh-disengagement-7196064

Scott, David. 2012. "Sino-Indian Territorial Issues: The Razor's Edge." In *The Rise of China: Implications for India*, edited by Harsh V. Pant, 195–217. New Delhi: Cambridge University Press.

Shankar, Mahesh. 2018. "Territory and China-India Competition: Mahesh Shankar." In *The China-India Rivalry in the Globalization Era*, edited by T.V. Paul, 27–54. Washington: Georgetown University Press.

Sidhu, Waheguru Pal Singh, and Jung-Dong Yuan. 2001. "Resolving the Sino-Indian Border Dispute: Building Confidence Through Co-operative Monitoring." *Asian Survey* 41, no. 2 (March/April): 351–376.

_____. 2003. *China and India: Cooperation or Conflict?* New Delhi: India Research Press.

Sikri, Rajiv. 2011. "The Tibet Factor in India-China Relations." *Journal of International Affairs* 64, no. 2: 55–71.

Stimson Centre. 1993. "Agreement on the Maintenance of Peace Along the Line of Actual Control in the India-China Border." Accessed March 25, 2021. https://www.stimson.org/1993/agreement-on-the-maintenance-of-peace-along-the-line-of-actual-control-in-t

United Nations. 1996. "Agreement Between India and China 1996." Accessed March 28, 2021. https://peacemaker.un.org/sites/peacemaker.un.org/files/CN%20IN_961129_Agreement%20between%20China%20and%20India.pdf

Vasudeva, Akriti. 2020. "Shedding the Dogmas in India's China Policy." South Asian Voices. Accessed June 27, 2020. https://southasianvoices.org/shedding-the-dogmas-in-indias-china-policy

Westcott, Stephen. 2017. "The intractable Sino-Indian Border Dispute: A Theoretical and Historical Account," PhD diss. Murdoch University.

Yuan, Jing-Dong. 2007. "The Dragon and the Elephant: Chinese-Indian Relations in the 21st Century." *The Washington Quarterly* 30, no. 3: 131–144.

10

Understanding China's 'New' Assertiveness from Resolved Territorial Questions

BHASO NDZENDZE

The assertiveness and aggression with which the People's Republic of China (PRC) has chosen to deal with the various territorial disputes in which it is currently engaged has ramped up in recent years, calling into question that regime's willingness to resolve these disputes with a diplomatic solution. In the past, however, this is precisely what leaders in Beijing have shown themselves capable of accomplishing. This chapter looks at the history of Chinese methods of dealing with disagreements over sovereignty by examining three distinct case studies: Mongolia, Shandong, and Macau. The Mongolian declaration of independence during the 1911 Xinhai Revolution, which brought down China's last imperial dynasty, remains the only successful case of secession by a former Chinese geographical entity. Moreover, the transfer of Shandong from Japan in 1922 and the transfer of Macau from Portuguese administration in 1999 through a process of bilateral negotiation, upon insistence of its removal from UN oversight and direct engagement with Lisbon instead, demonstrate that force need not be the only outlet for Beijing to settle its outstanding territorial disputes. This chapter highlights the need to look back at these revolved cases using a comparative perspective to understand China's current assertiveness and territorialism.

The chapter examines each case in its own domestic and international context and offers cross-case observations with regards to the more controversial questions of China's stance toward Taiwan, Hong Kong, Tibet, and Xinjiang in order to examine the differences in conditions for the successful secession and retention of international sovereignty by Mongolia compared to Tibet, Xinjiang, and even Taiwan; the relatively seamless takeover of Macau and Shandong compared to Hong Kong; and the relative lack of analysis that these cases engender in recent literature.

This chapter advances hypotheses to explain the differing approaches then and now, including the relative weakness of China in 1911, and of Portugal in the latter half of the 20th century, as well as lack of strategic value of the territories in question. It is asserted that the Mongolian case, coming at the height of the 'century of humiliation' and followed by perceived slights at the 1919 Paris Peace Conference that followed the First World War, has conditioned successive Chinese governments and nationalistic segments within the country's demographics to take advantage of key weaknesses in today's international system, and to be more proactive and unilateral in preventing secessionist movements and consolidating control over PRC territorial holdings, thereby problematising the newness of the assertiveness currently seen in Xi Jinping's China. This realisation slowly emerged after the Shandong transfer but was more effectively exercised in Tibet (1951) and over Macau. The current policy toward Hong Kong is thus merely a more recent incarnation of Chinese government proactiveness predicated on a Chinese Communist Party (CCP) leadership that is cognisant of these past lessons and the domestic audience costs, and the perceived permissiveness of the current international environment for such unilateral assertiveness.

The first section looks at the case of Mongolian independence and China's failure to reincorporate it into its territory. This is followed by a discussion of the difficulties around the return of Shandong following the First World War in the second section of the chapter. The third section examines the return of Macau. The fourth and final section consolidates the pattern seen across these cases and identifies the conditions behind China's modern-day assertiveness.

Mongolia

Mongolia has a long and illustrious history. The country as we know it today originated under the leadership of Genghis Khan in the 13th century. Eventually Genghis's grandson, Kublai Khan, consolidated his conquest of China and became emperor of China in 1271. He called his dynasty Yuan ('origin') and ruled in accordance with Chinese institutions and customs, which he retained. While the Yuan dynasty would eventually be replaced by the Ming in 1368, and then the ethnic Manchu Qing dynasty in 1644, the Mongolian territory remained part of China, and from 1691, northern Mongolia was effectively colonized by the Qing.

In 1911, the Qing dynasty collapsed, and Mongolia declared its independence from China on 1 December 1911. The leaders of this newly independent

Mongolia put in place a theocratic government led by the Bogd Khan, a monarchical position. Following a brief reincorporation in 1915, Russia, Mongolia, and the new Republic of China (ROC) signed an agreement that gave limited autonomy to Mongolia, though the ROC retained suzerainty over the nominally independent state. Nevertheless, in October 1919, the ROC revoked the autonomy of Outer Mongolia at the behest of local chieftains, whose power and influence had been greatly diminished by the imposition of a monarchical system of government. The ROC sent troops to garrison key areas of Mongolia, dethroning the Bogd Khan and occupying the country. This situation lasted until 1921 when the Chinese were driven out by a ragtag coalition of White Russians, Siberians, Japanese, and native Mongolians led the fanatically anti-communist Russian warlord, Baron Ungern-Sternberg. The baron, whose grand plan was to raise a cavalry of fighters to rout the communists out of Moscow, soon wore out his welcome, and a force of Mongolian soldiers, led by Damdin Sükhbaatar, sought the assistance of Russia's Red Army to oust Ungern (Palmer 2009).

Despite these tribulations and intrigues, Mongolian independence has stood since it was proclaimed in July 1921. While the Soviets, who exerted tremendous influence over the Mongolian state, were eager to rid the country of the Bogd Khan, he was demoted to a figurehead, and upon his death in 1924, the nation became the Mongolian People's Republic on the 26th of November that year. Brief diplomatic tussles would continue over the course of the 20th century, especially after the ROC was routed to Taiwan in 1949 and the CCP took power in Beijing and began to exhibit expansionary ambitions.

During the Sino-Soviet split, Mongolia predictably sided with the Union of Soviet Socialist Republics (USSR), expelled some Chinese citizens, and cut trade with China. In 1961, Mongolia gained entry into the United Nations as a member. In response to the weakening of the USSR before its final dissolution in 1991, Ulaanbaatar enacted social reforms in the mid- to late-1980s, and in 1989 established full diplomatic relations with the PRC.

The major source of diplomatic upheaval has been the Tibetan question. Mongolia and Tibet share strong religious bonds based on Tibetan Buddhism, and both view the Dalai Lama as a major religious leader. The Dalai Lama first visited Mongolia in 1979, and has been there eight times since. China sees the Dalai Lama as a politician intent on splitting the strategic Tibetan region away from the rest of China. Beijing has been occupying Tibet since 1951, and administering it as a special autonomous region since 1965 (Shakya 1999, 45). The Dalai Lama escaped into exile in India in 1959, in the wake of intense disagreements with the Beijing government over the status of Tibet and the level of autonomy that was promised under the controversial

17-Point Agreement, which he has subsequently renounced (Shakya 1999, 89, 124, 200).

Following the Dalai Lama's visit in 2002, the PRC government closed the border between the two countries for two days. Upon a subsequent visit in August of 2006, the PRC's Foreign Ministry reiterated to Mongolia that it should not have given the Dalai Lama a platform to spread his 'separatist' views (VOA 2009). In December 2016, there was yet another visit, amid the controversy over the Dalai Lama's being scheduled to chant special sutras 'at a large sports facility built by Chinese companies with Chinese aid' (Associated Press 2016). This time, however, it was widely known, and had been made clear by the Mongolian Foreign Minister, that the visit would be the last for the octogenarian Dalai Lama, not because of his age but because future visits would be barred by the government of Mongolia. That government had found itself in need of funds from Beijing. As the *Associated Press* (2016) reported, the country's leaders were under pressure as they were seeking a US$4.2 billion loan from the Chinese in order to offset a deep recession they were going through. Mongolia's exports are also heavily dependent on China, which accounts for 90% of the land-locked country's market (Associated Press 2016; Namjilsangarav, 2016).

Shandong

After the emergence of the Qing dynasty in 1644, China was the most powerful nation in East Asia for nearly three centuries (Boissoneault 2017). However, as its economic fortunes diminished and those of European states and neighbouring Japan grew with the innovations of the Industrial Revolution, the Qing Empire found itself at the mercy of these players. Starting in earnest around 1840, the heightening rivalry among the great powers in the scramble for spheres of influence and territories in Asia placed China in the crosshairs of Great Britain, Germany, France, Japan, Portugal, Russia, and the United States. A series of events took place following the Opium Wars of 1839–1842 and 1856–1860, setting in motion 'the establishment of foreign spheres of influence in prosperous Chinese provinces, the surrendering of colonial bases (Hong Kong, Qingdao, Port Arthur) and extraterritorial foreign settlements and concessions (Shanghai, Hankou, Tianjin) were violently pushed through despite Chinese resistance' (Mühlhahn 2016, 2). In the First Sino-Japanese War of 1895, China lost, and was forced to hand over Taiwan (also called Formosa) 'in perpetuity,' according to Article II of the Treaty of Shimonoseki. After the successful suppression of the Boxer Rebellion (1899–1901), Qing-ruled China was not only forced to pay additional reparations to the colonisers, but also had to agree to the stationing of their militaries in Beijing. These humiliations at the hands of external powers also laid bare the decline of the Qing Empire to

China's reform-minded intellectuals, who were increasingly republican in their disposition. Thus in 1911, the dynasty was overthrown, and revolutionary leader Dr Sun Yat-sen, serving as provisional president, proclaimed the Republic of China, but also acknowledged that this new political entity was unable to solve China's many pressing domestic and foreign policy problems (Mühlhahn 2016, 2). Among these was the continued presence of colonial outposts, including among them Germany. The country had made use of its military force to insert itself into China by capitalizing on the killing of two German missionaries, and attacking and invading the city of Qingdao in 1897. They then went about 'establishing what amounted to a German colony in Shandong province' (Boissoneault 2017, 1). The province was the historic centre of the Shang dynasty (1766–1122 BCE) and is the birthplace of China's greatest philosopher Confucius and military strategist Sun Tzu. In 1898, Kaiser Wilhelm II of Germany declared Qingdao a German colony. The city was then remodelled using German institutions and architecture as a template; 'a complete German system of administration was established. Public institutions such as banks, consulates, and schools were also built. The new upper class from Germany naturally required that German-style villas ought to be constructed as well' (Mühlhahn 2016, 2). Moreover, the Germans also brought with them a prejudicial outlook, with racism defining the daily interactions between coloniser and colonised. For example, the colonial system 'differentiated between the Chinese and European populations in a fundamental, but also spatial, way' and in proto-apartheid fashion, the Chinese required permits to move about and were from the onset 'prohibited from living within the European part of Qingdao' (Mühlhahn 2016, 2).

The prospect of expelling Germany from Qingdao and taking over the colony greatly interested the Japanese and led to them to join the fight against Germany in 1914, thereby rendering the Great War a global one. Within China, the newly established republican government was a tenuous one, by this time led by General Yuan Shikai, who had come into power in 1912. The ROC government had constant clashes with local warlords and did not enjoy the 'monopoly of violence' of the Weberian state. Though 'the Chinese people suffered political chaos, economic weakness, and social misery,' according to University of Hong Kong Professor Xu Guoqi, 'this was also a period of excitement, hope, high expectations, optimism and new dream,' principally due to a belief among the Chinese that they could 'use the war as a way to reshape the geopolitical balance of power and attain equality with European nations' (Xu 2011).

In this way, then, China also 'declared war on Germany in hopes of gaining regional dominance.' For political reasons, however, China's entry into the war on the side of the Allied Powers was deferred, and the ROC did not send conventional troops into battle (Boissoneault 2017). Although China had declared itself neutral at the start of the war in August 1914, Yuan Shikai had secretly offered the British some 50,000 troops to retake Qingdao. The British refused the offer, but Japan soon used its own army to eject the Germans from the city, and would stay there for the remainder of the war, and after.

'On 15 August 1914, Japan issued an ultimatum to the German Reich that its colony in Kiautschou had to be unconditionally vacated by 15 September. Japan declared war on the German Reich on 23 August. A few days later, Japanese and English ships started a naval blockade against Kiautschou' (Mühlhahn 2016, 2).

With the European Allies completely preoccupied with the war in Europe, Japan took the opportunity to annex Manchuria and North China as a Japanese protectorate. In January of the following year, the Japanese imposed upon China the Twenty-One Demands. These were 'political demands and considerable economic privileges for Japan, especially in Manchuria and Mongolia, as well as the lower reaches of Yangtze River and in the province of Fujian' (Mühlhahn 2016, 2). With no alternative, Yuan Shikai agreed to the demands on 25 May. He received little in the way of concessions in his negotiations with the Japanese, and indeed sparked public protests against his failure to safeguard Chinese sovereignty. This further weakened the government, and May 9 came to be known as a day of national humiliation, to be observed annually (later supplanted by May Fourth, described in detail below) (Mühlhahn 2016, 2).

By February 1916, however, as the death toll in Europe skyrocketed, the British became more amenable to the Chinese offer. British officials agreed that China could 'join with the Entente provided that Japan and the other Allies accepted her as a partner' (Mühlhahn 2016, 2). Japan in turn refused to allow Chinese soldiers to fight, for an armed China may have meant concessions would be granted, possibly including Qingdao, were it to contribute significantly to an Allied victory (Boissoneault 2017). If China could not fight directly, then, Yuan and his advisors decided that the next-best option 'was a secret show of support toward the Allies: they would send voluntary non-combatant workers, largely from Shandong, to embattled Allied countries' (Boissoneault 2017). Thus, the Chinese participated in auxiliary roles:

'Chinese workers dug trenches. They repaired tanks in Normandy. They assembled shells for artillery. They transported munitions in Dannes. They unloaded supplies and war material in the port of Dunkirk. They ventured farther afield, too. Graves in Basra, in southern Iraq, contain remains of hundreds of Chinese workers who died carrying water for British troops in an offensive against the Ottoman Empire' (Boehler 2019, 1).

Furthermore, since China was officially neutral, commercial businesses were formed to provide the labour (Jeffery 2017). The First World War is perhaps remembered primarily for the brutality of its trench warfare, and as Professor Bruce Elleman (2002, 33–34) notes, 'a lot of those trenches weren't dug by the [Allied] soldiers, they were dug by Chinese laborers.' This was 'one way for China to prove it deserved a seat at the table whenever the war ended and terms were agreed upon.' Alas, 'even after a year of supplying labor, their contribution remained largely unrecognized diplomatically' (Boissoneault 2017).

America's entry into the war represented a shift in the internal dynamics among the Allied powers, with US officials backing China's aim as the end of the war was nearing. US President Woodrow Wilson expected 'the Post-War conference to be able to resolve these diplomatic issues [of Shandong]' between China, Germany and Japan since he sought to frame and lead the post-war negotiations (Elleman 2002, 34). Further changes were brought by Germany's announcement of its strategy of unrestricted submarine warfare (Mühlhahn 2016, 2). Soon thereafter, 'more than 500 Chinese laborers aboard the French ship Athos were killed in February 1917 when a U-boat struck the ship.' At this point, China would be able to declare war on Germany, and did so on August 14th of that year, though in practice not much changed in the substance of Chinese involvement, 'since they had already been sending laborers' (Mühlhahn 2016, 2). Thus, Chinese hopes for territorial restoration experienced a substantial boost that, in failing to materialise, reaped generational consequences.

For a time, the Chinese government entertained the prospect of cooperating with Japan, as an equal and as a partner – spurred by power shifts in Japan, as well as pressing financial needs at home:

'Because "the domestic situation [was] overshadowed by dangers threatening from abroad," China's political parties decided that "a policy of friendly cooperation with Japan within limits [was] desirable," partly because the Terauchi cabinet, which came to power in Tokyo in October 1916, seemed likely to respond. Japan, however, was also a promising source of the foreign loans China needed to restore her financial stability and to enable the government to reassert its power. Of those in China who favoured closer ties with Japan, some favoured a permanent alliance, while others believed that China could be politically independent and financially dependent at the same time' (Craft 1994, 14).

Japan was therefore perceived by the Chinese authorities as a means to an end. According to one US official based in China, 'they appear to think that [Japan's domination] is more or less inevitable anyway, and that when Japan has nursed China back to strength the said country can be ejected' (Craft 1994, 14). Whilst there were different views on this, one man's decision ultimately mattered, and he was amenable to a rapprochement with Japan. 'Yuan and most of the cabinet opposed war because China was so weak militarily and could expect no support from the West' (Craft 1994, 10). In a similar vein, the Chinese foreign representative, Wellington Koo, suggested that, 'while China's army was being reorganized, the Waichiaopu should try to influence public opinion in Britain and the United States in order to drive a wedge between them and Japan. Once relations among the three became strained, China could try to persuade the West to protect her against Japan' (Craft 1994, 12).

Moreover, many Chinese public intellectuals gathered in Paris 'seeing it as a "once-in-a-thousand-years opportunity" for China to reclaim her rightful international standing and, more mundanely, to regain Tsingtao [Qingdao]' (Craft 1994, 22). The Chinese were optimistic that the Shantung Question would be answered favourably, leading to a feeling of betrayal when the former German colony was officially handed over to Japan. Notwithstanding vague promises that the Japanese would give Qingdao back to China sometime in the near future (a date of 1922 was suggested), the Chinese raised doubts over whether Japan would adhere to such commitments. Indeed, the Allies and Wilson had based this handover to Japan, *inter alia,* on the Twenty One Demands of 1915, in which China had 'gladly agreed' that Japan and Germany 'dispose of Shandong between them' (Craft 1994, 22). The period of the First World War and the attendant loss of Chinese territory and face was seen as yet an extension of the period of unequal treaties. Limited as their options were, however, Chinese authorities did not capitulate to the officiation of the transfer. It is no coincidence that this took place against the backdrop of a Chinese state in the form of a republic which was more susceptible to being influenced by the general populace. Wellington Koo, therefore, refused to sign the treaty, meaning that the Chinese delegation to the Peace Conference was the only one to not sign the Treaty of Versailles during the signing ceremony. In the words of Craft (1994, 22), 'although Peking wanted to sign the treaty notwithstanding, the May Fourth Movement sweeping the country at the time demanded reservations and, as the Allies and Wilson would not agree to them, the Chinese delegates chose not to sign.'

China's interwar period was, therefore, a significant period that coincides with China's complicated entry into multilateral frameworks, and yet it scarcely obtains much contemporary analysis. China's modern political history is inextricably linked to the foreign policy slights endured during this period and the domestic implications these brought about or at least catalysed, including the formation of the CCP. In other words, the century of humiliation, which is widely believed to be a principal narrative behind China's economic development–foreign policy nexus, is incomplete without a study of China's experiences in 1918 in Paris and the ramifications contained in the Versailles Treaty of 1919.

In retrospect, this refusal to sign the Treaty of Versailles marked sharply the single most identifiable point in Chinese political history in which, for the first time, domestic audience costs were a factor in its foreign policy. Unfair treaties had been a constant factor in China's recent memory, but this was the first such attempt to take place under the new republican government which was cognizant of the domestic political ramifications of showing weakness in foreign matters – an elemental feature which has only gained in importance, and indeed has become pronounced in China's post-1949 configuration. This is especially visible in the approach taken by the CCP regime toward issues such as the One China policy, the South China Sea, the Senkaku/Diaoyu Islands dispute, Tibet, and its insistence on non-interference in domestic affairs, buttressed by a civic nationalism toward foreign exploitation and territorial threats that is not only imposed from above but also generated from below, especially with the ability for online expressions of nationalistic sentiment to spread far and wide.

Macau

Diplomatic relations between contemporary China and Portugal were cemented in February of 1979. The lead up was based on three factors: the overthrow of Portugal's fascist government, events over Taiwan, and the return of Macau. Following the expulsion of the *Estado Novo* regime in Portugal in 1974, the Portuguese government recalled its soldiers from Macau and withdrew its formal diplomatic relations with the ROC on Taiwan. Following this, several conferences took place between June of 1986 and March of 1987, the end product of which was the Sino-Portuguese Joint Declaration of April 1987. The process was set in motion for Macau to be handed over to the PRC in 1999, to be governed as a special administrative region (SAR), concomitant with comparatively higher autonomy and its own legal code. The return of Macau involved several crucial factors. There was an unwillingness on the part of Portugal to retain the territory at all costs, and a general lack of interest by global players to stand in the way of the handover. There was also the issue of China's own power vis-à-vis Portugal. This was not the case compared to Britain vis-à-vis the Hong Kong handover, for example, and this asymmetry persists to this day. For example, Jochen Faget (2019) highlights the importance of the 2008 financial crisis and puts the importance of China to Portugal in the following terms: 'when Portugal was facing difficult times, the EU imposed tough austerity measures, while China pumped billions into the country.'

On the other hand, three main reasons underlie the Chinese interest in Portugal. Broadly, Portugal is the centre of a linguistic global population covering four continents consisting of some 260 million people, the majority of whom are in South America and Africa, and thus who are also of special interest to the CCP. Secondly, Portugal is also among the few countries in Western Europe to declare an interest in the Belt and Road Initiative, with its ambassador to China envisioning a value proposition for Portugal in its unparalleled proximity to Africa, North America, and Europe (Jose Augusto Duarte, 2018 Interview). This is also welcomed at the most senior levels of the Portuguese government, to the effect that 'over the past several years, Portugal's Prime Minister Antonio Costa has emerged as one of the staunchest supporters of Chinese investment in Europe,' even stating that Portugal's 'experience with Chinese investment is very positive,' and that the Chinese 'show total respect for our laws and market rules' (Faget 2019). On the other hand, according to a survey by Susi Dennison and Lívia Franco for the European Council on Foreign Relations, 'Portuguese citizens are becoming concerned about the government's policy on China. They believe that to become a stronger global player, the EU should make the limitation of Chinese economic leverage over Europe its second-highest priority – after efforts to strengthen European unity' (Dennison and Franco 2019, 14).

Nothing New: Patterns and Sources of China's Territorial Assertiveness

Beijing has recently been exerting increasing assertiveness over Hong Kong (most evident in the July 2020 National Security Law), Taiwan (seen in Xi's statements averring that use of force will remain an option), Tibet, and Xinjiang (Hass 2020; Su and Yi 2021). Moreover, Beijing has asserted claims over disputed islands in the South China Sea, as well as with Japan in the East China Sea. In recent years, there have been clashes with India over bilateral disputes (Ladakh), as well as over Doklam, which is disputed by China and Indian ally Bhutan. It is useful to place this in context. In essence, it is nothing new.

In the days before the formation of the PRC, republican Chinese diplomats targeted their activities in the League of Nations – the world's only truly multilateral institution at the time – toward two long-term Chinese national objectives. The first was obtaining formal legal equality with other states (and therefore putting an end to the disadvantageous treaty relations which had historically defined its relations with Western powers). The second was focused on gaining recognition for the country's 'self-assessed identity as a once and future great power' (Kaufman 2014, 605). On the first issue, these diplomats sought to goad the League to act indirectly on China's behalf, by supporting its diplomatic activities in other venues and upholding the effectiveness of international legal rules. On the second objective, the diplomats wanted the League's organisational structure to 'reflect China's self-perceived rightful status as an important nation' (Kaufman 2014, 605). However, these outcomes did not materialise, as the League failed to act against the Japanese annexation of Manchuria in 1931 the way it did against the Italian invasion of Ethiopia in 1935. Moreover, while Shandong had been returned in 1922, this was only accomplished through the United States strong-arming Japan.

As a result of this history, the PRC government has promoted a narrative of 'national humiliation' (Callahan 2006, 178). This discourse reiterates the humiliation of the Chinese people, the dismemberment of territory, and loss of sovereignty to foreign hands and domestic weakness and corruption. The so-called Century of Humiliation is largely conceived as having begun with the first Opium War in 1839, in which the Royal Navy opened up China to Western capitalism, and only ending in 1949, with the declaration of the PRC. According to Callahan, this may have worked too well:

'In the early twentieth century the political performances aimed to produce a proper Chinese nation out of the clashes between the Qing dynasty, northern warlords, and foreign empires. The goal was to construct a "China" worthy of being saved. When National Humiliation Day was revived in China at the turn of the twenty-first century, the political performances were more focused on containing the nation through a commemoration of the various crises of the early twentieth century' (Callahan 2006, 179).

While Callahan makes a strong case, he fails to take into consideration the earlier manifestation of this nationalism in the form of the May Fourth Movement against its own government, which was seen as weak and incapable of pursuing China's interests. Moreover, Chinese nationalism can equally be interpreted as a dispersed and bottom-up phenomenon, stemming not from government regulations and propaganda, but as a historically-derived civic practice rather than a set of artefacts to be consumed (Callahan 2006, 179).

The economist John Maynard Keynes, who was part of the British delegation to the Paris Peace Conference after the end of WWI, famously predicted in 1919 that the excessively punitive measures being taken against the defeated German state could lead to a resurgent Germany with a score to settle. In much the same way, contemporary analyses of China's foreign policy outlook ought to more accurately factor in the role of the slights suffered by China at the Paris Peace Conference, along with the territorial partitioning that accompanied them, as well as the impunity enjoyed by Japan even in the wake of the League of Nations, which the weaker nations of the world had looked to as an equaliser at the time. Far from being solely the product of

CCP propaganda, Chinese nationalism is also a bottom-up phenomenon that developed, perhaps inevitably, from the colonial encounter. In the words of Shameer Modongal (2016, 1), 'even though the communist party has [a] major role in creating a civic nationalism through its restriction on media and education system, the Chinese people show highly nationalist feeling even abroad where they can access international media.' Modongal further highlights the autonomous modes of expression of this nationalism, including most recently in the cyber sphere. Interestingly, though the PRC government exerts extensive control over the expression of political opinion through various forms of censorship (Freedom House 2021), much hypernationalist online content is allowed to stand. As a result, the intersection of top-down with bottom-up forms of nationalism create a self-reinforcing feedback loop in which foreign policy decision-making – traditionally the purview of elite politics in China – is increasingly being influenced by netizens in a networked world (Yang 2016, 355).

In the current era, 'the increased diversity, velocity and free flow of foreign policy information, has raised public attention to foreign policy' such that foreign policymaking sees substantial input from the public, even if informally (Yang 2016, 355). This phenomenon, wherein the public exerts pressure on the process of PRC foreign policymaking, was dubbed 'popular sovereignty' when the phenomenon became apparent through the seemingly grassroots response (in both China and South Korea) to Japan's effort to be granted a seat on the United Nations Security Council (Liu 2010). It would, argues Liu (2010, 73), have been an apparent endorsement of Japan's WWII-era aggressions in Asia. More recent work by Zhong and Hwang highlights findings which indicate that Chinese who are pro-democratic are also more likely to be nationalistic. 'Random survey data on Chinese urban residents in 34 Chinese cities reveal that democracy-oriented Chinese urbanites tend to show stronger nationalistic feelings,' and perhaps unexpectedly, the same study showed that 'people with more nationalistic feelings tend to be those who show less support for the current system in China' (Zhong and Hwang 2020). This may suggest that at least some of the voices among the autonomous and bottom-up proponents of Chinese nationalism make a distinction between the Chinese nation and the Chinese government – a distinction that the CCP has been keen to obscure.

In most cases, however, the ire of the populace is not directed toward the PRC regime, but the external world, with the Chinese diaspora being particularly active, including students in Western nations who actively defend Beijing's actions in academia and cyberspace, using the advantages of their proficiency with the English language, as well as the access they enjoy to digital platforms censored or banned in China itself (Modongal 2016, 5). This same grassroots enthusiasm toward territorial questions has extended toward

Hong Kong. While Westerners watched aghast as Chinese police brutally clamped down on democracy protests in the former British colony, counterprotests were organized by pro-CCP citizens of both China and Hong Kong to support the actions of the Beijing regime (Goh 2019; Shao 2019).

In 2012, as tensions rose over the disputed Senkaku/Diaoyu Islands, Chinese netizens organized boycotts of Japanese products as a form of protest, often through the Chinese microblogging website Weibo. In the words of one blogger: 'To those who say we shouldn't link buying Japanese goods to patriotism: if a seller bullied your ancestor, and plans to plunder your riches now, will you obediently pay him money to buy his goods?' Another common theme echoed by nationalistic bloggers is the Nanjing Massacre, as well as the continuing Japanese practice of honouring of its WWII martyrs at the Yasukuni Shrine (France 24 2012).

The vehemence of this anti-foreigner – especially anti-Japanese – sentiment online outstrips even the hardliners within the PRC government, serving to push policy further toward hawkishness, with netizens criticising their own country's policymakers for not being aggressive enough. If the perceived undermining of Chinese interests is expressed toward perceived foreign sources, it is carried out with the same vehemence toward China's own foreign policymakers, with the Chinese Ministry of Foreign Affairs (MFA) the subject of occasional ridicule. According to an MFA spokesperson, 'the ministry has been receiving calcium pills on a regular basis – a popular choice of insult from a public that sees the Chinese diplomats as spineless' (Jing 2017, 429). In the online world, the MFA has garnered the unofficial nickname 'the Ministry of Protests' due to its tendency to do little more than issue denouncements of unfavourable international developments (Jing 2017, 429).

Conclusion

Even prior to the founding of the PRC some 70 years ago, China has had a long history of territorial assertiveness. As examined above, this history introduces a critical stance into the debate today: namely, that such assertiveness has periodically appeared when conditions allow. Crucially, this assertiveness is neither fully top-down nor exclusively the result of CCP rule. Rather, it has its roots in popular sovereignty and is motivated by popular perceptions of international humiliation that took place long before the CCP came into being. Such a historical backdrop should give indication into the origins and contemporary social sources of China's foreign policy as far as territorial disputes are concerned.

References

Associated Press. 2016. "Dalai Lama to Visit Mongolia, Possibly Sparking China Anger." November 17, 2020. https://apnews.com/article/78a150f6ceb44d679b9347e3e2d55f5b

Boehler, Patrick. 2019. "The Forgotten Army of the First World War: How Chinese Labourers Helped Shape Europe." *South China Morning Post*. https://multimedia.scmp.com/ww1-china

Boissoneault, Lorraine. 2017. "The Surprisingly Important Role China Played in WWI." *Smithsonian Magazine*, August 17, 2017. https://www.smithsonianmag.com/history/surprisingly-important-role-china-played-world-war-i-180964532

Callahan, William A. 2006. "History, Identity, and Security: Producing and Consuming Nationalism in China." *Critical Asian Studies* 38, no. 2: 179–208.

Craft, Stephen G. 1994. "Angling for an Invitation to Paris: China's Entry Into the First World War." *The International History Review* 16, no. 1: 1–24.

Dennison, Susi, and Livia Franco. 2019. "The Instinctive Multilateralist: Portugal and the Politics of Cooperation." European Council on Foreign Relations, October 2, 2019. https://ecfr.eu/publication/instinctive_multilateralist_portugal_politics_cooperation

Duarte, Jose Augusto. 2018. CGTN Interview: "Portuguese Ambassador: We are not afraid of China's rise." *CGTN*, 13 June. https://news.cgtn.com/news/3d456a4d3530575a306c5562684a335a764a4855/share_p.html.

Elleman, Bruce. 2002. *Wilson and China: A Revised History of the Shandong Question*. New York: Routledge.

Faget, Jochen. 2019. "Portugal: A China-Friendly EU Nation Driven by Need." *DW*, March 12, 2019. https://www.dw.com/en/portugal-a-china-friendly-eu-nation-driven-by-need/a-47872582

France 24. 2012. "Chinese Debate Boycotting Japanese Products Over Islands Dispute." https://observers.france24.com/en/20120821-online-chinese-debate-boycotting-japanese-products-over-islands-dispute-protest-weibo-poll-censorship

Goh, Brenda. 2019. "'All the Forces': China's Global Social Media Push Over Hong Kong Protests." *Reuters*, August 22, 2019. https://www.reuters.com/article/us-hongkong-protests-china-socialmedia-idUSKCN1VC0NF

Hass, Ryan. 2020. "Why Now? Understanding Beijing's New Assertiveness in Hong Kong." Brookings Institution, July17, 2020. https://www.brookings.edu/blog/order-from-chaos/2020/07/17/why-now-understanding-beijings-new-assertiveness-in-hong-kong/

Jeffery, Keith. 2017. *1916: A Global History*. London: Bloomsbury.

Jing, Sun. 2017. "Growing Diplomacy, Retreating Diplomats – How the Chinese Foreign Ministry has been Marginalized in Foreign Policymaking." *Journal of Contemporary China* 26, no. 105: 419–433.

Kaufman, Alison Adcock. 2014. "In Pursuit of Equality and Respect: China's Diplomacy and the League of Nations." *Modern China* 40, no. 6: 605–638.

Liu, Shih-Diing. 2010. "Networking Anti-Japanese Protests: Popular Sovereignty Reasserted Since 2005. In *Online Chinese Nationalism and China's Bilateral Relations*, edited by Simon Shen and Shaun Breslin, 73–90. Plymouth: Lexington Books.

Modongal, Shameer. 2016. "Development of Nationalism in China." *Cogent Social Sciences* 2, no. 1: 1–7.

Mühlhahn, Klaus. 2016. "China, 1914-1918." International Encyclopedia of the First World War. https://encyclopedia.1914-1918-online.net/pdf/1914-1918-Online-china-2016-01-11.pdf

Namjilsangarav, Ganbat. 2016. "Mongolia Says Dalai Lama Will Not Be Allowed Future Visits." *Associated Press*, December 21, 2016. https://apnews.com/article/8c026337a97640309f4bdb530bf6cd07

Palmer, James. 2009. *The Bloody White Baron: The Extraordinary Story of the Russian Nobleman Who Became the Last Khan of Mongolia*. New York: Basic Books.

Shakya, Tsering. 1999. *The Dragon in the Land of Snows: A History of Modern Tibet Since 1947*. London: Pimlico.

Shao, Grace. 2019. "Social Media Has Become a Battleground in Hong Kong's Protests." *CNBC*, August 15, 2019. https://www.cnbc.com/2019/08/16/social-media-has-become-a-battleground-in-hong-kongs-protests.html

Su, Boyang, and Sophie Wushuang Yi. 2021. "Hong Kong: 'Patriotism Test' for Public Officials Shows China's Increasing Assertiveness." *The Conversation*, March 2, 2021. https://theconversation.com/hong-kong-patriotism-test-for-public-officials-shows-chinas-increasing-assertiveness-156070

Xu, Guoqi. 2011. *Strangers on the Western Front*. Cambridge: Harvard University Press.

Yang, Yifan 2016. "The Internet and China's Foreign Policy Decision-Making." *Chinese Political Science Review*, no. 1: 353–372.

Zhong, Yang, and Wonjae Hwang. 2020. "Why Do Chinese Democrats Tend to Be More Nationalistic? Explaining Popular Nationalism in Urban China." *Journal of Contemporary China* 29, no. 121: 61–74.

Note on Indexing

Our books do not have indexes due to the prohibitive cost of assembling them. If you are reading this book in paperback and want to find a particular word or phrase you can do so by downloading a free PDF version of this book from the E-International Relations website. View the e-book in any standard PDF reader and enter your search terms in the search box. You can then navigate through the search results and find what you are looking for. If you are using apps (or devices) to read our e-books, you should also find word search functionality in those.

You can find all of our books here: http://www.e-ir.info/publications

www.ingramcontent.com/pod-product-compliance
Lightning Source LLC
Chambersburg PA
CBHW060321030426
42336CB00011B/1156